VEGGIE
HOTELS

THE JOY OF
VEGETARIAN VACATIONS

VEGETARISCH-VEGAN
REISEN MIT GENUSS

EDITED AND COMPILED BY
HERAUSGEGEBEN UND ZUSAMMENGESTELLT VON
KAREN KLEIN, THOMAS KLEIN, PETER HAUNERT

teNeues

TABLE OF CONTENTS
INHALTSVERZEICHNIS

WHY VEGGIE?

For many years we traveled together for both business and pleasure. It was a dream existence, one would think, and yet something fundamental was missing. As travel writers and long-time vegetarians, we often had some difficulty finding good food on the road—for what use are beautiful rooms and enticing pools when all you can order in the restaurant are the side dishes?

Extensive research then brought us to the aha moment: they really do exist! Hotels where the staff are delighted and not confounded when you ask whether they have any vegetarian or vegan options. The chefs in these establishments cook with so much love and passion that their restaurants have become true finds. The hotels take care of everything a food lover could possibly want, bringing vacations back to what they were always supposed to be—a time to relax and enjoy yourself.

What began as a private pursuit grew into the two web portals, www.veggie-hotels.de and www.vegan-welcome.com. Established in 2011, VeggieHotels became the world's first directory of strictly vegetarian and vegan hotels, bed & breakfasts, as well as seminar and health centers. The listing now contains well over 500 hotels around the world. It represents a wide range of accommodations, from vegan surfing camps to five-star hotels, from luxurious Ayurvedic retreats to simple mountain chalets, and from Tuscan country estates to holistic wellness resorts on Bali. There is something for every (travel) preference. We added VeganWelcome in 2015, a hand-picked selection of especially vegan-friendly hotels, including a number of entirely vegan establishments.

The hotels presented in the book are dream destinations for fans of plant-based sustenance—and a whole lot more. They are also highly recommended for anyone interested in a healthy diet and lifestyle as well as sustainable travel. Those of a curious nature, who are open to exploring the world and would like to learn all about vegetarian and vegan gourmet cuisines, will find plenty of insider tips here.

All VeggieHotels share one thing in common: They do not serve any meat or fish, and their menus are one hundred percent vegetarian. Vegans will also find plenty of reasons to enjoy a stay in any VeggieHotel, as all of them also offer vegan options. As a rule, VeggieHoteliers are well prepared to welcome not only vegan guests but also those with food intolerances. Whole foods, celiac diet, clean eating, and raw foods are not foreign concepts here. Instead, these are all perfectly ordinary dietary choices.

More and more establishments whose menus traditionally feature meat and fish are embracing veganism and offering their guests excellent vegan meals alongside their conventional dishes. As a result, we created VeganWelcome as another web portal that lists highly recommended vegan-friendly hotels. The VeganWelcome properties are ideal places for families and friends to stay when not everyone has (yet) developed a passion for strictly vegetarian or vegan menus.

Every hotel presented in this book is unique, with a history entirely its own and often built on an intensely personal dream. In every establishment, guests come to enjoy new, creative, vegetarian, and vegan cuisines that will even satisfy the most selective gourmets.

To help you continue your culinary adventures after your vacation is over, on the following pages the veggie chefs have revealed some of their favorite recipes to try out at home.

And yet the VeggieHotels have much more to offer than just a healthy diet—they provide everything that does a body, mind, and spirit good: from cooking classes and holistic wellness packages to individual health and prevention programs.

We hope that you will enjoy exploring the world of vegetarian and vegan hotels. And if you set foot in a VeggieHotel or VeganWelcome establishment in the near future—inspired by this book, perhaps—have a great time and give your hosts our regards.

WELCOME – GRÜSS GOTT – NAMASTÉ

KAREN KLEIN, THOMAS KLEIN, PETER HAUNERT
FOUNDERS OF VEGGIEHOTELS® & VEGANWELCOME®

 100 % VEGAN

 GLUTEN-FREE MEALS POSSIBLE

 100 % VEGETARIAN

 RAW MEALS AVAILABLE

 VEGAN-FRIENDLY

 100 % CERTIFIED ORGANIC

 100 % VEGAN

 100 % VEGETARISCH

 VEGAN-FREUNDLICH

 GLUTENFREIE SPEISEN MÖGLICH

 ROHKOST-GERICHTE ERHÄLTLICH

 100 % BIO-ZERTIFIZIERT

WARUM VEGGIE?

Zusammen auf Reisen zu gehen war für uns viele Jahre Beruf und Hobby gleichermaßen. Ein Traum, sollte man meinen, doch wir vermissten dennoch etwas Grundsätzliches. Wir hatten es als Reisejournalisten und langjährige Vegetarier unterwegs oftmals nicht leicht mit der Verpflegung – denn was nützen die schönsten Zimmer und der lockende Pool, wenn man im Restaurant auf die Beilagen verwiesen wird?

Eine umfangreiche Recherche brachte dann das Aha-Erlebnis: Es gibt sie! Hotels in denen die Frage nach vegetarischen und veganen Speisen keine Verlegenheit auslöst, sondern Begeisterung. In diesen Häusern wird mit so viel Passion und Liebe gekocht, dass sie zu absoluten Entdeckungen geworden sind. Für Gaumenfreuden ist hier also gesorgt, und der Urlaub wird wieder zu dem, was er sein sollte – eine Zeit zum Genießen und Entspannen.

Aus dem anfangs privaten Anliegen entstanden die beiden Webportale www.veggie-hotels.de und www.vegan-welcome.com – 2011 gründeten wir mit VeggieHotels das weltweit erste Verzeichnis rein vegetarisch-veganer Hotels, Pensionen sowie Seminar- und Gesundheitszentren, welches mittlerweile bereits weit über 500 Häuser rund um den Globus umfasst. Das Angebot ist also groß, vom veganen Surfcamp bis zum Fünfsternehotel, vom luxuriösen Ayurveda-Retreat bis zum einfachen Bergchalet und vom toskanischen Landgut bis zum ganzheitlichen Wellnessresort auf Bali, für jeden (Reise-)Geschmack ist etwas dabei. 2015 folgte VeganWelcome als handverlesene Selektion besonders vegan-freundlicher Hotels, die natürlich auch einige komplett vegane Häuser einschließt.

Die in diesem Buch vorgestellten Hotels sind nicht nur Sehnsuchtsorte für Freunde der pflanzlichen Ernährung, sondern eine echte Empfehlung für alle, denen eine gesunde Ernährungs- und Lebensweise und nachhaltiges Reisen am Herzen liegen. Auch für Neugierige und Weltoffene, die einmal die vegetarisch-vegane Gourmetküche kennenlernen möchten, findet sich hier mancher Geheimtipp.

Eines haben alle VeggieHotels gemeinsam: Es kommen weder Fleisch noch Fisch auf den Tisch, das Speiseangebot ist zu einhundert Prozent vegetarisch. Vegan lebende Menschen werden in allen VeggieHotels ebenfalls glücklich, da immer auch vegane Optionen angeboten werden. Überhaupt sind VeggieHoteliers nicht nur bestens auf vegane Gäste eingestellt, sondern gleichermaßen auf solche mit Lebensmittelunverträglichkeiten. Vollwertkost, Zöliakie-Ernährung, Clean Eating oder Rohkost sind hier keine Fremdwörter, vielmehr handelt es sich um ganz selbstverständliche Ernährungsoptionen.

Immer mehr Häuser, in denen traditionell Fleisch und Fisch auf der Speisekarte stehen, wenden sich der veganen Ernährungsweise zu und bieten ihren Gästen neben ihren konventionellen Speisen eine ausgezeichnete vegane Küche an. Mit VeganWelcome haben wir deshalb folgerichtig ein weiteres Webportal mit empfehlenswerten vegan-freundlichen Hotels geschaffen. Die VeganWelcome-Häuser eignen sich ideal für Familien und Freunde, wenn sich (noch) nicht jeder für rein vegetarische oder vegane Menüs begeistert.

Jedes in diesem Buch vorgestellte Hotel ist ein Unikat, hat seine ganz eigene Geschichte, und oft steckt ein ganz persönlicher Traum dahinter. In allen Häusern kommen Gäste in den Genuss einer neuen, kreativen vegetarischen und veganen Küche, die auch Gourmets zufriedenstellt.

Damit die kulinarischen Urlaubserlebnisse auch zu Hause weitergehen können, verraten die Veggie-Küchenchefs auf den folgenden Seiten noch einige ihrer Lieblingsrezepte zum Nachkochen.

Doch bei den VeggieHotels geht es um mehr als nur Ernährung – alles, was Körper, Geist und Seele gut tut, wird angeboten. Von Kochkursen über ganzheitliche Wellnesspakete bis hin zu individuellen Gesundheits- und Präventionsprogrammen.

Wir hoffen, Sie genießen die Entdeckungsreise durch die Welt der vegetarisch-veganen Hotels und wenn Sie – vielleicht inspiriert von diesem Buch – bald zum ersten Mal den Fuß in ein VeggieHotel oder VeganWelcome-Haus setzen, lassen Sie es sich gut gehen und grüßen Sie recht herzlich von uns.

WELCOME – GRÜSS GOTT – NAMASTÉ

KAREN KLEIN, THOMAS KLEIN, PETER HAUNERT
GRÜNDER VON VEGGIEHOTELS® & VEGANWELCOME®

CAL REIET HOLISTIC RETREAT

SANTANYÍ, MALLORCA

Cal Reiet promises a unique vacation experience—and you can count on it providing a true alternative to the mass tourism otherwise found on the popular Balearic island of Mallorca. Built in 1881 as the summer residence of a prosperous family from Barcelona, this delightful estate is only a few minutes walk from the heart of the picturesque town of Santanyí.

When the current owners, Petra and Henning Bensland, bought the property in 2012 and restored it from the ground up, they started out with clear vision: to create a center for personal growth that simultaneously met the strictest standards of a first-class boutique hotel. However, Cal Reiet is not a classic hotel but rather a lovely oasis dedicated to holistic heath recovery and spiritual development, embedded in a lush Mediterranean garden. The stylish Mediterranean interior of the imposing country manor, with its tasteful décor, radiates a relaxing and uplifting atmosphere.

By combining yoga, meditation, nutrition, and other holistic therapies, the hotel aims to help its guests rediscover who they are inside, recharge their batteries, learn new things, grow as individuals, and return to their everyday lives with renewed energy.

High quality, vegetarian and vegan meals, filled with vitality, are an important part of this goal, food that cleanses the body and reinvigorates it with vibrant health. Many of the ingredients used are therefore harvested daily from the hotel garden or purchased from local farmers.

Cal Reiet is a magnificent holistic retreat, a wellness refuge where mindfulness in body and soul comes before all else.

Cal Reiet verspricht einzigartige Aufenthalte – und kann getrost als Gegenentwurf zum Massentourismus auf der beliebten Baleareninsel Mallorca bezeichnet werden. In nur wenigen Minuten Fußweg vom Zentrum des pittoresken Städtchens Santanyí ist dieses herrliche Anwesen zu erreichen, welches eine wohlhabende Familie aus Barcelona 1881 als Sommerresidenz erbauen ließ.

Als die jetzigen Besitzer Petra und Henning Bensland 2012 das Anwesen kauften und von Grund auf restaurierten, hatten sie eine klare Vision: Sie wollten ein Zentrum für persönliches Wachstum schaffen, das zugleich den höchsten Ansprüchen eines First-Class-Boutiquehotels genügt. Cal Reiet ist jedoch kein klassisches Hotel, vielmehr ist es eine wunderschöne Oase, die sich der ganzheitlichen Genesung und spirituellen Entfaltung widmet, und zwar eingebettet in einen üppigen Mittelmeergarten. Das stilvolle mediterrane Interieur des imposanten Landhauses mit seiner geschmackvollen Dekoration strahlt eine Atmosphäre von Entspannung und Unbeschwertheit aus.

Die Kombination aus Yoga, Meditation, Ernährung und weiteren holistischen Behandlungsformen soll die Gäste dabei unterstützen, sich selbst neu zu entdecken, zu regenerieren, zu lernen und zu wachsen sowie frische Kraft für den Alltag zu schöpfen. Dazu gehört als wichtiger Bestandteil auch eine vitale, vegetarisch-vegane Qualitätsküche, die dem Körper gesunde, reinigende Impulse vermittelt. Viele der verwendeten Zutaten kommen daher erntefrisch aus dem eigenen Garten oder von den Bauern aus der Umgebung. Mit Cal Reiet ist ein prachtvolles Holistic Retreat entstanden, ein Wellnessrefugium, in dem die Achtsamkeit für Körper und Seele über allem steht.

ROOMS: 15
SPECIALTIES: POOL, YOGA, MEDITATION, COOKING CLASSES, ACCESSIBLE FOR DISABLED PEOPLE, HOLISTIC WELLNESS RETREATS

CAL REIET HOLISTIC RETREAT
CARRER DE CAL REIET, 80
07560 SANTANYÍ
SPAIN (SPANIEN)
WWW.CALREIET.COM
+34 971 947 047

ZIMMER: 15
BESONDERHEITEN: POOL, YOGA, MEDITATION, KOCHKURSE, BEHINDERTENGERECHT, GANZHEITLICHE WELLNESSRETREATS

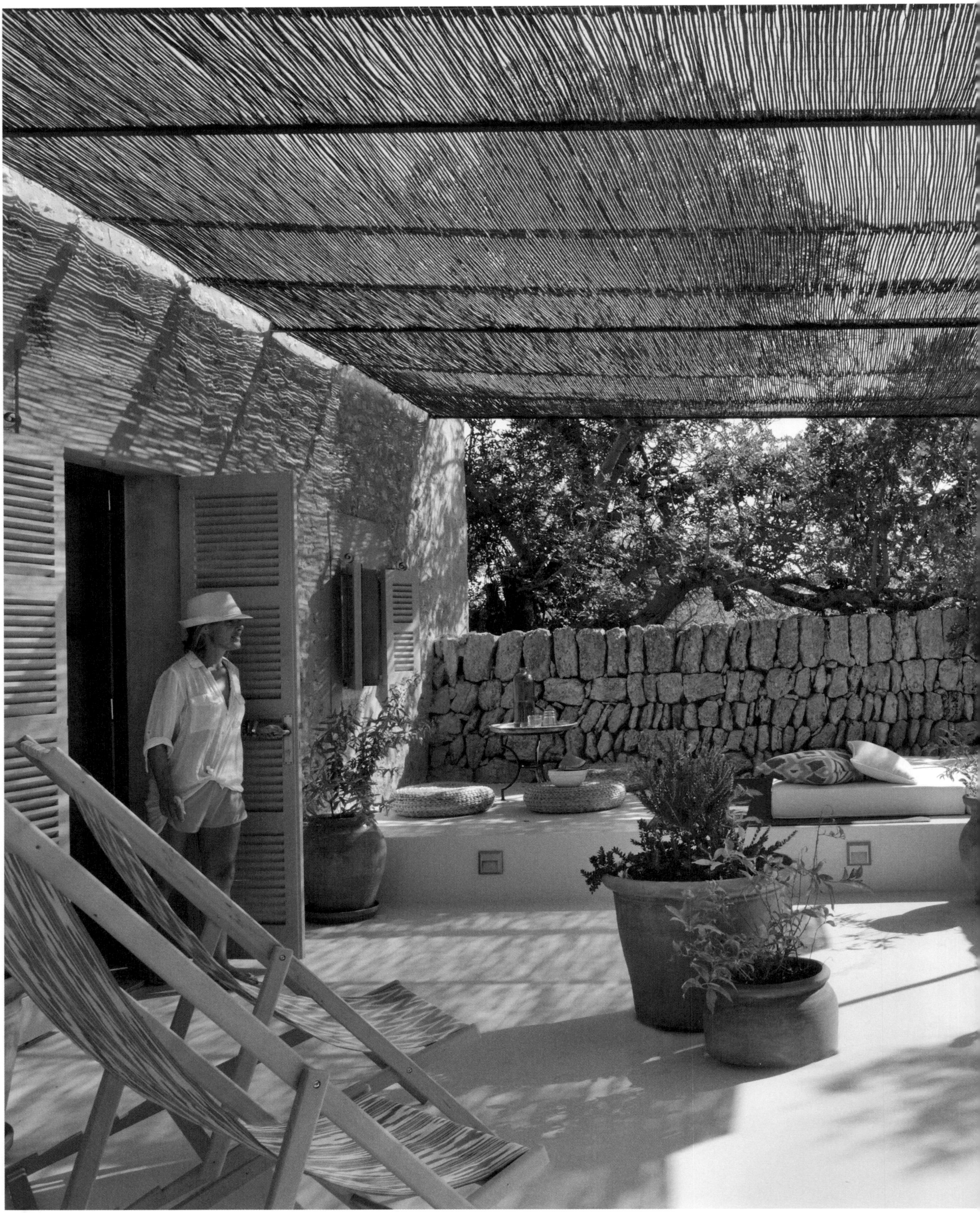

Cal Reiet was modeled after a retreat in Sweden built by a seriously ill Swedish entrepreneur. He was able to cure his illness with alternative therapies, yoga, and mindfulness, and he wished to pass on this life-saving knowledge to other people. Henning Bensland, who owns Cal Reiet, was so deeply moved by this story that he wanted to recreate the idea in a similar location. He ultimately found the ideal place on Mallorca and made his dream come true in 2015.

Vorbild für Cal Reiet war ein Retreat in Schweden, das ein schwer erkrankter schwedischer Unternehmer ins Leben gerufen hatte. Seine Krankheit konnte durch alternative Therapien, Yoga und Achtsamkeit geheilt werden, und diese für ihn lebensrettenden Erkenntnisse wollte er an andere Menschen weitergeben. Henning Bensland, Gastgeber des Cal Reiet, war von der Geschichte so tief beeindruckt, dass er einen ähnlichen Ort schaffen wollte. Auf Mallorca wurde er schließlich fündig, und 2015 wurde sein Traum Realität.

INGREDIENTS
SERVES 4

Carrot Aioli
6 medium carrots, peeled and cut into
  large pieces
3 tbsp/45 ml extra-virgin olive oil
1 large garlic clove, chopped
½ tsp Himalayan salt
½ tsp black pepper

Rice
4 cups/740 g Venere rice, rinsed
7 cups/1.7 l water
3 tbsp/45 ml extra-virgin olive oil
6 spring onions, diced
2 garlic cloves, chopped
2 cups/170 g portobello mushrooms, diced
1 cup/100 g green beans, chopped
½ tsp ground turmeric
½ tsp Tap de Corti paprika
½ tsp Himalayan salt
½ tsp black pepper
1 cup/240 ml coconut milk

ZUTATEN
FÜR 4 PERSONEN

Möhren-Aioli
6 mittelgroße Möhren, geschält und
  in große Stücke geschnitten
3 EL natives Olivenöl extra
1 große Knoblauchzehe, gehackt
½ TL Himalajasalz
½ TL schwarzer Pfeffer

Reis
740 g schwarzer Reis
3 EL natives Olivenöl extra
6 Frühlingszwiebeln, gehackt
2 Knoblauchzehen, gehackt
170 g Champignons, in Würfel geschnitten
100 g grüne Bohnen, gehackt
½ TL gemahlene Kurkuma
½ TL Tap-de-Corti-Paprikapulver
½ TL Himalajasalz
½ TL schwarzer Pfeffer
240 ml Kokosmilch

BLACK VENERE RICE
WITH CARROT AIOLI

SCHWARZER REIS
MIT MÖHREN-AIOLI

METHOD
Carrot Aioli: Boil the carrots until soft, drain, and transfer to a blender. Add the oil, garlic, salt, and pepper and blend until you get an emulsion. Transfer to a bowl and set aside.
Rice: Combine the rice and water in a pot, cover, and bring to a boil. Reduce the heat to low and cook until all the water has been absorbed, the rice is cooked, about 35 minutes. Reserve in a pan.
Heat the oil in a large skillet, add the onions and garlic, and sauté for 5 minutes.
Add the mushrooms and green beans and sauté for 10 to 12 minutes.
Add the turmeric, paprika, salt, and pepper and sauté for 5 more minutes.
Stir in the cooked rice and the coconut milk. Serve with the carrot aioli.

ZUBEREITUNG
Für die Aioli die Möhren in wenig Wasser weich kochen. Dann in ein Sieb abgießen und abtropfen lassen. Die Möhren mit Öl, Knoblauch, Salz und Pfeffer in einem Mixer cremig pürieren. Die Aioli in eine Schüssel füllen und beiseitestellen.
Den Reis in einem Sieb unter fließendem Wasser abspülen, bis das Wasser klar abläuft. Den Reis dann mit 1,7 l Wasser in einem Topf aufkochen und zugedeckt bei schwacher Hitze etwa 35 Minuten garen, bis er das Wasser vollständig aufgenommen hat. Beiseitestellen.
Das Öl in einer großen Pfanne erhitzen. Frühlingszwiebeln und Knoblauch darin 5 Minuten glasig dünsten. Pilze und Bohnen zugeben und 10–12 Minuten mitdünsten. Mit Kurkuma, Paprikapulver, Salz und Pfeffer würzen und 5 Minuten braten.
Gekochten Reis und Kokosmilch einrühren und mit der Möhren-Aioli servieren.

ECOCIRER B&B & ART HOTEL
SÓLLER, MALLORCA

Mallorca in the Balearic Islands has its very own Wild West: it's called Serra de Tramuntana and is a UNESCO World Heritage Site. The mountain range, with its steep serpentine roads, picturesque towns, and countless numbers of spectacular vista points, extends over the island's entire northwest. While tour groups rarely venture into this region, travelers who appreciate sustainable tourism and the unspoiled nature on this side of Mallorca can be found here. Many find their way over the hazardous winding roads that lead from the island's capital of Palma to Sóller, the "town of oranges." Situated in a green valley between tall mountains, Sóller is surrounded by orange groves. Ecocirer Bed & Breakfast and the Art Hotel, two related ecological inns, stand on a narrow side street just outside the busy downtown.

Old Mallorquin town houses, recycled items, along with art and design, combine to create a very special holiday experience. The inn throws away as little as possible, and everything is checked to see whether it can be repurposed and enhance the Ecocirer in slightly modified form. The fresh, organic breakfast with vegan and vegetarian options changes daily. Innkeeper Bárbara is always coming up with new dishes that can be prepared from her home-grown varieties of fruit and vegetables. The hotel doesn't only guarantee culinary diversions. The Ecocirer team is also happy to organize outings for its guests, including special tours all over the island. And if you're looking forward to a fun day at the beach, never fear: An ancient wooden tram runs at a leisurely pace to Port de Sóller, two and a half miles (four kilometers) away, where you can plunge into the blue-green Mediterranean right from the tram stop.

Die Baleareninsel Mallorca hat einen wilden Westen: das UNESCO-Weltnaturerbe Serra de Tramuntana. Die Gebirgskette mit ihren steilen Serpentinenstraßen, malerischen Städtchen und unzähligen spektakulären Aussichtspunkten erstreckt sich über den gesamten Nordwesten der Insel. Pauschalurlauber verirren sich nur selten in diese Gegend, dafür aber Reisende, die sanften Tourismus und die ursprüngliche Seite Mallorcas zu schätzen wissen. Viele führt der Weg über eine der abenteuerlich-kurvigen Straßen von der Inselhauptstadt Palma nach Sóller. Die „Orangenstadt" liegt zwischen hohen Bergen in einem grünen Tal, umgeben von Orangenhainen. Ein wenig abseits des quirligen Zentrums stehen in einer schmalen Seitenstraße die beiden ökologischen Gästehäuser Ecocirer Bed & Breakfast und das dazugehörige Art Hotel.

Hier verbinden sich alte mallorquinische Stadthäuser, recycelte Einzelstücke, sowie Kunst und Design zu einem ganz besonderen Urlaubserlebnis. Es wird so wenig wie möglich weggeworfen sowie jedes einzelne Teil daraufhin überprüft, ob es nicht umfunktioniert und leicht verändert das Ecocirer bereichern kann. Das frische vegan-vegetarische Biofrühstück wechselt täglich sein Gewand: Hotelchefin Bárbara lässt sich immer etwas Neues einfallen, das sich aus den selbst angebauten Obst- und Gemüsesorten zubereiten lässt. Nicht nur kulinarische Abwechslung ist garantiert: Das Team des Ecocirer organisiert für seine Gäste gerne Ausflüge und spezielle Touren über die ganze Insel. Auf Badefreuden muss man ebenso wenig verzichten, wenn man mit einer alten Holztram gemächlich ins vier Kilometer entfernte Port de Sóller fährt, wo man sich direkt von der Straßenbahnhaltestelle ins türkisblaue Mittelmeer stürzen kann.

ROOMS: 8
SPECIALTIES: AYURVEDA, YOGA, PILATES, MEDITATION, COOKING CLASSES, ART CLASSES, CYCLING, HIKING

ECOCIRER B&B & ART HOTEL
CAMÍ DES FOSSARET, 16
07100 SÓLLER
SPAIN (SPANIEN)
WWW.ECOCIRER.COM
+34 672 411 227

ZIMMER: 8
BESONDERHEITEN: AYURVEDA, YOGA, PILATES, MEDITATION, KOCHKURSE, MALKURSE, FAHRRADFAHREN, WANDERN

INGREDIENTS
SERVES 8

Pumpkin Pie Spice
1½ tbsp ground cinnamon
1 tbsp ground ginger
2 tsp ground nutmeg
1 tsp ground allspice
1 tsp ground cloves

Waffles
½ cup/120 ml oat drink
5 tbsp/75 g pumpkin puree
2 tbsp brown sugar
1 tbsp coconut oil, melted
2 tsp powdered egg replacer
  or 1 ripe banana, mashed
1½ cups/180 g all-purpose flour
1 tbsp baking powder
Pinch salt

ZUTATEN
FÜR 8 STÜCK

Pumpkin Pie Spice
1 ½ EL gemahlener Zimt
1 EL gemahlener Ingwer
2 TL gemahlene Muskatnuss
1 TL gemahlener Piment
1 TL gemahlene Gewürznelken

Waffeln
120 ml Haferdrink
75 g Kürbispüree
2 EL Rohrzucker
1 EL Kokosöl, zerlassen
2 TL Ei-Ersatzpulver
180 g Mehl
1 EL Backpulver
Salz

Außerdem
Waffeleisen

PUMPKIN WAFFLES
WITH HOMEMADE PUMPKIN PIE SPICE

KÜRBIS-GEWÜRZWAFFELN
MIT HAUSGEMACHTEM PUMPKIN PIE SPICE

METHOD

Pumpkin Pie Spice: Combine ground cinnamon, ginger, nutmeg, allspice, and cloves in a small bowl.

Waffles: Preheat a waffle iron according to the manufacturer's directions.

In a large bowl, whisk the oat drink, pumpkin puree, sugar, melted oil, and egg replacer together until smooth. Add 1 teaspoon pumpkin pie spice and stir. In a separate bowl, whisk the flour, baking powder, and salt together. Stir the flour mixture into the pumpkin mixture until just combined. (The batter will be thick.)

Spoon some batter into the waffle iron according to the manufacturer's directions and cook until crisp and lightly browned, 3 to 5 minutes. Repeat with the remaining batter. Serve with your favorite toppings.

Tip: This makes about ¼ cup pumpkin pie spice; keep the extra in a small jar, and use for quick breads, lattes, and anything else that calls for a blend of warm spices. If you don't want to make your own spice, you can find it at the store.

ZUBEREITUNG

Für das Pumpkin Pie Spice alle Zutaten in einer kleinen Schüssel mischen.

Für die Waffeln Haferdrink, Kürbispüree, Zucker, Öl und Ei-Ersatzpulver in einer großen Schüssel cremig rühren. 1 TL Pumpkin Pie Spice unterrühren. In einer zweiten Schüssel Mehl, Backpulver und 1 Prise Salz vermischen. Die Mehlmischung in die Kürbismischung einrühren, bis ein dickflüssiger Teig entsteht.

Das Waffeleisen gemäß Gebrauchsanweisung vorheizen. Einen Löffel Teig auf die untere Backfläche geben, das Eisen schließen und die Waffel in 3–5 Minuten knusprig und gold-braun backen. Herausnehmen und mit dem restlichen Teig wiederholen. Die Waffeln nach Belieben garnieren und servieren.

Tipp: Das restliche Pumpkin Pie Spice füllen Sie am besten in ein Schraubglas und würzen damit Lebkuchen, Latte und andere Köstlichkeiten, die nach warm-aromatischen Gewürzen verlangen. Wenn Sie das Pumpkin Pie Spice nicht selbst mischen möchten, verwenden Sie stattdessen einfach Lebkuchengewürz.

KALIYOGA RETREATS

ÓRGIVA, ANDALUSIA

When the pace of everyday life keeps speeding up and you have lost the ability to unwind, it can do you a lot of good to withdraw to an oasis of peace and tranquility. Kaliyoga is exactly this kind of oasis—a retreat in Andalusia, surrounded by the striking mountain landscape of the Sierra Nevada. You will discover picturesque, white mountain villages here, along with vineyards, forests, enchanting valleys, waterfalls, clear streams, and 325 days of sunshine per year. Best of all, the region has not yet been overrun by mass tourism. All of these attributes go a long way toward helping you quiet the never ending merry-go-round of thoughts in your head, to take deep breaths, and to embark on a journey of self-discovery, perhaps by taking long walks or mountain hikes. Not to mention the authentic Kaliyoga retreats, where you will find first-rate yoga classes and healing treatments.

A stay at this hotel has more to offer than just a vacation with a bit of yoga and meditation thrown in. For many people, the hotel is where they go through life-changing experiences and form life-long friendships with help from the passionate, highly trained staff, who offer every guest entirely personalized care and advice. The chic hotel itself takes care of the rest, with its fabulous location and mountain views, and the cleansing meals served by the Kaliyoga kitchen staff, with plenty of raw superfoods. At the end of your stay, you will return home with your batteries recharged.

Instead of sleeping in one of the lovingly furnished rooms, you also have the option of spending a night outdoors in a traditional Indian teepee—and feel free to turn off your phone.

Wenn die Geschwindigkeit des täglichen Lebens stetig zunimmt und Abschalten kaum mehr möglich ist, dann tut es gut, sich in eine Oase der Stille und des Friedens zurückziehen zu können. Genau so eine Oase ist Kaliyoga – ein Retreat in Andalusien, eingerahmt von der beeindruckenden Berglandschaft der Sierra Nevada. Pittoreske weiße Bergdörfer entdeckt man hier, aber auch Weinberge, Wälder, zauberhafte Täler, Wasserfälle, klare Flüsse und 325 Sonnentage im Jahr – die Region ist zudem noch nicht vom Massentourismus überrannt worden. Das alles trägt positiv dazu bei, das individuelle Gedankenkarussell anzuhalten, tief durchzuatmen und zu sich zu kommen, etwa bei langen Spaziergängen oder Bergwanderungen und natürlich nicht zuletzt bei den authentischen Kaliyoga-Retreats mit seinen Yogaklassen und Heilanwendungen auf allerhöchstem Niveau.

Ein Aufenthalt hier ist mehr als ein Urlaub mit ein wenig Yoga und Meditation, für viele Menschen bedeutet er, lebensverändernde Erfahrungen zu machen und lebenslange Freundschaften zu schließen. Dafür sorgt das leidenschaftliche, hochqualifizierte Team, das jeden Gast ganz persönlich berät und betreut. Die fantastische Lage des stilvollen Hauses mit Blick auf die Berge und das reinigende Essen der Kaliyoga-Küche mit viel Rohkost-Superfood tun ihr Übriges. Am Ende kehrt man mit aufgeladenen Batterien heim.

Wer mag, kann nicht nur in einem der liebevoll eingerichteten Zimmer, sondern auch draußen im traditionellen Indianertipi schlafen – und das Mobiltelefon darf gerne mal ausgeschaltet bleiben.

ROOMS: 10
SPECIALTIES: SWIMMING POOL, YOGA, HEALTH TREATMENTS, MASSAGES, MEDITATION, COOKING CLASSES, HIKING

KALIYOGA RETREATS SPAIN
LAS BARRERAS
18400 ÓRGIVA
SPAIN (SPANIEN)
WWW.KALIYOGA.COM
+34 858 995 890

ZIMMER: 10
BESONDERHEITEN: SCHWIMMBAD, YOGA, HEILANWENDUNGEN, MASSAGEN, MEDITATION, KOCHKURSE, WANDERN

HOTEL AÑATERVE

VALLEHERMOSO, LA GOMERA

More than twenty years ago, Amala and Herman, the owners of Hotel Añaterve, discovered a long-forgotten and abandoned building situated high above the valley of Vallehermoso (which fittingly means "beautiful valley" in Spanish). They began to dream of the possibilities offered by this location, marveling at the fantastic views it offered of the village, valley, and ocean. They recognized that the building was in a terrific spot on the magical island of La Gomera thanks to its central location between the warmer southern region and the green northern region with its lush vegetation. They simply fell in love with the place. Following a careful renovation, the family-run hotel is now a place where guests can feel right at home. It also happens to be a perfect starting point for guests to explore the mountainous island of La Gomera, one of Spain's Canary Islands. La Gomera is a green oasis with rugged cliffs, volcanic mountains, and cloud forests. With more than 250 miles (400 kilometers) of trails, it is a paradise for hikers. In addition, the island is home to Garajonay National Park, a UNESCO World Heritage Site filled with numerous indigenous plants.

The hotel's five lovingly decorated rooms blend authentic style with modern comforts—and all feature an ocean view. In the restaurant, an old wine press dating back to 1900 pays tribute to the original use of the room as the "casa de vino." Today the room accommodates guests who come to enjoy the vegetarian and vegan specialties. Afterwards guests can either relax on the rooftop terrace or in the flower-filled garden, practice yoga, or set out on an extended hike on the most exotic of the Canary Islands. Amala and Herman run Hotel Añaterve as a place that respects what the island stands for: nature, tranquility, and rugged beauty.

Als Amala und Herman, die Betreiber des Hotels Añaterve, vor über 20 Jahren das längst verlassene und vergessene Gebäude hoch über dem Tal von Vallehermoso („schönes Tal") entdeckten, begannen sie zu träumen. Sie sahen die Möglichkeiten, die dieser Ort bot, seine fantastische Aussicht über Dorf, Tal und Meer, seine großartige Lage auf der magischen Insel La Gomera, zentral zwischen dem wärmeren Süden und dem grünen Norden mit seiner reichen Vegetation. Sie hatten sich in den Ort verliebt. Heute ist das mit viel Hingabe renovierte, familiär geführte Hotel ein Platz an dem man sich zu Hause fühlen kann. Gleichzeitig ist es der perfekte Ausgangspunkt, die bergige Kanareninsel zu entdecken – eine grüne Oase mit schroffen Klippen, Vulkanbergen und Nebelwäldern. Ein Paradies für Wanderer mit über 400 Kilometern Wanderpfaden und dem Garajonay-Nationalpark, einem UNESCO-Weltnaturerbe, welches viele indigene Pflanzen beheimatet.

Die fünf liebevoll gestalteten Zimmer bieten eine Mischung aus authentischem Stil und modernem Komfort – und haben allesamt Meerblick. Im Restaurant zeugt die alte Weinpresse von 1900 noch von der ursprünglichen Verwendung des Raumes als *Casa de vino*. Hier genießt man heute vegetarische und vegane Spezialitäten. Wer mag, entspannt anschließend auf der Dachterrasse oder im blumenreichen Garten, praktiziert Yoga oder bricht zu einer ausgedehnten Wanderung über die exotischste Kanareninsel auf. Amala und Herman führen ihr Hotel Añaterve als einen Ort, der dazu passt, wofür die Insel steht: Natur, Ruhe und schroffe Schönheit.

ROOMS: 5
SPECIALTIES: HIKING TRAILS DIRECTLY FROM THE HOTEL, YOGA, BIKE RENTAL, LIBRARY

HOTEL AÑATERVE
CALLE LA RODADERA S/N
38840 VALLEHERMOSO
CANARY ISLANDS | SPAIN (SPANIEN)
WWW.ANATERVE.COM
+34 922 800 330

ZIMMER: 5
BESONDERHEITEN: WANDERWEGE DIREKT VORM HOTEL, YOGA, FAHRRADVERLEIH, BIBLIOTHEK

VEGAN LIFE BEACH BREAKS

DÉNIA, ALICANTE

Vegan Life Beach Breaks welcomes everyone—human, dog, and chicken—and all other animals too, of course. Some of them even live here, such as the dogs named Happy and Monkey and the hens who go by Pili and Mili, who enjoy receiving visitors and don't mind being petted. Tanya, the charming innkeeper, is truly multi-talented: she's a mindfulness and happiness coach, an animal rights activist, a dietary consultant, and a trained raw foods chef. The food here is therefore one hundred percent vegan, much of it even raw vegan. Tanya is happy to offer raw vegan cooking workshops to anyone who's interested.

Although the popular tourist town of Dénia is right nearby, the hotel's garden with its ocean view is the perfect place to spend an idle morning or afternoon. A marvelous sandy beach is only a few steps away—chirping birds and the crash of ocean waves guaranteed. In good weather—and the weather here is almost always good—dinner is served and enjoyed in the garden. Once a week, innkeeper Eduardo usually prepares his vegan version of paella *el fuego*, Spain's national dish.

During the mild winter months, Vegan Life Beach Breaks organizes the "University of Happyland," which combines seminars and classes on a healthy diet, mindfulness, and meditation with delicious food.

Im Vegan Life Beach Breaks ist jeder gern gesehen – egal ob Mensch, Hund oder Huhn. Und alle anderen Tiere natürlich auch. Einige leben sowieso schon hier, wie etwa die Hunde Happy und Monkey und die Hennen Pili und Mili, die sich über Besuch und ein paar Streicheleinheiten freuen. Die charmante Gastgeberin Tanya ist ein echtes Multitalent: Achtsamkeits- und Glückscoach, Tierrechtsaktivistin, Ernährungsberaterin und ausgebildete Rohkostköchin. Selbstverständlich ist die Verpflegung daher auch zu einhundert Prozent vegan und häufig sogar rohvegan. Für Interessierte bietet Tanya mit Vergnügen rohvegane Kochworkshops an. Obwohl der beliebte Touristenort Dénia gleich in der Nähe ist, lädt der eigene Garten, mit Blick auf das Meer, wunderbar zum Faulenzen ein. Und der herrliche Sandstrand liegt nur wenige Schritte entfernt – Vogelgezwitscher und Meeresrauschen gibt es garantiert dazu. Das Abendessen wird bei gutem Wetter – und das Wetter ist hier fast immer gut – im Garten serviert und genossen. Üblicherweise bereitet Gastgeber Eduardo einmal in der Woche seine vegane Version des spanischen Nationalgerichts Paella *el fuego* zu.

In den milden Wintermonaten veranstaltet das Vegan Life Beach Breaks die sogenannte University of Happyland, bei der Seminare und Kurse zu gesunder Ernährung, Achtsamkeit, Yoga und Meditation mit köstlichem Essen kombiniert werden.

ROOMS: 6
SPECIALTIES: VEGAN ROOM FACILITIES, YOGA, MEDITATION, COOKING CLASSES, KAYAK AND BIKE RENTAL, SEMINARS ON MINDFULNESS

VEGAN LIFE BEACH BREAKS
16 CALLE MUSSOLA
03700 LES MARINES, DÉNIA
SPAIN (SPANIEN)
WWW.VEGANLIFEBEACHBREAKS.COM
+34 634 354 892

ZIMMER: 6
BESONDERHEITEN: VEGANE RAUM-AUSSTATTUNG, YOGA, MEDITATION, KOCHKURSE, KAYAK- UND FAHRRAD-VERLEIH, MINDFULNESS SEMINARE

VELONA'S JUNGLE LUXURY SUITES

FLORENCE, TUSCANY

No one who stays at Velona's Jungle needs to fear encountering wild animals. It is the furniture, artworks, and décor of the elaborately furnished rooms that create a jungle atmosphere—including rainwater showers in the bathrooms. Leopard-patterned seat upholstery, floral decorations, and animal portraits on the walls bring the wilderness into the elegant and luxuriously furnished suites. The stylish boutique hotel is situated right in the historic heart of Florence, one of Italy's most glamorous cities. It is a designer oasis—packed with art objects that the family patriarch and art dealer, Pasquale Velona, has been collecting on his travels throughout Europe since the 1950s. The artworks perfectly complement the antique and contemporary furniture from the owner's gallery. The hotel is a visual feast for the eyes—of special fascination for any traveler who is always on the lookout for unusual and unforgettable lodgings.

Velona's Jungle also offers warm hospitality, a bountiful vegetarian and vegan breakfast made from local organic ingredients, and innkeeper Veronica's tireless efforts to make everything sustainable can be seen on all levels. She will also be happy to give environmentally conscious guests the best tips on how to reach the Renaissance city on foot or explore it by bike, and where they can find the best local products and antique treasures. Incidentally, the hotel also extends a warm welcome to four-legged guests—but if you plan to bring along an elephant or tiger, best let Veronica know ahead of time.

Angst vor wilden Tieren braucht im Velona's Jungle niemand haben. Dschungelgefühl vermitteln eher Möbel, Kunst und Dekoration in den aufwendig gestalteten Räumlichkeiten – Regenwaldduschen in den Bädern inklusive. Leopardenmuster auf Sesseln, florale Dekors und Tierportraits an den Wänden bringen die Wildnis in die anspruchsvoll und luxuriös ausgestatteten Suiten. Das stylishe Boutiquehotel liegt mitten im historischen Zentrum von Florenz, einer der glanzvollsten Städte Italiens, und ist eine wahre Designeroase – vollgepackt mit Kunstobjekten, die der Familienpatriarch und Kunsthändler Pasquale Velona auf seinen Reisen durch Europa seit den 1950er-Jahren gesammelt hat. Die Kunstgegenstände korrespondieren hervorragend mit den antiken und zeitgenössischen Möbeln aus der Galerie des Besitzers. Das Haus ist ein visueller Augenschmaus, der vor allem Reisende fasziniert, die immer auf der Suche nach ungewöhnlichen und unvergesslichen Unterkünften sind.

Zu Velona's Jungle gehört auch ganz selbstverständlich die herzliche Gastfreundlichkeit, ein üppiges vegetarisch-veganes Frühstück aus lokalen Biozutaten und das große Bemühen der Gastgeberin Veronica um Nachhaltigkeit auf allen Ebenen. Von ihr erhalten Besucher auch die besten Tipps, wie man die Renaissancestadt umweltfreundlich zu Fuß oder auf dem Rad erobert und wo man die besten lokalen Produkte und alten Schätze entdeckt. Übrigens sind tierische Gäste ebenfalls herzlich willkommen – das Mitbringen eines Elefanten oder Tigers sollte man aber besser vorher mit Veronica besprechen.

ROOMS: 4 SUITES
SPECIALTIES: CENTRAL LOCATION, CONSERVATION OF RESOURCES, CYCLING

VELONA'S JUNGLE LUXURY SUITES
VIA MONTEBELLO 86
50123 FIRENZE
ITALY (ITALIEN)
WWW.VELONASJUNGLE.COM
+39 055 27 41 536

ZIMMER: 4 SUITEN
BESONDERHEITEN: ZENTRALE LAGE, RESSOURCENSCHONUNG, FAHRRADFAHREN

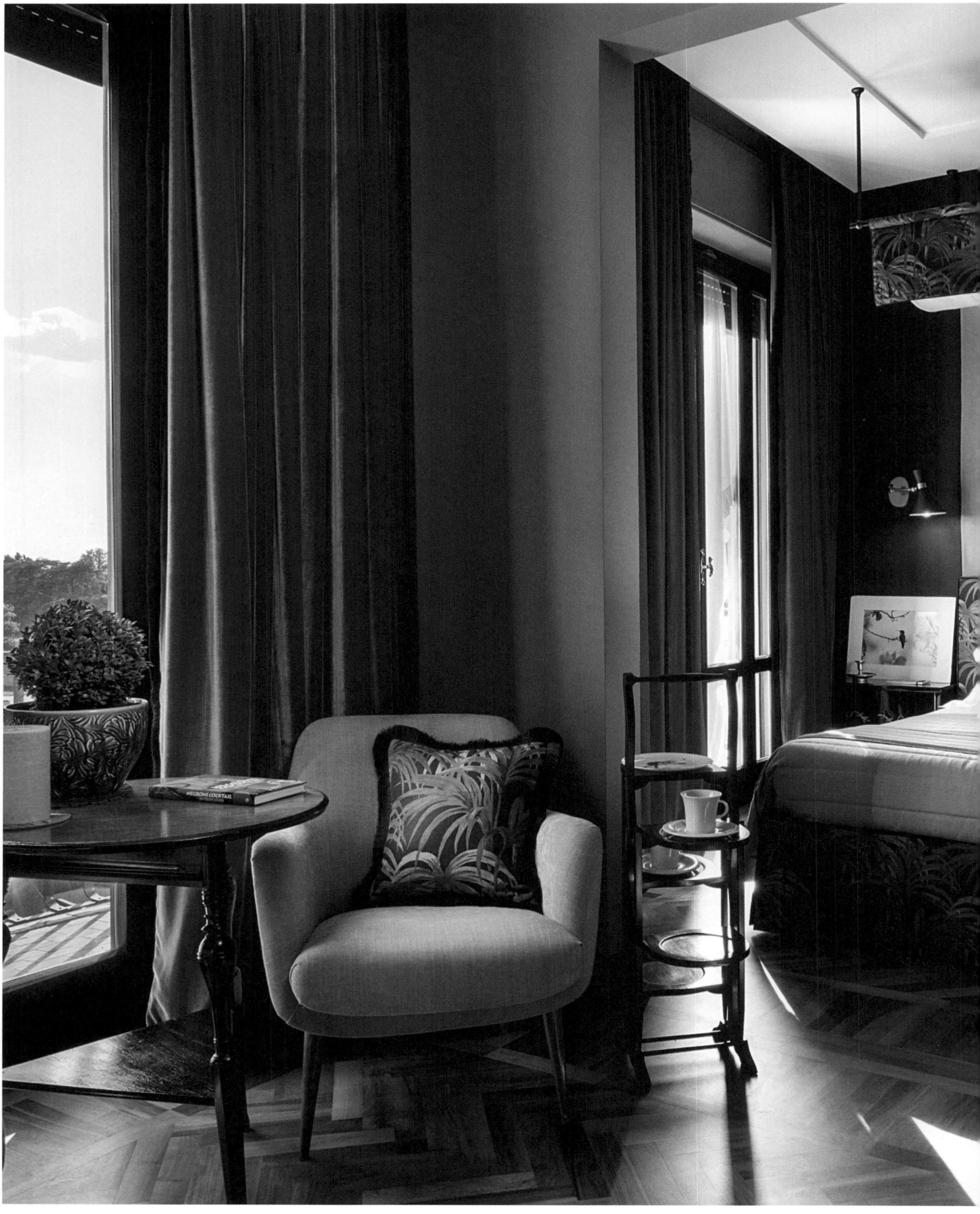
NEGRONI COCKTAIL

The luxurious suites in Velona's Jungle are unique and absolutely spectacular. Countless numbers of art objects that owner Veronica's grandfather brought home from trips to Rome, Naples, Paris, and Vienna, combine with antique furniture, contemporary art, fabrics, and decorative elements created by Veronica's favorite designers to form an ambience that you just can't stop admiring. Each of the spacious suites is a work of art all its own.

Die luxuriösen Suiten im Velona's Jungle sind wahrlich spektakulär und einzigartig. Zahllose Kunstobjekte, die der Großvater von Betreiberin Veronica aus Rom, Neapel, Paris oder Wien mitbrachte, sorgen zusammen mit antiken Möbeln, zeitgenössischer Kunst, Stoffen und Dekorationselementen von Veronicas Lieblingsdesignern für ein Ambiente, von dem man einfach nicht genug bekommt. Jede der großzügigen Suiten ist ein Kunstwerk für sich.

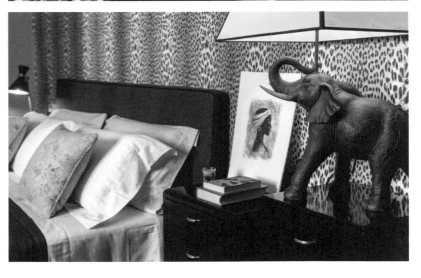

CRUMBLE
WITH PEACHES AND THYME

PFIRSICH-THYMIAN-CRUMBLE
MIT HAFER-NUSS-STREUSELN

"This fresh and easy recipe was created for us by Chiara Gianelli, nutritional advisor at *amatterofnourishment.com*. It is 100 percent vegan and contains only the natural sugar of the fruit. The seeds and spices, like thyme and fennel, are typical of Tuscany; no ingredient in this recipe had to travel thousands of miles to arrive at our table!" *Veronica, proprietor of Velona's Jungle*

„Dieses frische, leicht zuzubereitende Rezept hat Chiara Gianelli (Ernährungsberaterin bei *amatterofnourishment.com*) für uns entwickelt. Es ist vegan und enthält nur den natürlichen Fruchtzucker des Obstes. Die verwendeten Nüsse, Kerne, Samen und Gewürze sind typisch für die Toskana. Keine Zutat für diesen Crumble musste Tausende von Kilometern reisen, um auf unseren Teller zu gelangen."
Veronica, Besitzerin von Velona's Jungle

INGREDIENTS
SERVES 4 TO 5

Crumble

1½ cups/120 g rolled oats (gluten-free
  if needed)
⅔ cup/80 g walnuts, finely chopped
3 tbsp whole-grain spelt flour
2 tbsp pumpkin seeds, finely chopped
1½ tbsp extra-virgin olive oil
Pinch salt
7–8 tbsp/105–120 ml lukewarm water

Filling

3 ripe peaches
1 tbsp extra-virgin olive oil
1 tbsp chopped fresh thyme
  or 1 tsp dried thyme
1 tsp fennel seeds, crushed
Handful of strawberries, hulled and
  chopped (optional)
Juice of ½ lemon

ZUTATEN
FÜR 4–5 PERSONEN

Streusel

120 g zarte Haferflocken (Kleinblatt,
  nach Belieben glutenfrei)
80 g Walnusskerne, fein gehackt
3 EL Vollkornmehl
2 EL Kürbiskerne, fein gehackt
1 ½ EL natives Olivenöl extra
Salz

Crumble

3 reife Pfirsiche
1 EL natives Olivenöl extra
1 EL frisch gehackter Thymian
  oder 1 TL getrockneter
1 EL Fenchelsamen, zerstoßen
1 Handvoll Erdbeeren, entkelcht
  und gehackt (nach Belieben)
Saft von ½ Zitrone

METHOD

Crumble: Preheat the oven to 350°F/180°C. Line a rimmed baking sheet with parchment paper. In a bowl, combine the oats, walnuts, flour, pumpkin seeds, 1½ tablespoons of the oil, and the salt. Add the water slowly, mixing with your hands and adding just enough water so that the mixture holds together when pressed but doesn't form one big clump. Spread into an even layer on the baking sheet and bake until dry and golden brown, 15 to 20 minutes, stirring once or twice. (Keep an eye on the mixture, since it tends to burn easily.)

Filling: While the crumble is baking, wash the peaches, pit them, and chop them into large chunks, leaving the skins on. Heat the oil in a large skillet over medium heat, add the thyme and fennel seeds, and cook for a few seconds until fragrant. Add the peaches and cook for 3 to 4 minutes, stirring gently. Add the strawberries, if desired, and cook for about 30 seconds, just until they release their juices but are not cooked. Off the heat, add the lemon juice and stir to combine. Add the crumble mixture and let cool completely before serving.

Tips: You can eat this for breakfast or as a snack, served at room temperature. If you'd like to, add some extra fresh fruit or a dollop of plant-based yogurt. When peaches are not in season, use pears for a delicious alternative.

ZUBEREITUNG

Für die Streusel den Backofen auf 180 °C vorheizen, ein tiefes Backblech mit Backpapier belegen. Haferflocken, Nüsse, Mehl, Kürbiskerne, Öl und 1 Prise Salz in einer Schüssel mischen. Dann alles mit den Händen verkneten und dabei langsam 105–120 ml lauwarmes Wasser dazugießen, bis die Masse zu Streuseln zusammenhält. Die Streusel gleichmäßig auf dem Blech verteilen und im Ofen in 15–20 Minuten goldbraun backen. Dabei ein- bis zweimal durchrühren, damit die Streusel nicht verbrennen.

Inzwischen für den Crumble die Pfirsiche waschen, entsteinen und in große Stücke schneiden. Das Öl bei mittlerer Hitze in einer Pfanne erhitzen. Thymian und Fenchelsamen darin einige Sekunden rösten, bis sie anfangen zu duften. Die Pfirsiche zugeben und 3–4 Minuten braten, dabei vorsichtig rühren. Nach Belieben die Erdbeeren zufügen und etwa 30 Sekunden mitbraten, bis ihr Saft austritt. Die Pfanne vom Herd nehmen und den Zitronensaft unter die Früchte heben. Die Früchte in vier bis fünf Schälchen verteilen, die Streusel daraufgeben und den Crumble vor dem Servieren vollständig auskühlen lassen.

Tipp: Servieren Sie den Crumble mit Zimmertemperatur zum Frühstück oder als Snack zwischendurch. Auch mit etwas frischem Obst oder einem Klecks veganem Joghurt macht er sich hervorragend. Außerhalb der Pfirsichsaison schmeckt er mit Birnen sehr köstlich.

I PINI BIOTIQUE WINERY

SAN GIMIGNANO, TUSCANY

Rolling green hills, ancient cities, Mediterranean cypresses as tall as a house, and vineyards steeped in tradition combine with picturesque beaches and coastal towns to create the utmost in desirable travel destinations: Tuscany. For many Italy fans, the region is the epitome of vacation, culture, and leisure. The little town of San Gimignano, dubbed "Medieval Manhattan" because of its many towers, is not only one of Tuscany's most representative locations but has also been a UNESCO World Heritage Site since 1990.

The biodynamic and vegan i pini agriturismo and vineyard stands on a hill less than 1.2 miles (two kilometers) from downtown, surrounded by cypresses and with a priceless view of San Gimignano. The historic villa was carefully restored in typical Tuscan style and now welcomes its guests with vegan, organic agriturismo hospitality. Sustainability was a top priority during the renovations. The mattresses are biodegradable, the toiletries in the rooms are completely vegan, the linens are washed only with organic products, and guests will find all kinds of sweet and salty treats made from regional ingredients for breakfast. You can enjoy Tuscany with all your senses here. The vegan wines as well as the premium-quality olive oil and vegetables, all from the own garden, delight your palate, while the perfume of oranges and cypresses tickles your nose and your eyes take in the broad expanse of the hilly landscape that stretches to the famous towers of San Gimignano. Whether you splash about comfortably in the hotel's salt water pool, enjoy the magical light, or explore the region on foot or a bike, you won't be able to get enough of enchanting Tuscany!

Sanfte grüne Hügel, uralte Städte, haushohe Säulenzypressen und traditionsreiche Weinberge stehen zusammen mit malerischen Stränden und Küstenorten für eine absolute Sehnsuchtsregion: die Toskana. Für viele Italienliebhaber der Inbegriff von Urlaub, Kultur und Muße. Und das Städtchen San Gimignano, das dank seiner vielen Türme auch gerne „Manhattan des Mittelalters" genannt wird, ist nicht nur eines der Aushängeschilder der Region, sondern seit 1990 auch UNESCO-Weltkulturerbe.

Keine zwei Kilometer vom Zentrum der Stadt entfernt, liegt das biodynamisch und vegan geführte Agriturismo und Weingut i pini auf einem Hügel, umrahmt von Zypressen und mit unbezahlbarem Blick auf San Gimignano. Die historische Villa wurde behutsam im typischen toskanischen Stil restauriert und heißt nun seine Gäste als veganes Bio-Agriturismo willkommen. Besonderes Augenmerk wurde bei den Umbauten auf Nachhaltigkeit gelegt. Die Matratzen sind ökologisch abbaubar, die Kosmetikprodukte auf den Zimmern konsequent vegan, die Bettwäsche wird nur mit Bioprodukten gewaschen – und zum Frühstück erwarten den Gast allerlei süße und salzige Köstlichkeiten aus regionalen Zutaten. Hier kann man die Toskana mit allen Sinnen genießen. Die hauseigenen veganen Weine sowie hochwertiges Bio-Olivenöl und Gemüse aus eigenem Anbau erfreuen den Gaumen, während einem der Duft von Orangen und Zypressen in die Nase steigt und die Augen über die hügelige Weite zu den berühmten Türmen von San Gimignano wandern. Egal, ob man sich im Salzwasserpool gemütlich treiben lässt, das märchenhafte Licht genießt oder die Gegend zu Fuß oder mit dem Fahrrad erkunden will: Mehr Toskana geht nicht!

ROOMS: 11 ROOMS & SUITES
SPECIALTIES: SALTWATER POOL, IN-HOUSE WINE CRAFTING, WINE TASTING, CONSERVATION OF RESOURCES (E.G. SOLAR POWER, RAINWATER CONSERVATION), KIDS AGE 12 ALLOWED

AGRITURISMO I PINI
LOC. SANTA MARGHERITA 37
53037 SAN GIMIGNANO
ITALY (ITALIEN)
WWW.IPINITOSCANA.COM
+39 0577 940 650

ZIMMER: 11 ZIMMER & SUITEN
BESONDERHEITEN: SALZWASSER-POOL, HAUSEIGENE WEINKELTEREI, WEINVERKOSTUNG, RESSOURCEN-SCHONUNG (U.A. SOLARENERGIE, REGENWASSERAUFFANGSTATION), KINDER AB 12 JAHREN ERLAUBT

FATTORIA SAN MARTINO

MONTEPULCIANO, TUSCANY

"Nature is a powerful magician and a wise healer. All vital energy comes from her and her fruits," say Karin and Antonio, the innkeepers of Fattoria San Martino. For more than ten years, they have been resolutely growing biodynamic produce in the fattoria's fields, and their vegetarian/vegan restaurant, Al N°3 Cucina di Verdure, serves meals made entirely of seasonal ingredients grown on the premises or nearby farms. Even the pasta so popular in Italy is made by hand from home-grown grain. Karin cooks with a great deal of devotion and expertise and serves meals in the restaurant, with its innovative interior design, or in the secluded garden, with its wonderful panoramic view of Tuscany's beautiful nature.

Not only can you get a good meal here, but you can also sleep soundly—in spacious rooms, furnished with natural materials, on the upper floor of the villa, which was renovated according to organic principles. Handmade decorations and furniture display gorgeous details wherever you look—it therefore comes as no surprise that Karin was once a fashion designer and continues to practice this profession today. The innkeepers would like to give their guests the opportunity to feel one with nature, to gain inspiring insight into the healthy relationship between people and the environment, to touch, smell, and enjoy vegetables, herbs, and fruits they planted themselves. It's hard to believe that the vibrant tourist city of Montepulciano lies waiting only ten minutes away, while Florence and Rome are also close enough for a day trip.

„Die Natur ist ein mächtiger Magier und ein weiser Heiler; alle Energie kommt von ihr und ihren Früchten", so die Gastgeber der Fattoria San Martino, Karin und Antonio. Die Felder der Fattoria bewirtschaften sie daher auch seit über zehn Jahren konsequent biodynamisch, und selbstverständlich werden in ihrem vegetarisch-veganen Restaurant Al N°3 Cucina di Verdure nur saisonale Zutaten aus dem eigenen Anbau oder der Umgebung verwendet. Sogar die in Italien so beliebte Pasta wird hier aus eigens angebautem Getreide handgemacht. Die Hausherrin kocht mit viel Hingabe und Expertise, serviert wird anschließend im originell eingerichteten Restaurant oder im lauschigen Garten, mit fantastischem Rundumblick in die schöne Natur der Toskana.

Und es lässt sich hier nicht nur gut essen, sondern auch ganz hervorragend schlafen – in großzügig und natürlich gestalteten Zimmern im Obergeschoss der nach biologischen Grundsätzen renovierten Villa. Wunderschöne Details, wohin man schaut, handgemachte Dekoration und Möbel – dass Karin auch Designerin ist, überrascht nicht. Die Gastgeber möchten ihren Besuchern die Möglichkeit geben, Naturverbundenheit zu spüren, inspirierende Einblicke in eine gesunde Beziehung zwischen Mensch und Umwelt zu gewinnen und selbst gepflanztes Gemüse, Kräuter und Früchte zu berühren, zu riechen und zu genießen. Kaum zu glauben, dass nur zehn Minuten entfernt die lebhafte Touristenstadt Montepulciano auf einen Besuch wartet, aber auch Florenz und Rom sind nicht zu weit für einen Ausflug.

ROOMS: 4
SPECIALTIES: ECOLOGICAL SWIMMING POND, COOKING CLASSES, ORGANIC FARMING, (E-)BIKE RENTAL, DYEING CLASSES WITH HERBS AND FLOWERS

FATTORIA SAN MARTINO
VIA MARTIENA, 3
53045 MONTEPULCIANO
ITALY (ITALIEN)
WWW.FATTORIASANMARTINO.IT
+39 0578 717463

ZIMMER: 4
BESONDERHEITEN: NATUR-BADETEICH, KOCHKURSE, BIODYNAMISCHE BEWIRT-SCHAFTUNG, (E-)FAHRRADVERLEIH, FÄRBEKURSE MIT KRÄUTERN UND BLUMEN

CHICKPEA OMELET
WITH CREAMED CARROT AND SPINACH

KICHERERBSEN-OMELETT
MIT MÖHRENCREME UND SPINAT

The chickpea flour needs to be hydrated for at least 4 hours ahead of preparation.

Das Kichererbsenmehl muss mindestens 4 Stunden vor der Zubereitung quellen und trocknen.

INGREDIENTS
SERVES 4

ZUTATEN
FÜR 4 PERSONEN

Creamed Carrot
3 tbsp extra-virgin olive oil, plus extra to taste
1 onion, chopped
1 medium potato, peeled and chopped
1¼ tbsp/20 g fresh ginger, minced
4 large carrots, peeled and chopped
Salt and pepper
10 lemon verbena leaves, cut in thin strips

Möhrencreme
3 EL natives Olivenöl extra, plus mehr zum Abschmecken
1 Zwiebel, gehackt
1 mittelgroße Kartoffel, geschält und gehackt
20 g frisch geriebener Ingwer
4 große Möhren, geschält und gehackt
Salz, Pfeffer
10 Blätter Zitronenverbene, fein geschnitten

Omelet
1 cup/115 g chickpea flour, combined with 1½ cups/350 ml water and left to rest at least 4 hours or up to overnight
5 tbsp/75 ml extra-virgin olive oil
5 tbsp/20 g chopped fresh parsley
Salt and pepper

Omelett
5 EL natives Olivenöl extra, plus mehr zum Beträufeln
115 g Kichererbsenmehl, mindestens 4 Stunden oder über Nacht in 350 ml Wasser eingeweicht
5 EL frisch gehackte Petersilie
Salz, Pfeffer

Spinach
7 oz/200 g spinach
1 garlic clove, chopped
1 tbsp extra-virgin olive oil
Pinch salt

Extra-virgin olive oil

Spinat
200 g Spinat
1 Knoblauchzehe, gehackt
1 EL natives Olivenöl extra
Salz

natives Olivenöl extra zum Servieren

METHOD

Creamed carrot: Heat the oil in a large saucepan over medium heat; add the onion, potato, and ginger and cook until softened. Add the carrots and stir well. Reduce the heat to low and cook, stirring in water as necessary to keep the vegetables moist, until all are completely softened. Whisk in salt, pepper, and additional oil to taste. The mixture should be creamy; if it is too liquid, continue to heat gently on the stove and keep whisking. Add the lemon verbena leaves, cover, and remove from the heat.

Omelet: Heat the oven to 390°F/200°C. While the carrot mixture is cooking, add 2½ tablespoons of the oil and the parsley to the chickpea flour mixture and stir to combine. Season with salt and pepper to taste. Line a 7 by 7 inch/20 x 15 cm baking dish with parchment paper, grease with the remaining 2½ tablespoons oil, and pour the chickpea mixture into the dish. Bake for 5 to 10 minutes. Let cool completely and cut the omelet into squares. Do not turn the oven off.

Spinach: While the omelet is cooling, cook the spinach in boiling water for about 3 minutes and then quickly place it in cold water. Let cool, drain it thoroughly, and combine it in a dish with the garlic, olive oil and salt.

To assemble: Drizzle the omelets with a drop of oil and heat in the oven for 5 minutes. For each serving, spoon some creamed carrot and spinach onto one side of a plate. Place the omelet square in the middle of the plate, and sprinkle with olive oil. Serve.

ZUBEREITUNG

Für die Möhrencreme das Öl bei mittlerer Hitze in einem Topf erhitzen. Zwiebel, Kartoffel und Ingwer darin weich garen. Die Möhren einrühren und das Gemüse bei schwacher Hitze köcheln lassen, bis es weich und cremig ist. Bei Bedarf etwas Wasser zugeben. Ist das gekochte Gemüse zu flüssig, unter Rühren noch etwas länger köcheln lassen. Mit Salz, Pfeffer und Öl abschmecken, die Zitronenverbene einrühren und zugedeckt beiseitestellen.

Inzwischen für das Omelett den Backofen auf 200 °C vorheizen. Eine Backform (20 x 15 cm) mit Backpapier auslegen und mit 2 ½ EL Öl bestreichen. Restliches Öl, eingeweichtes Kichererbsenmehl und Petersilie verrühren. Mit Salz und Pfeffer abschmecken. Die Mischung in der Form verteilen und im Ofen 5–10 Minuten backen. Vollständig abkühlen lassen, danach in vier Quadrate schneiden. Den Ofen nicht ausschalten.

Während das Omelett abkühlt, den Spinat etwa 3 Minuten in kochendem Wasser garen. Dann sofort in kaltem Wasser abschrecken, in einem Sieb abtropfen und abkühlen lassen. Den Spinat in einer Schüssel mit Knoblauch, Öl und 1 Prise Salz mischen. Die Omelettquadrate jeweils mit 1 Tropfen Öl beträufeln und im heißen Ofen nochmals 5 Minuten backen.

Jeweils einen Löffel Möhrencreme und Spinat an den Rand von vier Tellern setzen. Die Omelettquadrate in die Mitte der Teller legen, mit Olivenöl beträufeln und sofort servieren.

AGRITURISMO CORONCINA

MACERATA, MARCHE

Coroncina welcomes its guests to the special ambience of Italy's Marche region. Surrounded by rich green meadows and a hilly landscape, this genuine farmhouse is where people come for rest and relaxation, serenity, peace, and the opportunity to connect with nature. Eight hundred olive trees of the "coroncina" cultivar frame the once abandoned farmhouse and serve as the inspiration for its name. Melania, the heart and soul of the establishment, purchased the property in 2003 with the intention of making it her home and refuge. She renovated the house with care, largely preserving its original character and designing the interior with the complementary look and feel of Provence—the fact that she used to work in her family's world famous furniture company may well have contributed to this success. While her farmhouse was always a beautiful home, Melania began to dream of bigger things: to establish the first vegetarian agritourism program in a region where most people had no clear idea of what it actually means to be a "vegetarian." And so she opened her vegetarian restaurant in 2007. As of 2012, her guests have also been able to spend the night in her charmingly furnished rooms; on request, they can even have a bathtub right next to the bed.

Melania uses half of her twenty-acre (eight-hectare) property as a vegetable garden, which fills the pantry of what is now a purely vegan restaurant with seasonal delicacies. This bounty also forms the basis for her ever changing, imaginative menu. She views food as an emotional experience, one that combines tastes, scents and colors. And she has indeed made her dream come true.

Für Ruhe, Gelassenheit, Frieden und die Verbundenheit mit der Natur ist an diesem besonderen Ort gesorgt. Inmitten sattgrüner Wiesen und Hügel heißt das authentische Landhaus Coroncina seine Gäste in den italienischen Marken willkommen. 800 Olivenbäume der Gattung Coroncina rahmen das ehemals verlassene Landhaus ein und inspirierten die Namensgebung. Melania, die Besitzerin und gute Seele des Hauses, kaufte es 2003, um es zu ihrem Heim und Wohlfühlort zu machen. Sie renovierte es behutsam, bewahrte den ursprünglichen Charakter weitestgehend und stattete es mit dem passenden Interieur im provenzalischen Stil aus – dabei dürfte geholfen haben, dass sie vorher in der weltweit bekannten Möbelfirma ihrer Familie tätig war. Und während ihr Landhaus ein immer schöneres Zuhause wurde, erwuchs in ihr ein weiterer Traum: Sie wollte in einer Region, in der die Menschen zumeist keine richtigen Vorstellungen haben, was „vegetarisch" tatsächlich bedeutet, den ersten vegetarischen Agrotourismus anbieten. 2007 eröffnete sie schließlich ihr vegetarisches Restaurant. Seit 2012 können Gäste hier auch in charmant eingerichteten Zimmern übernachten, auf Wunsch sogar mit einer Badewanne direkt neben dem Bett.

Die Hälfte ihres acht Hektar großen Grundstücks nutzt Melania als Gemüsegarten, der die Speisekammer ihres inzwischen rein veganen Restaurants mit saisonalen Köstlichkeiten füllt und Grundlage ihrer wechselnden fantasievollen Menüs ist. Für sie bedeutet Essen eine emotionale Erfahrung, die Geschmäcker, Gerüche und Farben verbindet. Und ihr Traum ist tatsächlich wahr geworden.

ROOMS: 2 ROOMS, 1 APARTMENT, 1 CAMPING TUN
SPECIALTIES: COOKING CLASSES, INFRARED SAUNA, THERMOSAUNA, MASSAGES, HYDROMASSAGE TUB

AGRITURISMO CORONCINA
VIA FOSSA, 2
62020 BELFORTE DEL CHIENTI
ITALY (ITALIEN)
WWW.AGRITURISMOCORONCINA.IT
+39 366 923 8075

ZIMMER: 2 ZIMMER, 1 APPARTEMENT, 1 SCHLAFFASS
BESONDERHEITEN: KOCHKURSE, INFRAROTSAUNA, THERMOSAUNA, MASSAGEN, HYDROMASSAGE-BECKEN

The vegan restaurant in the Coroncina is furnished in classic country cottage style, decorated with the pastel wall murals, wooden beams, and terracotta roof tiles typical of the region. In the morning, guests can look forward to a bountiful breakfast buffet that features many local products. And in the evening, the establishment serves a wonderful five-course dinner. The view from the restaurant opens right onto the hotel's own vegetable and herb garden—where the ingredients for seasonally inspired dishes grow and thrive.

Das vegane Restaurant im Coroncina ist im klassischen Landhausstil eingerichtet und mit den für die Region typischen Pastellwandmalereien, Holzbalken und Terrakottadachziegeln verziert. Gäste können sich morgens auf ein reichhaltiges Frühstücksbuffet mit vielen lokalen Produkten freuen. Am Abend wird ein herrliches Fünf-Gänge-Menü serviert. Direkt vom Restaurant aus hat man einen Blick auf den hauseigenen Gemüse- und Kräutergarten – hier wächst und gedeiht die Grundlage für die saisonal inspirierten Gerichte.

PASTA
FLAVORED WITH NUTS AND LEMON

SCHNELLE PASTA
MIT NÜSSEN UND ZITRONE

INGREDIENTS
SERVES 4

1 lb/400 g pasta
1 tsp sesame oil
1 tbsp pumpkin seeds
1 tbsp almonds
1 tbsp pine nuts
1 tbsp pistachio nuts
1 tbsp sunflower seeds
1 tbsp flaxseeds
2 tbsp extra-virgin olive oil
Zest and juice of 1 lemon

ZUTATEN
FÜR 4 PERSONEN

400 g Pasta (Hartweizennudeln)
Salz
1 TL Sesamöl
1 EL Kürbiskerne
1 EL Mandeln
1 EL Pinienkerne
1 EL Pistazien
1 EL Sonnenblumenkerne
1 EL Leinsamen
2 EL natives Olivenöl extra
abgeriebene Schale und Saft
  von 1 Bio-Zitrone

This dish is quick and easy, and very tasty.
Use any shape of pasta you like.

METHOD
Bring a large pot of water to a boil, add the pasta, and cook until
al dente. Meanwhile, combine the sesame oil, pumpkin seeds,
almonds, pine nuts, pistachios, sunflower seeds, and flaxseeds in
a large skillet over medium heat and toast just until fragrant. Let cool
slightly, then transfer the mixture to a food processor and pulse
until blended. Drain the pasta and return it to the pot. Add the nut
mixture and the olive oil to the pasta and stir.
Stir in the lemon zest and juice, and serve.

ZUBEREITUNG
In einem großen Topf Wasser aufkochen und salzen. Die Pasta
hineingeben und nach Packungsangabe bissfest kochen.
Inzwischen Sesamöl, Kürbiskerne, Mandeln, Pinienkerne, Pistazien,
Sonnenblumenkerne und Leinsamen in einer Pfanne bei
mittlerer Hitze rösten, bis sie duften. Etwas abkühlen lassen,
dann in einer Küchenmaschine in Intervallen fein hacken.
Die Nudeln in ein Sieb abgießen und in den Topf zurückgeben.
Nussmischung und Olivenöl darübergeben und unterrühren.
Zitronenschale und -saft unterheben und die Pasta sofort servieren.

Tipp: Die duftende Nuss-Zitronen-Sauce ist schnell und unkompliziert
zubereitet. Sie schmeckt zu jeder Art von Pasta, ob kurz oder lang,
dick oder dünn.

MONTALI COUNTRY HOUSE

PERUGIA, UMBRIA

Situated right in the center of the famous "boot," Umbria is the green heart of Italy. In the 1980s, Malu and Alberto Musacchio opened the first vegetarian restaurant in the Umbrian capital of Perugia. And as if that weren't adventurous enough, a short time later they bought a dilapidated estate surrounded by a large olive grove, which they renovated little by little with a great deal of love and attention to detail. The result is the Montali Country House—a romantic oasis of relaxation and culinary experiences. Malu and Alberto tirelessly refine and expand their prize-winning gourmet menu. The hotel's restaurant is now considered one of the world's best vegetarian restaurants and draws patrons from all over the globe.

Guests enjoy fine food and select wines while savoring a breathtaking panoramic view of the surrounding landscape. The olive grove, with its 1,500 gnarly trees, whose fruits supply the hotel's own olive oil, call you to come out for a stroll. If you venture beyond the olive grove, the path leads to Lake Trasimeno with its Maggiore and Minore islands. As your gaze sweeps over the calm water, you will finally discover the true secret of the Italian lifestyle. *La dolce far niente*—the sweet art of doing nothing.

Umbrien ist das grüne Herz Italiens und es liegt genau im Zentrum des berühmten „Stiefels". Hier, in der umbrischen Hauptstadt Perugia, eröffnete das Ehepaar Malu und Alberto Musacchio in den 1980er-Jahren das erste vegetarische Restaurant der Stadt. Und als wäre das noch nicht abenteuerlich genug, kauften sie wenig später ein verfallenes Anwesen inmitten eines weitläufigen Olivenhains, welches sie Stück für Stück und mit viel Liebe zum Detail selbst sanierten. Das Ergebnis ist das Montali Country House – ein romantischer Ort der Erholung und kulinarischer Erlebnisse. Malu und Alberto verfeinern und erweitern ihre preisgekrönte Gourmetküche unermüdlich. Das Restaurant des Hauses gilt heute als eines der besten vegetarischen Restaurants der Welt und zieht Gäste aus allen Teilen des Globus an.

Bei atemberaubenden Ausblicken auf das landschaftliche Panorama lassen sich feine Speisen und erlesene Weine besonders genießen. Der Olivenhain mit seinen 1500 knorrigen Bäumen, deren Früchte auch das hauseigene Olivenöl liefern, fordert zum Lustwandeln auf. Spaziert man über die Grenzen des Hains hinaus, führt einen der Weg zum Trasimenischen See mit seinen Inseln Maggiore und Minore. Während der Blick über das ruhige Wasser wandert, spürt man das Geheimnis italienischer Lebensart wie an kaum einem anderen Ort: *La dolce far niente* – das süße Nichtstun.

ROOMS: 9
SPECIALTIES: POOL, HOMEMADE OLIVE OIL PRODUCTION, POOL TABLE, HIKING, COOKING CLASSES

COUNTRY HOUSE MONTALI
VIA MONTALI, 23
06068 PERUGIA
ITALY (ITALIEN)
WWW.MONTALIONLINE.COM
+39 075 835 0680

ZIMMER: 9
BESONDERHEITEN: POOL, HAUSEIGENE OLIVENÖL-PRODUKTION, BILLARDTISCH, WANDERN, KOCHKURSE

BIPARMENTIER
A VELVETY COMBINATION OF TWO CLASSIC SOUPS

BIPARMENTIER –
SAMTIGES SUPPENDUETT

INGREDIENTS
SERVES 6

Croutons
6 slices day-old bread, cut into ½-inch cubes
2 tbsp olive oil
1 tbsp chopped mixed herbs (parsley, sage, thyme, rosemary)
Salt and black pepper

Potato-Leek Soup
1 tbsp extra-virgin olive oil
1 tbsp butter
1 leek, white and light green parts only, cleaned and coarsely chopped
2 cups/500 ml vegetable broth
2 small potatoes (10 oz/300 g), peeled and thinly sliced
1 oz/30 g green olives, coarsely chopped
1 tbsp coarsely chopped fresh parsley
1 tbsp heavy cream
Salt and black pepper

Pumpkin Soup
1 tbsp extra-virgin olive oil
1 tbsp butter
1 small shallot, finely chopped
1 leek, white and light green parts only, cleaned and coarsely chopped
2 cups/500 ml vegetable broth
9 oz/250 g pumpkin, peeled and cut in ½-inch cubes
1 small potato (5 oz/150 g), peeled and thinly sliced
3 sage leaves
2 tsp chopped fresh parsley
Ground nutmeg
1 tbsp heavy cream
Salt and black pepper

ZUTATEN

FÜR 6 PERSONEN

Croûtons

6 Scheiben hartes Brot, in 1 cm große
  Würfel geschnitten
2 EL Olivenöl
1 EL gemischte Kräuter (Petersilie,
  Salbei, Thymian, Rosmarin)
Salz, schwarzer Pfeffer

Kartoffel-Lauch-Suppe

1 EL natives Olivenöl extra
1 EL Butter
1 Stange Lauch, weißer und hellgrüner
  Teil grob gehackt
500 ml Gemüsebrühe
300 g kleine Kartoffeln, geschält und in
  dünne Scheiben geschnitten
30 g grüne Oliven, grob gehackt
1 EL frisch gehackte Petersilie
1 EL Sahne
Salz, schwarzer Pfeffer

Kürbissuppe

1 EL natives Olivenöl extra
1 EL Butter
1 kleine Schalotte, fein gehackt
1 Stange Lauch, weißer und hellgrüner
  Teil grob gehackt
500 ml Gemüsebrühe
250 g Kürbis, geschält und in 1 cm große
  Würfel geschnitten
150 g kleine Kartoffeln, geschält und in
  dünne Scheiben geschnitten
3 Salbeiblätter
2 TL frisch gehackte Petersilie
frisch geriebene Muskatnuss
1 EL Sahne
Salz, schwarzer Pfeffer

METHOD

Croutons: Heat the oven to 350°F/180°C. Toss the bread cubes with the oil and herbs and season with salt and pepper. Spread out on a baking sheet and bake for 5 minutes, or until golden brown and crispy on the outside and soft in the middle. Let cool.

Potato-leek soup: Heat the oil and butter in a large pot over medium heat, add the leek, and cook until tender but not browned, about 2 minutes. Add the vegetable broth, potatoes, olives, and parsley and cook until the potatoes are tender.

Remove from the heat. Puree in batches in a blender until the soup is completely smooth. Pour through a strainer into a clean pot. Stir in the cream and season with salt and pepper to taste. Cover and set aside until ready to serve.

Pumpkin soup: Heat the oil and butter in a large pot over medium heat, add the shallot, and cook until translucent. Add the leek and continue to cook slowly until tender but not browned. Add the vegetable broth, pumpkin, potato, sage, parsley, and nutmeg to taste and cook until the potato and pumpkin are tender.

Remove from the heat and discard the sage leaves. Puree in batches in a blender until the soup is completely smooth. Pour through a strainer into a clean pot. Stir in the cream and season with salt and pepper to taste. Cover and set aside until ready to serve.

To serve: Heat the soups and check the consistency of each. If one is too thick, add a small amount of broth until equal consistency is achieved. For each serving, scoop 4 ounces/125 ml of each soup into two equal-sized ladles. Holding one ladle in each hand, slowly pour both soups at the same time into a serving bowl, starting at the center. Serve immediately with croutons on the side or on top of the soup.

ZUBEREITUNG

Für die Croûtons den Backofen auf 180 °C vorheizen. Brotwürfel, Öl und Kräuter mischen und mit Salz und Pfeffer würzen. Auf einem Backblech verteilen und im Ofen in 5 Minuten knusprig goldbraun rösten. Abkühlen lassen.

Für die Kartoffel-Lauch-Suppe Öl und Butter in einem Topf bei mittlerer Hitze erhitzen. Den Lauch darin weich dünsten, jedoch nicht bräunen lassen. Brühe, Kartoffeln, Oliven und Petersilie zugeben und köcheln lassen, bis die Kartoffeln weich sind. Die Suppe dann im Mixer cremig pürieren und durch ein Sieb in einen sauberen Topf passieren. Sahne einrühren, mit Salz und Pfeffer abschmecken und zugedeckt beiseitestellen.

Für die Kürbissuppe Öl und Butter in einem Topf bei mittlerer Hitze erhitzen. Die Schalotte darin glasig dünsten. Den Lauch zugeben und mitdünsten, bis er weich, jedoch nicht braun ist. Brühe, Kürbis, Kartoffeln, Salbei, Petersilie und Muskat zugeben und köcheln lassen, bis das Gemüse weich ist. Den Salbei entfernen, die Suppe im Mixer cremig pürieren und durch ein Sieb in einen sauberen Topf passieren. Sahne einrühren, mit Salz und Pfeffer abschmecken und zugedeckt beiseitestellen.

Zum Servieren die Suppen wieder erhitzen und bei Bedarf mit etwas Gemüsebrühe verdünnen. Pro Portion von jeder Suppe 125 ml mit zwei gleich großen Schöpfkellen abnehmen. Jede Kelle in eine Hand nehmen und in der Mitte beginnend beide Suppen gleichzeitig in eine Suppenschale gießen. Sofort mit den Croûtons servieren.

LA VIMEA BIOTIQUEHOTEL
NATURNS, SOUTH TYROL

It goes without saying that people who follow a vegan lifestyle are not the only vacationers welcome to stay at LA VIMEA—and yet even aficionados of a purely plant-based cuisine will be astonished by the place and unable to stop raving about it. After all, LA VIMEA is Italy's very first entirely vegan hotel. Not only the creative, organic food but the entire hotel is vegan—down to the very last detail. It all starts with the room furnishings. You will not find any leather seat coverings or down comforters here. Instead, the furniture and floors is made from wood from the nearby alps, cut under the right moon sign, while organic fair trade cotton was used for the duvets. The complementary toiletries are, of course, vegan, organic, and not tested on animals. Even behind the scenes, the hotel uses exclusively vegan products, for example cleansers and detergents.

Anyone who dedicates themselves to a holistic lifestyle does so out of conviction—as do the owners of the biotique hotel. To the Posch family, holistic management means not only treating animals with respect but also avoiding the use of plastic whenever possible. The hotel uses only green energy and solar power, and the owners make every effort to buy the establishment's food locally in order to support the small farms that have always thrived in South Tyrol. The kitchen, with its untreated work surfaces, creates light vegan specialties, such as Heusuppe (hay soup), wild herb salads, sage gnocchi, and lemon risotto. LA VIMEA is a vegan dream come true in Naturno/Naturns, where the quintessentially Italian southern mellowness meets alpine hospitality.

Selbstverständlich dürfen nicht nur vegan lebende Menschen im LA VIMEA ihre Urlaubstage verbringen – doch gerade die Freunde einer rein pflanzlichen Küche kommen aus dem Staunen und Schwärmen sicher gar nicht mehr heraus, denn LA VIMEA ist das erste komplett vegane Hotel Italiens. Nicht nur die biologische Kreativküche ist vegan, sondern das gesamte Hotel, bis ins kleinste Detail. Das beginnt schon bei der Zimmereinrichtung: Lederbezüge oder Daunendecken sind hier nicht zu finden, stattdessen wurde für Möbel und Böden mondgeschlagenes Vollholz aus den umliegenden Alpen und für Bettdecken FAIRTRADE-Biobaumwolle verwendet. Naturgemäß sind auch die bereitgestellten Kosmetika vegan, tierversuchsfrei und bio. Selbst in den Bereichen, wo man es als Gast nicht einmal merken würde, wie bei Reinigungs- und Waschmitteln, werden ausschließlich vegane Produkte benutzt, die biologisch abbaubar sind.

Wer Ganzheitlichkeit so konsequent vorlebt, der macht das aus Überzeugung – so wie das Betreiberpaar des Biotiquehotels. Für Familie Posch bedeutet ganzheitliches Wirtschaften nicht nur Tiere zu achten, sondern auch auf Plastik zu verzichten, wo es nur geht. Sie nutzen Ökostrom und Sonnenenergie zur Versorgung des Hotels und beziehen die verwendeten Lebensmittel möglichst aus der Region, um kleinste bäuerliche Strukturen, wie sie in Südtirol seit jeher gewachsen sind, zu unterstützen. In der naturbelassenen Küche werden leichte vegane Spezialitäten wie Heusuppe, Wildkräutersalate, Salbeinocken oder Zitronenrisotto kreiert. LA VIMEA ist ein wahr gewordener Vegantraum in Südtiroler Natur, wo die Milde des Südens mit ihrem italienischen Lebensstil auf die Herzlichkeit der Alpen trifft.

ROOMS: 4 LOFTS, 8 SUITES, 28 ROOMS
SPECIALTIES: YOGA, MEDITATION, AYURVEDA, ECOLOGIAL SWIMMING POND, SALT WATER INDOOR SWIMMING POOL, HOT STONE LOUNGE, SAUNA, ACCESSIBLE FOR DISABLED PEOPLE, KIDS AGED 12 ALLOWED

LA VIMEA BIOTIQUE HOTEL
AUGUST KLEEBERG 7
39025 NATURNS
ITALY (ITALIEN)
WWW.LAVIMEA.COM
+39 0473 055 035

ZIMMER: 4 LOFTS, 8 SUITEN, 28 ZIMMER
BESONDERHEITEN: YOGA, MEDITATION, AYURVEDA, NATUR-BADETEICH, SALZWASSER-HALLENBAD, HOT-STONE-LOUNGE, SAUNA, BEHINDERTENGERECHT, KINDER AB 12 JAHREN ERLAUBT

TWO-TONE NETTLE RAVIOLI
ON A BED OF TOMATO COULIS

ZWEIFARBIGE BRENNNESSEL-RAVIOLI
AUF TOMATEN-COULIS

INGREDIENTS
SERVES 4

Dough
2 cups/400 g organic semolina,
  plus 1 cup/200 g for dusting
1½ tbsp olive oil
½ cup/100 g cooked organic spinach
Food-grade rock salt

Filling
1 bunch nettles
½ cup/100 g spelt drink
5 oz/150 g walnuts
2 oz/50 g brined capers

3½ oz/100 g Taggiasca olives, pitted
5 sprigs of oregano, leaves only

Tomato coulis
4 sprigs of oregano
4 tbsp olive oil
1 shallot, chopped
4 ripe tomatoes, cubed
Salt
16 olives for garnish

ZUTATEN
FÜR 4 PERSONEN

Teig
400 g Bio-Hartweizengrieß,
  plus 200 g für die Arbeitsfläche
1½ EL Olivenöl
100 g gekochter Bio-Blattspinat
Steinsalz

Füllung
1 Bund Brennnesseln
100 g Dinkeldrink
150 g Walnusskerne
50 g gesalzene Kapern
100 g Taggiasche-Oliven, entsteint
5 Zweige Oregano, Blättchen abgezupft

Tomaten-Coulis
4 Zweige Oregano
4 EL Olivenöl
1 Schalotte, gehackt
4 reife Tomaten, in Würfel geschnitten
Salz
16 Oliven zum Dekorieren

METHOD

Dough: Combine 1 cup/200 g semolina with ¾ tablespoon oil and a scant ½ cup/100 ml lukewarm water and knead to form an elastic dough. To make the green dough, combine 1 cup/200 g semolina with the spinach, the remaining oil, and a scant ½ cup/100 ml water and also knead to form an elastic dough. Cover the two doughs and let rest in the refrigerator for 1 hour.

Filling: Place the nettles, spelt drink, nuts, capers, olives, and oregano in a blender and puree until smooth.

Tomato coulis: Wash the oregano and shake dry. Set aside the tips of the twigs for garnish and remove the leaves from the rest of the twigs. Heat the oil in a pot and lightly sauté the shallots. Add the tomato cubes and oregano leaves and simmer for around 15 minutes. Puree the coulis with an immersion blender to the desired consistency.

Roll out both doughs to a thickness of ⅛ inch/5 mm with a rolling pin. Cut out 12 white and 12 green circles with a drinking glass. Place 1 tablespoon of filling in the center of each white circle and cover with the green circles. Press the edges together to seal. Make sure that there are no air bubbles in the pockets of dough. Cook the ravioli in boiling water for 3 minutes until done. Remove and drain. Divide the tomato coulis between four plates and arrange the ravioli on top. Garnish with the olives and oregano tips.

ZUBEREITUNG

Für den hellen Teig 200 g Grieß mit ¾ EL Öl und 100 ml lauwarmem Wasser zu einem elastischen Teig verkneten. Für den grünen Teig 200 g Grieß mit Spinat, restlichem Öl und 100 ml Wasser ebenfalls zu einem elastischen Teig verkneten. Beide Teige im Kühlschrank zugedeckt 1 Stunde ruhen lassen.

Für die Füllung Brennnesseln, Dinkeldrink, Nüsse, Kapern, Oliven und Oregano im Standmixer zu einer glatten Masse pürieren.

Für das Tomaten-Coulis den Oregano waschen und trocken schütteln. Die Spitzen der Zweige für die Deko beiseitelegen, die Blättchen abzupfen. Das Öl in einem Topf erhitzen und die Schalotte darin sanft erhitzen. Tomatenwürfel und Oreganoblättchen zugeben, salzen und etwa 15 Minuten köcheln lassen. Das Coulis nach Belieben mit dem Stabmixer pürieren.

Beide Teige mit dem Nudelholz 5 mm dick ausrollen. Mit einem Glas 12 weiße und 12 grüne Kreise ausstechen. Jeweils 1 TL Füllung in die Mitte der weißen Kreise setzen, mit den grünen Kreisen abdecken und am Rand festdrücken. Dabei darauf achten, dass keine Luftbläschen in den Teigtaschen sind. Die Ravioli in kochendem Wasser 3 Minuten garen. Herausheben und abtropfen lassen.

Das Tomaten-Coulis auf vier Teller verteilen und die Ravioli darauf anrichten. Mit den Oliven und den Oreganospitzen dekorieren.

ECO PARK HOTEL AZALEA

TRENTINO-SOUTH TYROL

Benvenuti to picturesque Cavalese, a village in the Dolomites that feels as though it could be set on the Mediterranean coast. Its atmosphere is friendly and unspoiled, with a southern European flair. This ambience as also found in the Eco Park Hotel Azalea, whose stylish interior, with bright modern rooms, is furnished with natural materials and many classic design elements. You will find nature inside and out, as every uniquely styled room is named after the flowers that grow in the garden. The color green repeats throughout the hotel—even in the form of many green ideas that turn the establishment into a multi-prize-winning ecohotel.

Owner and architect Manuela Demattio obviously cares a great deal about the environment. After all, the enchanting landscape of Trentino-South Tyrol is a nature conservation area. Beautiful cities such as Trento/Trient and Rovereto/Rofreit, Bozen/Bolzano and Meran/Merano have historic centers, churches, and museums just waiting to be explored. Vacationers who enjoy an active lifestyle will also rejoice, since the Fiemme Valley is known not only for its ski slopes but also for its wide range of sports and leisure activities at any time of the year. Wherever you go here, you will always encounter clear, healthy mountain air and a heavenly panoramic view. On returning from one of these excursions, you can unwind marvelously by relaxing in the hotel's wellness zone and sampling its experimental cuisine with a candlelight dinner, accompanied by a glass of vintage Trentino wine. At the Eco Park Hotel Azalea, the use of fresh, regional, organic ingredients is as much a matter of course as the blend of traditional Italian and vegetarian/vegan cuisine.

Benvenuti im malerischen Cavalese, einem mediterran anmutenden Dorf mitten in den Dolomiten. Freundlich, ursprünglich und mit südeuropäischem Flair – genauso geht es im Eco Park Hotel Azalea zu. Das stylishe Interieur mit den hellen, modernen Zimmern ist mit natürlichen Materialien und vielen Designklassikern ausgestattet. Die Natur wird hier ins Haus geholt, denn jedes Zimmer ist nach den Blumen benannt, die man auch im Garten findet, und hat seinen eigenen Stil. Besonders die Farbe Grün wird immer wieder verwendet – auch in Form von vielen grünen Ideen, die das Hotel zu einem mehrfach ausgezeichneten Ecohotel machen.

Die Umwelt liegt der Besitzerin und Architektin Manuela Demattio ganz offensichtlich am Herzen, die bezaubernde Landschaft Trentino-Südtirols will schließlich geschützt sein. Wunderschöne Städte wie Trento oder Rovereto, Bozen oder Meran laden mit ihren historischen Stadtkernen, Kirchen und Museen zum Bummeln ein. Aktivurlauber können sich ebenfalls freuen, denn das Fleimstal ist nicht nur für seine Skipisten, sondern auch für seine vielfältigen Sport- und Freizeitangebote zu jeder Jahreszeit bekannt. Stete Begleiter: klare, gesunde Bergluft und ein traumhaftes Panorama. Vortrefflich erholen kann man sich nach solchen Ausflügen im Wellnessbereich des Hauses und im Rahmen der servierten kulinarischen Experimente bei Kerzenschein und einem erlesenen Glas Wein aus dem Trentino. Die Verwendung von frischen regionalen Biozutaten ist im Eco Park Hotel Azalea ebenso selbstverständlich wie die Verbindung der traditionell italienischen mit der vegetarisch-veganen Küche.

ROOMS: 34 ROOMS & SUITES
SPECIALTIES: BAKING CLASSES, NATURE KIDS CHILD CARE, (KIDS) YOGA, ART CLASSES, SHIATSU TREATMENTS, AYURVEDA WEEKENDS, ACCESSIBLE FOR DISABLED PEOPLE

ECO PARK HOTEL AZALEA
MANUELA DEMATTIO
VIA DELLE CESURE 1
38033 CAVALESE – TRENTO
ITALY (ITALIEN)
WWW.ECOPARKHOTELAZALEA.IT
+39 0462 340109

ZIMMER: 34 ZIMMER & SUITEN
BESONDERHEITEN: BROTBACKKURSE, NATUR-KINDERBETREUUNG, (KINDER-) YOGA, MALKURSE, SHIATSU-BEHANDLUNGEN, AYURVEDA-WOCHENENDEN, BEHINDERTENGERECHT

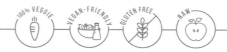

VALE DE MOSES

CASTELO BRANCO, CENTRAL PORTUGAL

The landscape is wild and yet oddly intimate. It lies deep in the Portuguese mountains, scattered with olive and madrone trees, vibrant green fields, rugged mountain slopes, and gentle streams that wind through the valleys. Here and there, you encounter small villages with a handful of inhabitants and nothing else but the sounds of nature and a peaceful ambience. Along the way to Vale de Moses, you pass the village of Ameira. Twisting, tree-lined roads take you ever higher into the mountains until you finally reach yoga paradise. People come here to withdraw into nature for a week or more and recharge their batteries. To finally leave the treadmill behind, perhaps their smart phones and obligations as well—to relax and devote themselves entirely to their own wellbeing.

This gorgeous retreat is the best place to do all these things. Vonetta and Andrew Winter discovered the once abandoned farm in 2007 while on an adventure trip through Europe with their children and the family dog. Was it just a coincidence that the old farmhouse situated on the side of a mountain had the same name as their dog, Moses?

They stayed and built a retreat for yogis who appreciate mountain air, walks in the forest, riverside mud baths, and delicious, healthy food as well as deep, restful sleep. And they built it for everyone else who wants to deepen their love of yoga practice, no matter their level of proficiency. Guests have the option of spending the night in tipis situated among the trees and taking showers in mountain water—you don't get any closer to nature than this.

Wild und doch vertraut wirkt die Landschaft tief in den portugiesischen Bergen, mit seinen Oliven- und Erdbeerbäumen, dem satten Grün der Felder, seinen rauen Berghängen und ruhigen Bächen, die die Täler durchziehen. Vereinzelt tauchen kleine Dörfer mit einer Handvoll Einwohnern auf, ansonsten gibt es nur Naturgeräusche und Frieden. Auf dem Weg zum Vale de Moses passiert man das Dörfchen Ameira, auf verschlungenen, von Bäumen gesäumten Wegen fährt man immer höher in die Berge, bis man schließlich auf das Yogaparadies stößt. Wer sich hierher aufmacht, tut dies, um sich für eine oder mehrere Wochen in die Natur zurückzuziehen und die Batterien aufzuladen. Endlich raus aus dem Hamsterrad, mal ohne Smartphone und Verpflichtungen etwas für sich allein tun und entspannen.

Dieses wunderschöne Retreat stellt die besten Voraussetzungen dazu bereit. Die ehemals verlassene Farm wurde von Vonetta und Andrew Winter, ihren Kindern und ihrem Hund 2007 auf einem Abenteuertrip durch Europa entdeckt. War es wirklich nur ein Zufall, dass der alte Bauernhof an einem Berghang so hieß, wie ihr Hund Moses?

Sie blieben hier und schufen einen Rückzugsort für Yogis, die Bergluft, Waldspaziergänge, Schlammbäder in den Flüssen und gesund-köstliches Essen sowie tiefen Schlaf zu schätzen wissen – und einfach für alle, die ihre Liebe zum Yoga vertiefen wollen, egal auf welchem Level sie praktizieren. Wer mag, übernachtet in Tipis zwischen den Bäumen und duscht mit Bergwasser – naturverbundener geht es kaum.

ROOMS: 2 STONE HOUSES, 3 ROOMS, 3 TENTS
SPECIALTIES: YOGA, MASSAGES, ACUPUNCTURE, TUI NA MASSAGE, MEDITATION, COOKING CLASSES, POOL, MUD BATH, HIKING, CLIMBING

VALE DE MOSES
AMIEIRA/OLEIROS
6160-052 CASTELO BRANCO
PORTUGAL
WWW.VALEDEMOSES.COM
+351 272 634006

ZIMMER: 2 STEINHÄUSER, 3 ZELTE, 3 ZIMMER
BESONDERHEITEN: YOGA, MASSAGEN, AKUPUNKTUR, TUINA-MASSAGE, MEDITATION, KOCHKURSE, POOL, SCHLAMMBAD, WANDERN, KLETTERN

Many forms of yoga are practiced at Vale de Moses, from Ashtanga and
Vinyasa Flow to Dynamic Hatha and even Yin Yoga and Acro Yoga.
But don't let yourself feel pressured by the sheer variety of styles—after
all, yoga means "unity." Experienced yoga instructors help you deepen
your love of yoga and embark on a journey of self-discovery without
distractions. A desire for a whole lot of yoga and meditative mindfulness
will remain with you long after you return home—along with the wish
to return to the Portuguese mountains someday.

Im Vale de Moses werden viele Arten des Yoga praktiziert, von Ashtanga
und Vinyasa Flow über Dynamic Hatha bis hin zu Yin Yoga oder
Acro Yoga. Man sollte sich aber nicht durch die Vielfalt der Stile
unter Druck gesetzt fühlen, schließlich heißt Yoga „Einheit".
Erfahrene Yogalehrer helfen, die Liebe zum Yoga weiter zu vertiefen und
ohne Ablenkung zu sich selbst zu finden. Was auch nach der Heimkehr
bleibt, ist sicher die Lust auf ganz viel Yoga und meditative Achtsamkeit –
und der Wunsch, in die portugiesischen Berge zurückzukehren.

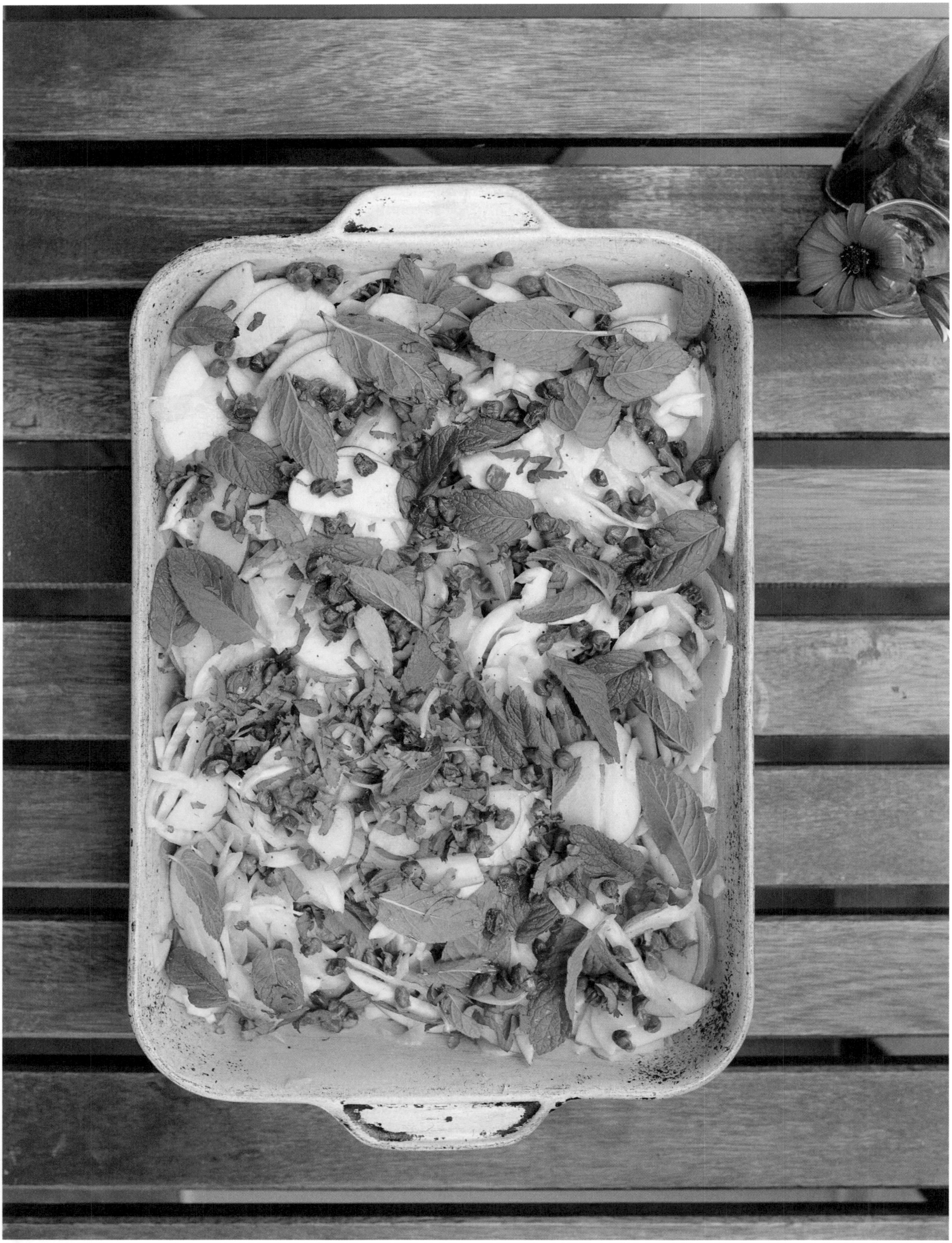

FENNEL, AND APPLE SALAD
WITH MINT LEAVES

FENCHEL-APFEL-SALAT
MIT MINZE

INGREDIENTS
SERVES 2

1 fennel bulb, sliced
3 apples, cored and sliced
Juice of 2 lemons
1 tsp olive oil
2 tbsp capers
Handful fresh mint leaves

METHOD
Combine the fennel and apple slices in a bowl, add the lemon juice, and marinate for 2 hours to help draw out the aniseed flavor in the fennel. Drain the juice from the fennel and apples.

Heat the oil in a small skillet, add the capers, and fry them gently. Sprinkle the capers over the fennel and apples.

Garnish with mint leaves and serve.

ZUTATEN
FÜR 2 PERSONEN

1 Fenchelknolle, in Scheiben geschnitten
3 Äpfel, entkernt und
  in Scheiben geschnitten
Saft von 2 Zitronen
1 TL Olivenöl
2 EL Kapern
1 Handvoll frische Minzeblätter

ZUBEREITUNG
Fenchel- und Apfelscheiben in eine Schüssel geben. Den Zitronensaft untermischen und alles 2 Stunden durchziehen lassen, um den Anisgeschmack aus dem Fenchel zu ziehen. Danach den Saft, der sich in der Schüssel gebildet hat, abgießen.

Das Öl in einer kleinen Pfanne erhitzen und die Kapern darin leicht anbraten. Herausnehmen und über den Fenchel und die Äpfel streuen.

Den Salat auf zwei Tellern anrichten, mit Minzeblättern bestreuen und servieren.

BOUTIQUE HOTEL VIVENDA MIRANDA

LAGOS, ALGARVE

As soon as you enter the Vivenda Miranda Boutique Hotel, you will feel the flair and magic of bygone centuries. After all, this former private residence of a 17th-century aristocratic family is filled with original elements, all preserved or lovingly restored. Nothing here is ordinary and much is handmade—from the wall paintings to the restored antiques. The Moorish architecture, with façades in warm earth tones, blends perfectly with tables made from logs and headboards made from antique cabinet doors. Every room is unique and radiates Portuguese charm.

Situated right on the coastal cliffs of Portugal's Algarve region and only two kilometers from downtown Lagos, the hotel offers balcony views of the sea and the impressive coast line. The establishment's extensive, lush garden also offers a wonderful refuge.

The boutique hotel takes a holistic approach to health, which includes yoga and tai chi workshops. It also pays attention to mindful amenities and respect for nature. Not to mention its fabulous location. The in-house spa uses only the organic, vegan products of Neal's Yard Remedies in London. The gourmet artisan meals served in the Mirandus Restaurant also complement the hotel's style and are prepared to meet the tastes of guest who follow a vegan, raw foods, or gluten-free lifestyle.

Schon beim Betreten des Boutique Hotels Vivenda Miranda spürt man das Flair und die Magie der vergangenen Jahrhunderte, denn im ehemaligen Privathaus einer Adelsfamilie aus dem 17. Jahrhundert wurden so viele Originalelemente wie möglich erhalten oder liebevoll restauriert. Nichts ist hier gewöhnlich, vieles handgemacht – von der Wandbemalung bis zu den restaurierten Antiquitäten. Die maurische Bauart mit ihren Fassaden in warmen Erdtönen passt wunderbar zu Tischen aus Baumstämmen oder Kopfenden aus antiken Schranktüren. Jedes Zimmer ist ein Unikat mit portugiesischem Charme.

Unmittelbar an der Steilküste der portugiesischen Algarve gelegen und nur zwei Kilometer von der Altstadt Lagos entfernt, führt der Blick vom Balkon direkt auf das Meer und die beeindruckende Küste. Natürlich ist auch der weitläufige und üppig bepflanzte Garten des Hauses ein wunderbarer Ruhepol.

Der Fokus des Boutiquehotels liegt auf holistischer Gesundheit, einem ganzheitlichen Ansatz, zu dem Yoga- oder Tai-Chi-Workshops ebenso zählen, wie die achtsame Ausstattung und der respektvolle Umgang mit der Natur – nicht zu vergessen die fantastische Lage. Im hauseigenen Spa werden exklusiv die veganen Bioprodukte von Neal's Yard Remedies aus London verwendet. Und auch die kulinarisch anspruchsvollen Gerichte der Artisan Gastronomy im Restaurant Mirandus treffen den Stil und werden wahlweise vegan, rohköstlich oder glutenfrei zubereitet.

ROOMS: 24 ROOMS & SUITES
SPECIALTIES: POOL, JACUZZI, SAUNA, STEAM BATH, YOGA, MEDITATION, AYURVEDA, DETOX, TAI CHI, QI GONG, GOLF, ACCESSIBLE FOR DISABLED PEOPLE

BOUTIQUE HOTEL VIVENDA MIRANDA
RUA DAS VIOLETAS
8600-282 LAGOS
PORTUGAL
WWW.VIVENDAMIRANDA.COM
+351 282 763 222

ZIMMER: 24 ZIMMER & SUITEN
BESONDERHEITEN: POOL, JACUZZI, SAUNA, DAMPFBAD, YOGA, MEDITATION, AYURVEDA, DETOX, TAI-CHI, QIGONG, GOLF, BEHINDERTENGERECHT

OMASSIM GUESTHOUSE

E R I C E I R A – S A N T O   I S I D O R O ,   L I S B O A

Yoga mats and surfboards. As different as they may be, these items form a perfect pair at the omassim Surf & Yoga guesthouse, which is located just about 22 miles (35 kilometers) north-west of Lisbon, Portugal. Ericeira, a fishing village of narrow streets and a welcoming atmosphere, is situated on a seven-mile (eleven-kilometer) strip of coastline renowned as Europe's first and only surfing reserve. The area attracts surfers from all over the world—all of them determined to catch "the perfect wave" and discover the most beautiful beaches.

At a destination that could easily be called a "mecca" for surfers, the owners of omassim guesthouse, Lia and Eduardo, created a temporary home not only for surfers, but also for yogis, beach and veggie lovers or people who simply want to enjoy life. Omassim's guests get to learn why yoga, meditation, and surfing complement each other so perfectly, both physically and spiritually. The guesthouse offers more dynamic yoga classes in the morning, such as Vinyasa Flow or Hatha Yoga, as well as a more relaxing "After-Surf-Yoga", which mostly includes Yin Yoga. And that is not all by a long shot: The area of Ericeira-Ribamar offers the perfect spot for long and beautiful hiking or mountain bike tours, SUP or even SUP-Yoga. And the guesthouse itself is able to top that, with Ayurvedic massages, reiki, sweat lodges and glass walking. Naturally, an active vacation makes you hungry, and the guesthouse has this detail covered as well with an international, vegetarian/vegan gourmet menu made from fresh, mostly regional ingredients, some of them from the guesthouse's own garden—prepared with love, care and creativity. So it hardly matters whether you want to catch the famous waves of Ericeira or get some rest and relaxation— whether your favorite accessory is a surfboard or a yoga mat—you have certainly come to the right place, omassim has it all.

Yogamatte und Surfbrett – obwohl so unterschiedlich, passen sie im omassim Surf & Yoga Guesthouse, das etwa 35 Kilometer nordwestlich von Lissabon, Portugal, entfernt liegt, perfekt zusammen. Der Fischerort Ericeira mit seinen engen Gassen und seiner einladenden Atmosphäre liegt an einem elf Kilometer langen Küstenstreifen, der als Europas erstes und einziges Surfschutzgebiet anerkannt wurde und Wellenreiter aus der ganzen Welt magisch anzieht – immer auf der Suche nach der „perfekten Welle" und den schönsten Stränden.

An einem Ort also, den man leicht als „Surf-Mekka" bezeichnen kann, kreierten Lia und Eduardo, die Betreiber von omassim, ein Zuhause auf Zeit, jedoch lange nicht nur für Surfer, sondern ebenso für Yogis, Strandfans, Veggies oder Leute, die einfach das Leben genießen wollen. Im omassim lernt man, warum Yoga, Meditation und das Surfen eine perfekte Einheit bilden und sich gegenseitig positiv aufeinander auswirken – körperlich wie geistig. Im Guesthouse werden sowohl dynamischere Morgen-Yoga-Klassen, wie Vinyasa-Flow oder Hatha Yoga angeboten, als auch entspannendes „After-Surf-Yoga", das unter anderem aus Yin Yoga besteht. Und das ist längst nicht alles: das Gebiet um Ericeira-Ribamar bietet die perfekte Grundlage für lange und wunderschöne Wanderungen oder Moutainbike-Touren und ist optimal zum Stand-Up-Paddeln oder um SUP-Yoga zu praktizieren. Für das i-Tüpfelchen sorgt wiederum das Guesthouse selbst, durch ayurvedische Massagen, Reiki Schwitzhütten und sogar Glasläufe. Ganz klar: Aktivurlaub macht hungrig, und auch darum wird sich hier bestens gekümmert, mit einer internationalen vegetarisch-veganen Gourmetküche, mit frischen, meist regionalen Zutaten – teilweise sogar aus dem eigenen Garten –, die mit viel Liebe, Sorgfalt und Kreativität zubereitet werden. Egal also ob man die berühmten Wellen Ericeiras surfen möchte oder die perfekte Entspannung sucht, ob Surfbrett oder Yogamatte – hier ist man ganz sicher am richtigen Ort, denn omassim bietet all dies.

ROOMS: 8
SPECIALTIES: YOGA, SURFING, MASSAGES (E.G. PINDA), REIKI, AYURVEDA TREATMENTS, POOL, SWEAT LODGE

OMASSIM GUESTHOUSE
RUA DAS TAIPAS, N°2, PALHAIS
2640-068 ERICEIRA, SANTO ISIDORO
PORTUGAL
WWW.OMASSIM.COM
OMASSIM@GMAIL.COM

ZIMMER: 8
BESONDERHEITEN: YOGA, WELLENREITEN, MASSAGEN (U.A. PINDA), REIKI, AYURVEDA-BEHANDLUNGEN, POOL, SWEAT LODGE

AYURVEDA PARKSCHLÖSSCHEN
TRABEN-TRARBACH, RHINELAND-PALATINATE

Ayurveda Parkschlösschen looks back upon a long tradition of health. Nestled in an extensive park, this health resort is surrounded by old trees, vineyards, and a softly murmuring stream. Traben-Trarbach, a small town known for its many art nouveau buildings, is situated on a picturesque loop of the Mosel River. Here, everything began in 1800 with a modest bathhouse that evolved into a spacious spa building, which experienced a number of changes over the years before it was eventually brought back to life by Wolfgang Preuß in 1993. For the entrepreneur, the transforming experience of an Ayurvedic cure was a milestone in his life. From that point on, his vision was to establish the principles of Ayurveda at the highest level in Germany.

Today, under the leadership of his wife Brigitte and his daughter Carina Preuß, the motto at Parkschlösschen is: Everything is Ayurveda. Ayurveda Parkschlösschen is the only five-star health resort in Europe to fully and exclusively implement the Ayurvedic philosophy. Since 1993 the Parkschlösschen focuses on the Ayurvedic detox cure Panchakarma, under the supervision of experienced Ayurvedic practitioners. Everything—from the food to the therapies and treatments, exercise, yoga, and meditation—is based on the millennia-old principles of holistic Ayurvedic medicine. The same holds true for the cuisine, because Ayurveda views an appropriate diet as a means of promoting health and wellbeing. Parkschlösschen offers vegetarian Ayurveda Cuisine made of fresh ingredients, most of which are organic. Vegan options as well as a vegan version of the Panchakarma cure and all other Ayurveda programs are also available upon request. This unique place of holistic regeneration and healing has all the amenities of a five-star hotel. For guests, Ayurveda at Parkschlösschen means rediscovering their lightness, regenerating body and mind, and strengthening their body's own healing powers. It is only logical that the resort's vision is "To make the world healthier, one person at a time!"

Gesundheit hat eine lange Tradition im Ayurveda Parkschlösschen, das eingebettet in einer großzügigen Parkanlage liegt, umgeben von alten Bäumen, Weinbergen und einem leise flüsternden Bach. Hier, im historischen Jugendstilstädtchen Traben-Trarbach an einer der malerischen Moselschleifen, entstand bereits 1800 ein Badehaus, später ein großzügiges Kurhaus, welches wechselhafte Zeiten erlebte, bevor es 1993 nach langem Dornröschenschlaf von Wolfgang Preuß wieder zum Leben erweckt wurde. Für den Unternehmer war die transformierende Erfahrung einer Ayurveda-Kur ein Meilenstein in seinem Leben, und seine Vision war es fortan, die Prinzipien des Ayurveda auf höchstem Niveau auch in Deutschland zu etablieren.

Heute, unter der Leitung von Ehefrau Brigitte und Tochter Carina Preuß, lautet das Motto im Parkschlösschen: Alles wirkt. Alles ist Ayurveda. Es ist das einzige mit Fünf Sternen ausgezeichnete Kurhotel in Europa, das die ayurvedische Philosophie ganzheitlich und ausschließlich umsetzt. Seit 1993 konzentriert sich das Parkschlösschen dabei auf die ayurvedische Detoxkur Panchakarma, die von erfahrenen Ayurveda-Medizinern begleitet wird. Hier basiert alles – von der Ernährung, über die Therapien und Behandlungen, Bewegung, Yoga und Meditation – auf den jahrtausendealten Prinzipien der ganzheitlichen ayurvedischen Heilkunst.

Das gilt auch für die Küche, denn im Ayurveda wird eine typgerechte Ernährung als heilende Medizin betrachtet. Das Parkschlösschen bietet eine vegetarische Ayurveda Cuisine aus frischen, vorwiegend biologischen Zutaten, auf Wunsch immer auch vegan. Selbst eine vegane Variante der Panchakarma-Kur und aller anderen Ayurveda-Programme ist bei Bedarf möglich. Dieser einzigartige Ort der ganzheitlichen Regeneration und Heilung bietet alle Annehmlichkeiten eines Fünfsternehotels. Ayurveda im Parkschlösschen bedeutet: seine Leichtigkeit wiederzuentdecken, Körper und Geist zu regenerieren und seine Selbstheilungskräfte zu stärken. Die Vision des Hauses lautet folgerichtig: „To make the world healthier, one person at a time!"

ROOMS: 43 ROOMS, 15 SUITES
SPECIALTIES: AYURVEDA COOKING WORKSHOPS, LIFESTYLE COACHING & TREATMENTS UNDER SUPERVISION OF EXPERIENCED AYURVEDIC PRACTITIONERS, POOL, SAUNA, YOGA, MEDITATION

AYURVEDA PARKSCHLÖSSCHEN
WILDBADSTRASSE 201
56841 TRABEN-TRARBACH
GERMANY (DEUTSCHLAND)
WWW.AYURVEDA-PARKSCHLOESSCHEN.DE
+49 6541 7050

ZIMMER: 43 ZIMMER, 15 SUITEN
BESONDERHEITEN: AYURVEDA-KOCHWORKSHOPS, -LIFESTYLE-COACHING, -BEHANDLUNGEN UNTER MEDIZINISCHER ANLEITUNG POOL, SAUNA, YOGA, MEDITATION

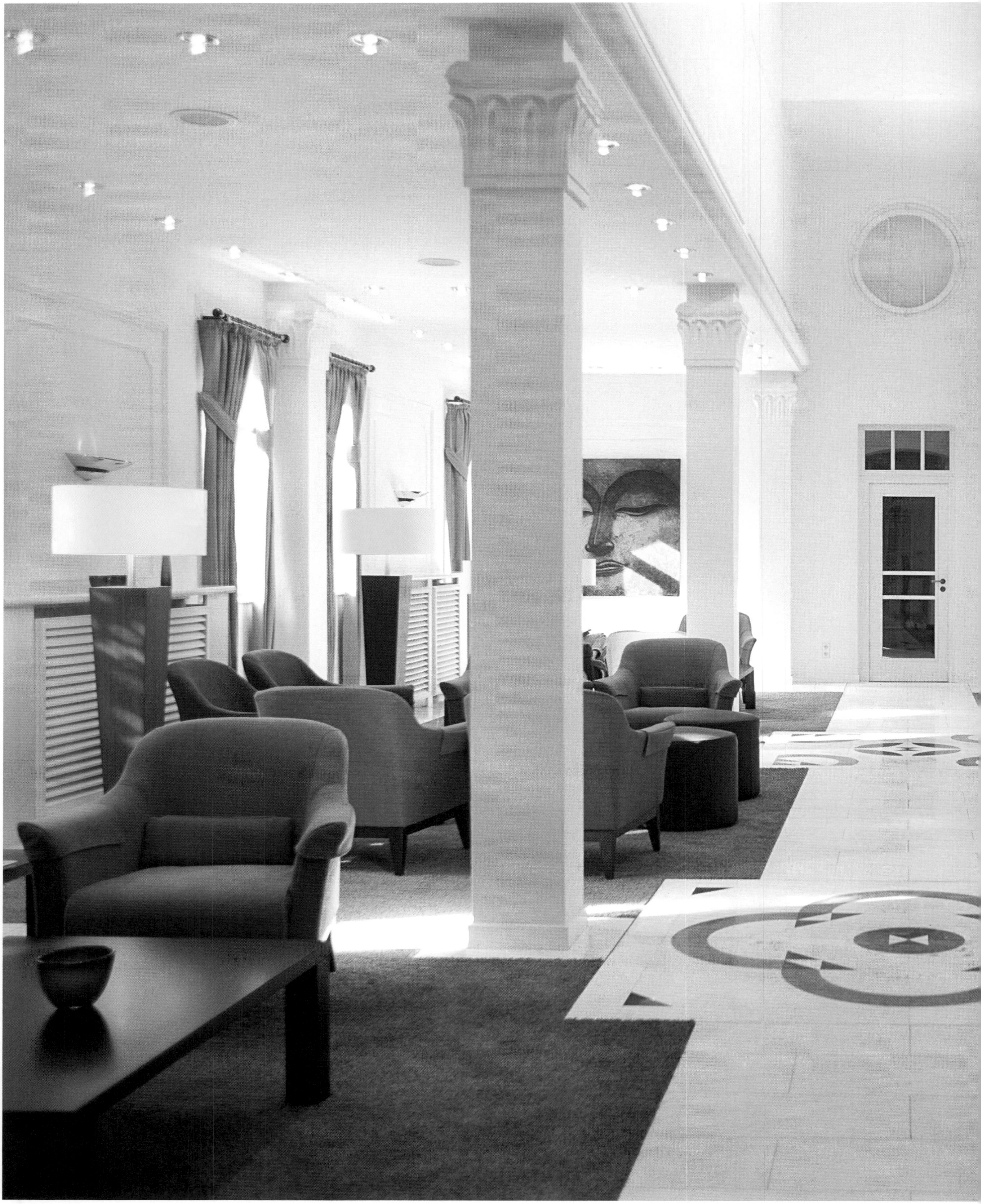

Ayurveda Parkschlösschen has a therapy department dedicated to Ayurveda that features thirteen therapy rooms and eleven quiet rooms in accordance with the traditional Ayurveda principle of separate areas for men and women. In addition, a 21,500 square feet (2,000 square meter) wellness area offers a thermal pool, two saunas, a fitness studio, cosmetic studio, a yoga and exercise area, and interiors which follow the ancient Indian principles of Vastu architecture featuring minimal electrosmog and WiFi-free.

Das Ayurveda Parkschlösschen verfügt über einen rein ayurvedischen Therapiebereich mit dreizehn Behandlungs- und elf Ruheräumen, gemäß des traditionellen Ayurveda nach Männern und Frauen getrennt. Zudem bietet der 2000 Quadratmeter große Wellnessbereich ein Thermalbad, zwei Saunen, Fitnessstudio, Kosmetikstudio, Yoga- und Gymnastikbereich und außerdem eine natürliche baubiologische Einrichtung nach der altindischen Architekturlehre Vastu mit sehr geringem Elektrosmog und ohne WLAN.

SESAME-CRUSTED EGGPLANT PATTIES
WITH PARSLEY RICE AND WARM TOMATO CUCUMBER SALAD

AUBERGINENBRATLINGE IN SESAMKRUSTE
AN PETERSILIENREIS UND TOMATEN-GURKEN-GEMÜSE

INGREDIENTS
SERVES 4

Eggplant patties

2 eggplants

1 tbsp sun-dried tomatoes, chopped

2 tbsp sunflower seeds

1 tsp mustard

1 tbsp capers

1 tbsp freshly chopped parsley

Salt, pepper, ground coriander,
  ground sweet paprika, dried marjoram

Balsamic vinegar

4 tbsp breadcrumbs

1 tbsp sesame seeds

1 tbsp olive oil

Parsley rice

2 cups basmati rice

1 bunch Italian parsley, stems removed

2 tbsp olive oil

Salt

Tomato cucumber salad
3½ oz/200 g tomatoes, peeled,
  seeds removed, and quartered
1 cucumber, halved lengthwise,
  seeds removed
1 tbsp ghee
Salt, pepper
1 tsp mustard
1 bunch dill (fresh or freeze-dried),
  chopped

ZUTATEN
FÜR 4 PERSONEN

Auberginenbratlinge
2 Auberginen
1 EL getrocknete Tomaten, gehackt
2 EL Sonnenblumenkerne
1 TL Senf
1 EL Kapern
1 EL frisch gehackte Petersilie
Salz, Pfeffer, gemahlener Koriander,
  edelsüßes Paprikapulver,
  getrockneter Majoran
Aceto balsamico
4 EL Paniermehl
1 EL Sesamsamen
1 EL Olivenöl

Petersilienreis
2 Tassen Basmatireis
1 Bund glatte Petersilie,
  Blätter abgezupft
2 EL Olivenöl
Salz

Tomaten-Gurken-Gemüse
200 g Tomaten, gehäutet, entkernt
  und geviertelt
1 Gurke, längs halbiert und entkernt
1 EL Ghee
Salz, Pfeffer
1 TL Senf
1 Bund Dill (frisch oder gefrier-
  getrocknet), gehackt

METHOD

Eggplant patties: Preheat the oven to 375°F/200°C. Puncture the eggplants all over with a fork and bake in the oven for 20 minutes until very soft. Allow to cool and then cut in half and scoop out the flesh with a spoon. Roughly chop the eggplant flesh and mix in a bowl with the tomatoes, sunflower seeds, mustard, capers, parsley, spices, and a little vinegar. Generously season the mixture and blend in 3 tablespoons of breadcrumbs. If the mixture is not firm enough, add the rest of the breadcrumbs. Form 12 small patties and dredge in the sesame seeds. Heat the oil in a pan and sear the patties on both sides.

Parsley rice: Rinse the rice in a sieve under warm, running water and drain well. Blend the parsley leaves with 1 tablespoon of oil and the same amount of water in a container, using an immersion blender. Set aside. Heat the rest of the oil in a pot and toast the rice without browning it. Add salt and 4 cups of water, cover the pot and bring the rice to a boil. Lower the heat, pull the pot partway off the burner, replace the lid, and allow the rice to steam for 15 to 20 minutes. Then fold in the parsley puree.

Tomato cucumber salad: Cut the tomato quarters and cucumber halves into strips, taking care not to make them too thin. Heat the ghee in a pan, add the vegetables, and season with salt, pepper, and mustard. Add the dill and briefly sauté the vegetables. Arrange the eggplant patties, parsley rice, and vegetables on four warmed plates and serve.

ZUBEREITUNG

Für die Bratlinge den Backofen auf 200 °C vorheizen. Die Auberginen mit einer Gabel rundum mehrmals einstechen und im Ofen etwa 20 Minuten sehr weich garen. Abkühlen lassen, dann halbieren und das Fruchtfleisch mit einem Löffel herausschaben. Das Fruchtfleisch grob hacken und in einer Schüssel mit Tomaten, Sonnenblumenkernen, Senf, Kapern, Petersilie, Gewürzen und etwas Essig vermischen. Die Masse kräftig abschmecken und 3 EL Paniermehl untermischen. Ist die Masse nicht fest genug ist, das restliche Paniermehl untermengen. Aus der Masse 12 Bratlinge formen und im Sesam wenden. Das Öl in einer Pfanne erhitzen und die Bratlinge darin von beiden Seiten leicht anbraten.

Für den Petersilienreis den Reis in einem Sieb unter fließend warmem Wasser abspülen und gut abtropfen lassen. Die Petersilienblätter mit je 1 EL Öl und Wasser in einem Rührbecher mit dem Pürierstab mixen, beiseitestellen. Das restliche Öl in einem Topf erhitzen und den Reis darin hell anbraten. Salz und 4 Tassen Wasser zugeben und den Reis zugedeckt aufkochen. Dann die Hitze reduzieren, den Topf etwas von der Herdplatte ziehen und den Reis zugedeckt 15–20 Minuten ausquellen lassen. Zuletzt das Petersilienpüree unterheben.

Für das Gemüse Tomatenviertel und Gurkenhälften in nicht zu dünne Streifen schneiden. Das Ghee in einer Pfanne erhitzen, die Gemüse hineingeben und mit Salz, Pfeffer und Senf würzen. Dill zufügen und das Gemüse kurz durchschwenken. Auberginenbratlinge, Petersilienreis und Gemüse auf vier vorgewärmten Tellern anrichten und servieren.

LANDHAUS BECKMANN

KALKAR, NORTH RHINE-WESTPHALIA

The Lower Rhine region may not be one of the most visited vacation destinations in Germany, but the region bordering the Netherlands is growing in popularity—for very good reason. The landscape is flat and yet not the least bit boring. Cyclists, in particular, love the diverse routes that cross green meadows and pass through forest and charming towns, often right along the Rhine. Day-trippers will find many interesting sights, from historic Roman cities such as Xanten, with its archeological park, to top-class museums and amusement parks.

The four-star Landhaus Beckmann is an excellent place to stay while you explore the Lower Rhine region. Not only does it win points for its commitment to sustainability, for which it has received the GreenSign seal from InfraCert, but it is also absolutely vegan-friendly—from its cuisine to its skin care products to its minibars. The hotel uses only vegan cleansers and toiletries.

In the very spot where the residents of the former farmhouse used to serve schnapps after church on Sunday, you can now enjoy dishes typical of the Lower Rhine region in the Tellerrand restaurant. Made from high quality regional ingredients, the meals include many vegan options. Don't let anyone tell you that the locals are stolid and close-minded! The hotel also has a spacious spa and wellness area, where you can relax luxuriously, perhaps after a long bike ride through this green landscape. Perhaps it is high time you discovered the Lower Rhine region.

Der Niederrhein gehört vielleicht nicht zu den am meisten besuchten Urlaubsregionen in Deutschland, aber der Landstrich an der Grenze zu den Niederlanden wird stets beliebter – und das nicht ohne Grund. Flach ist die Landschaft, und doch nicht langweilig. Besonders Radfahrer lieben die vielfältigen Routen über grüne Wiesen, durch Wälder und charmante Städtchen, oft direkt am Rhein entlang. Ausflugsziele gibt es reichlich, von historischen Römerstädten wie Xanten mit seinem archäologischen Park über hochkarätige Museen bis zu Freizeitparks.

Eine empfehlenswerte Unterkunft für die Entdeckung des Niederrheins ist das Viersterne-Landhaus Beckmann, das nicht nur in puncto Nachhaltigkeit überzeugt und dafür bereits mit dem Siegel „GreenSign" von InfraCert ausgezeichnet wurde, sondern auch absolut *vegan-friendly* ausgerichtet ist – von der Küche über Pflegeprodukte bis hin zur Minibar. Es werden ausschließlich vegane Reinigungsmittel und Kosmetika verwendet.

Genau dort, wo früher auf dem ehemaligen Bauernhof nach dem Gottesdienst Schnaps ausgeschenkt wurde, kann man heute im Restaurant Tellerrand typische niederrheinische Gerichte mit hervorragenden Erzeugnissen aus der Region genießen – mit vielen veganen Optionen. Soll noch mal einer sagen, der Niederrheiner sei stur und schaue nicht über den Tellerrand! Zum Hotel gehört außerdem ein großzügiger Spa- und Wellnessbereich, in dem man nicht nur nach einer ausgiebigen Radtour quer durch diese grüne Region vortrefflich relaxen kann. Es ist wohl an der Zeit, endlich mal den Niederrhein zu entdecken!

ROOMS: 41
SPECIALTIES: SAUNA, WHIRLPOOL, MASSAGES, INFRARED LOUNGER, GYM

LANDHAUS BECKMANN
RÖMERSTRASSE 1
47546 KALKAR
GERMANY (DEUTSCHLAND)
WWW.LANDHAUS-BECKMANN.DE
+49 2824 962 566 66

ZIMMER: 41
BESONDERHEITEN: SAUNA, WHIRLPOOL, MASSAGEN, INFRAROTLIEGEN, FITNESSRAUM

HOTEL NICOLAY 1881

ZELTINGEN-RACHTIG, RHINELAND-PALATINATE

Steep vineyards, charmingly cozy half-timber houses, a wide river, and plenty of hearty food—this is what most people think of when they picture the Moselle region, that strip of land where Germany, Luxembourg, and France come together. But who would have thought to find a vegan oasis in this very place?

The Hotel Nicolay 1881 is situated right on a loop of the Moselle River, not far from the famous town of Bernkastel-Kues. Run by the same family for five generations, the establishment is currently in the capable hands of Chef Johannes Nicolay. The former post office blends traditional hospitality with the finest vegan cuisine. Two vegan restaurants, complete with the hotel's own mushroom farm, along with a fully vegan wellness zone invite guests to let themselves be pampered and leave their everyday stress behind.

The Moselle Valley is the ideal place to do this, since it seems almost as though time has stood still in its tiny villages and historic towns. The famous Moselle Riesling, whose vines grown on steep, green slopes all around the hotel and whose fruit is often still picked by hand, determines the rhythm of life here, which is more in tune with the moods of nature than anywhere else. Guests are invited to stroll a short way along the Moselstieg trail and marvel at the various views of the ancient landscape. The 227-mile (365-kilometer) hiking trail was recently crowned the prettiest path anywhere in Germany.

Steile Weinberge, charmant-heimelige Fachwerkhäuser, ein breiter Fluss und ganz viel deftiges Essen – das verbinden die meisten Menschen mit dem Moselgebiet, jenem Landstrich, in dem sich Deutschland, Luxemburg und Frankreich treffen. Doch wer hätte gedacht, dass sich ausgerechnet hier eine vegane Oase befindet?

Unweit der berühmten Stadt Bernkastel-Kues – direkt an einer Moselschlaufe – liegt das Hotel Nicolay 1881, das bereits in fünfter Generation, heute von Küchenchef Johannes Nicolay, geführt wird. In der ehemaligen Poststation treffen traditionelle Gastlichkeit und feinste vegane Küche aufeinander. Gleich zwei vegane Restaurants, inklusive eigener Pilzzucht sowie ein komplett veganer Wellnessbereich, laden den Besucher ein, sich verwöhnen zu lassen und den Alltagsstress abzuschütteln.

Das Moseltal ist hierfür der ideale Ort, denn ein wenig scheint es, als sei die Zeit in den kleinen Dörfern und historischen Städten stehen geblieben. Der berühmte Moselriesling, dessen Weinreben rund um das Hotel auf den grünen Steilhängen wachsen und oftmals noch von Hand gepflückt werden, bestimmt hier den Rhythmus der Menschen, der viel stärker an die Launen der Natur geknüpft ist, als anderswo. Die Besucher sind eingeladen, ein Stück den Moselstieg entlang zu streifen und sich von den verschiedenen Aussichten auf die uralte Landschaft fesseln zu lassen – der 365 Kilometer lange Wanderweg wurde unlängst zum schönsten seiner Art in Deutschland gekürt.

ROOMS: 34
SPECIALTIES: TWO VEGAN RESTAURANTS, YOGA, MEDITATION, HIKING, MOUNTAINBIKE TOURS, SAUNA, DETOX AND BEAUTY TREATMENTS, MASSAGES

HOTEL NICOLAY 1881
UFERALLEE 7
54492 ZELTINGEN
GERMANY (DEUTSCHLAND)
WWW.HOTEL-NICOLAY.DE
+49 6532 93910

ZIMMER: 34
BESONDERHEITEN: ZWEI VEGANE RESTAURANTS, YOGA, MEDITATION, WANDERN, MOUNTAINBIKE-TOUREN, SAUNA, DETOX- UND BEAUTY-BEHANDLUNGEN, MASSAGEN

But don't just admire the Moselle wine on the vine, for you can enjoy it in abundance in the hotel as well, along with delicious
meals. From vegan fast food at the "Sonnenuhr" to high-quality, plant-based gourmet cuisine at "Restaurant Weinstube,"
all dishes are always freshly prepared without any additives. According to ancient tradition, wherever wine grows, celebrations are
soon to follow. At the Hotel Nicolay 1881, you can not only enjoy some much needed R&R but also join as many as 90 guests
in vegan feasts served at festive events such as weddings and birthdays.

Natürlich darf man den Moselwein nicht nur in Rebenform bestaunen, im Hotel kann er auch ausgiebig genossen werden,
zusammen mit den köstlichen Speisen – ob veganes Fastfood in der Sonnenuhr oder hochklassige pflanzliche Gourmetküche
im Restaurant Weinstube – alle Gerichte werden immer frisch zubereitet und sind frei von Zusatzstoffen. Wo Wein wächst,
da wird gefeiert, das war schon immer so. Im Hotel Nicolay 1881 kann man sich nicht nur eine Auszeit gönnen, sondern auch
mit bis zu 90 Gästen rein vegane Feste wie Hochzeiten und Geburtstage feiern.

INGREDIENTS
SERVES 4

Flaxseed patties (makes 8 patties)
1 lb/500 g golden flaxseeds
1 tbsp/20 g sea salt
1½ tsp/3 g black pepper, coarsely ground
1 scant tsp/2 g ground paprika
1¼ tsp/5 g cane sugar
1 shallot, finely diced
Seeds scraped from inside 1 vanilla bean
1 garlic clove
1 oz/20 g curly parsley
½ tbsp/8 g coconut oil

Fakeon (makes 5 strips of fakeon)
1 tbsp/15 g water
2 tsp/10 g BBQ seasoning (or sauce,
  but then leave out the saffron sauce)
½ tsp/10 g tomato paste
1 tsp/5 g Danish smoked salt
2 sheets of rice paper, softened in water
½ tbsp/8 g coconut oil

Caramelized nuts
3 tbsp/40 g sugar
¼ cup/30 g walnuts

Spinach and rhubarb
2 tsp/8 g walnut oil
1 oz/20 g shallots, finely diced
½ garlic clove
½ cup/50 g rhubarb, julienned
1½ cup/50 g fresh spinach, washed and drained
1 pinch nutmeg & salt each

Potatoes
2 tbsp/20 g vegan margarine
6 oz/180 g potatoes, cooked, peeled,
  and cut into ½-inch/1-cm cubes

Saffron sauce
2 tbsp/30 g vegan margarine
1 oz/30 g shallots, finely dices
1 garlic clove
1 pinch saffron threads
1 vanilla bean
2 bay leaves
2 tbsp/200 ml Riesling or another
  dry white wine
Zest of ½ organic lemon
1 splash lemon juice
½ cup/100 g plant-based cream substitute

GOLDEN FLAXSEED PATTIES ON A BED OF RHUBARB AND SPINACH
WITH FAKEON, CARAMELIZED NUTS, AND POTATO CUBES IN SAFFRON SAUCE

METHOD

Flaxseed patties: Blend golden flaxseeds with 2 cups/500 ml of water. Add salt, pepper, paprika, sugar, shallots, vanilla, garlic clove, and parsley and continue to mix thoroughly. Let the finished mixture rest for around 15 minutes. Preheat the oven to 350°F/180°C. Form patties, sear on both sides in a pan with a little coconut oil. Bake for 15 minutes.

Fakeon: Mix the water and tomato paste with the BBQ seasoning and Danish smoked salt and brush onto one of the softened sheets of rice paper. Place the second sheet of rice paper on top and press them together. Cut into strips and fry in the coconut oil.

Caramelized nuts: Caramelize the sugar and add the walnuts.

Spinach and rhubarb: In a pot, sweat the shallots and garlic cloves in the walnut oil until translucent. Add the rhubarb and spinach to the pot and season with salt and nutmeg.

Potatoes: Sweat the potato cubes in the margarine until golden brown. Season to taste with fresh, chopped herbs or a little salt.

Saffron sauce: Sweat the shallots, garlic clove, and saffron threads in the vegan margarine. Add the vanilla bean, bay leaf, Riesling, lemon zest, and lemon juice. Bring to a boil and reduce to approximately a scant ½ cup/100 ml. Add the plant-based cream substitute. Pass the sauce through a sieve, stir to mix.

To serve, arrange the drained rhubarb/spinach mixture on a plate. Stir the saffron sauce again until combined and drizzle it around the vegetables. Place the flaxseed patties and fakeon on top of the vegetables and add the golden brown potatoes to the plate. To garnish, deep-fry a leaf of spinach or ramsons (wild garlic), or dry it in the oven at low heat and drape it over the patties.

Tip: It's a good idea to place each component of this dish in an oven preheated to 200°F/70°C as each one is prepared so that the entire dish can be served hot.

GOLDLEINSAMENBRATLINGE AUF RHABARBER-BLATTSPINAT

MIT FAKEON, KARAMELLNÜSSEN UND KARTOFFELWÜRFELN AN SAFRANSAUCE

ZUTATEN
FÜR 4 PERSONEN

Goldleinsamenbratlinge
500 g Goldleinsamen
20 g Meersalz
3 g schwarzer Pfeffer, grob gemahlen
2 g Paprikapulver
5 g Rohrzucker
Mark von 1 Vanilleschote
1 Schalotte, fein gehackt
1 Knoblauchzehe
20 g krause Petersilie
8 g Kokosfett

Fakeon-Streifen
10 g Tomatenmark
10 g BBQ-Gewürz
5 g dänisches Rauchsalz
2 Reispapierblätter,
 in Wasser eingeweicht
8 g Kokosfett

Karamellnüsse
40 g Zucker
30 g Walnusskerne

Spinat und Rhabarber
8 g Walnussöl
20 g Schalotten, fein gehackt
½ Knoblauchzehe
50 g Rhabarber, in Stifte geschnitten
50 g Blattspinat, gewaschen,
 und abgetropft
1 Prise Muskatnuss
1 Prise Salz

Kartoffeln
20 g Bio-Margarine (z. B. Alsan)
360 g Pellkartoffeln, abgekühlt und
 in 1 cm große Würfel geschnitten

Safransauce
30 g Bio-Margarine (z. B. Alsan)
30 g Schalotten, fein gehackt
1 Knoblauchzehe
1 Prise Safranfäden
1 Vanilleschote
2 Lorbeerblätter
200 ml Riesling oder
 trockener Weißwein
abgeriebene Schale von ½ Bio-Zitrone
1 Spritzer Zitronensaft
100 g Soja-Kochcreme

ZUBEREITUNG

Für die Bratlinge Leinsamen und 500 ml Wasser im Standmixer fein verquirlen. Salz, Pfeffer, Paprikapulver, Zucker, Vanille, Schalotte, Knoblauch und Petersilie untermixen. Die Masse 15 Minuten ruhen lassen, dann zu 8 Bratlingen formen. Den Backofen auf 180 °C vorheizen. Das Kokosfett in einer Pfanne erhitzen und die Bratlinge darin von beiden Seiten anbraten. Im Ofen in 15 Minuten fertig backen.

Für die Fakeon-Streifen Tomatenmark, Gewürz, Salz und 1 EL Wasser verrühren. Ein Reisblatt damit bestreichen, das zweite Blatt darauflegen und andrücken. In fünf Streifen schneiden und im heißen Kokosfett braten.

Für die Karamellnüsse den Zucker in einer Pfanne schmelzen und karamellisieren lassen. Die Nüsse im heißen Karamell schwenken.

Für Spinat und Rhabarber das Walnussöl in einem Topf erhitzen und Schalotten und Knoblauch glasig anschwitzen. Rhabarber und Spinat zugeben und mit Muskat und Salz würzen.

Die Margarine in einer Pfanne erhitzen und die Kartoffelwürfel darin goldbraun braten. Nach Geschmack frische, gehackte Kräuter oder etwas Salz hinzugeben.

Für die Safransauce die Margarine in einem Topf erhitzen. Schalotten, Knoblauch und Safranfäden darin anschwitzen. Vanille, Lorbeer, Riesling, Zitronenschale und -saft zugeben, aufkochen und auf etwa 100 ml einkochen lassen. Die Kochcreme einrühren, die Sauce durch ein Sieb passieren und mit dem Pürierstab schaumig aufmixen.

Zum Anrichten den abgetropften Rhabarber-Spinat auf einen Teller geben. Die Safransauce nochmals aufmixen und darum herum verteilen. Die Bratlinge und den Fakeon darauflegen und die goldbraunen Kartoffeln hinzugeben. Als Dekorationselement kann ein Spinatblatt oder ein Blatt Bärlauch bei niedriger Temperatur im Backofen getrocknet oder frittiert und auf den Bratlingen drapiert werden.

Tipp: Es empfiehlt sich die Einzelkomponenten bei 70 °C im vorgeheizten Backofen zu „sammeln", damit auch alles schön heiß auf den Teller kommt.

HAUS AM WATT

HERINGSAND, SCHLESWIG-HOLSTEIN

Paradise doesn't always mean palm trees, coconuts, coral reefs and a blue-green sea. It can also look like this: mudflats and meadows, thatched roofs and fruit trees, homemade cakes, and a comfortable, old vestibule. On arriving in this peaceful idyll, you take a deep breath. A really deep one. And then another. Beyond the dike stands Haus am Watt, a certified organic bed and breakfast. Embedded in a landscape of meadows and fields, only a few minutes from the North Sea coast, the 250-year-old thatched roof farmhouse is steeped in tradition. Furnished with antiques in the style of a country cottage, the house has retained its original charm.

After rising from a restful sleep, you are met with the scent of freshly baked rolls, with a breakfast of regional organic foods waiting in the large vestibule. In the evening, you are once again pampered with a three-course vegetarian or vegan meal, always prepared from organic and seasonal ingredients, a good many of them from the own garden. With its ancient fruit trees and lawns perfect for sunbathing, a pond ecosystem, a fire pit, and a rustic barrel sauna—not to mention chickens, cats and horses—the large estate offers a perfect spot for every guest, whether they want to curl up with a book in the shade of a tree or relax in a yoga class in the light-flooded seminar house. The Wadden Sea—which was named a UNESCO World Heritage Site in 2009—lies a short kilometer away. Enjoy a lazy stroll along the beach, hike through the mudflats, take long walks, go on an excursion or take a boat to the Hallig Islands or to view the seal colonies—the marvelous sea air will have you taking deep breaths until you leave your everyday cares behind.

Es braucht nicht unbedingt Palmen, Kokosnüsse, türkisblaues Meer und ein Korallenriff – das Paradies kann auch genau so aussehen: Wattenmeer und Weiden, Reetdach und Obstbäume, hausgebackener Kuchen und eine gemütliche alte Diele. Wer in dieser Ruhe ankommt, darf durchatmen. Ganz tief. Und noch einmal. Hinter dem Deich liegt die biozertifizierte Pension Haus am Watt, ein 250 Jahre alter Reetdachhof mit langer Tradition, eingebettet in eine Landschaft aus Wiesen und Feldern, nur wenige Minuten von der Nordseeküste entfernt. Der ursprüngliche Charakter wurde erhalten und das Haus mit alten Landhausmöbeln ausgestattet.

Steht man hier nach einem erholsamen Schlaf auf, riecht es nach frisch gebackenen Brötchen, denn das Frühstück aus regionalen Bioprodukten wartet bereits in der großen Diele. Am Abend wird man mit einem vegetarischen oder veganen Drei-Gänge-Menü noch einmal verwöhnt – die Zutaten sind dabei immer ökologisch und saisonal aus dem eigenen Garten. Das große Anwesen mit alten Obstbäumen und Liegewiesen, Teichbiotop und Feuerplatz, uriger Fasssauna sowie Hühnern, Katzen und Pferden hält für jeden Gast einen Lieblingsplatz bereit – ganz egal, ob man es sich mit einem Buch im Schatten eines Baumes bequem macht oder im lichtdurchfluteten Seminarhaus beim Yoga entspannt.

Nur einen Kilometer entfernt beginnt das Wattenmeer, seit 2009 UNESCO-Weltnaturerbe. Faulenzen am Strand, Wattwanderungen, Spaziergänge, Exkursionen oder Schifffahrten zu Halligen und Seehundbänken – die herrliche Meeresluft lässt einen immer wieder tief durchatmen und den Alltag komplett vergessen.

ROOMS: 13
SPECIALTIES: SAUNA, MASSAGES, YOGA SEMINARS, AYURVEDA, BIKE RENTAL, COOKING CLASSES, CREATIVE CLASSES, HIKING

HAUS AM WATT
HERINGSANDER STRASSE 4
25764 HERINGSAND
GERMANY (DEUTSCHLAND)
WWW.HAUSAMWATT.DE
+49 4833 424 274

ZIMMER: 13
BESONDERHEITEN: SAUNA, MASSAGEN, YOGASEMINARE, AYURVEDA, FAHRRADVERLEIH, KOCHKURSE, KREATIVKURSE, WANDERN

BIOHOTEL CARPE DIEM

OSTSEEBAD PREROW, MECKLENBURG-VORPOMMERN

A stay at the Carpe Diem would be best described as an opportunity to slow down. Take it easy. Don't worry about anything other than yourself for once. This is very easy to do in this Mediterranean-styled establishment situated in the Baltic coastal town of Prerow. The Poppe family runs the small hotel with a great deal of passion and a personal touch. People come to Carpe Diem from all over Germany to enjoy the therapeutic treatments offered by owner and osteopath Mario Poppe. Of course, they also come for the gourmet and health weeks that are regularly held here. Filled with a meditative ambience, the hotel is a peaceful oasis, where you can leave all your cares behind—in the wellness area, a yoga class, or relaxing on a sun lounge in the vast garden. Indoors and outdoors, guests encounter artworks that demand undisturbed contemplation.

The innkeepers' passion can also be found in the hotel's culinary offerings, as the bountiful organic, vegetarian and vegan breakfast buffet is anything but standard fare, with homemade spreads and wholegrain breads baked on the premises. You can also pamper yourself with delicious whole foods in the afternoons and evenings. Preferably paired with a glass of homemade elderflower lemonade.

When the immediate surroundings beckon, you can go on long, restorative walks and explore the wildly romantic Darß Peninsula, with its kilometers of beaches and deep forests.

When it comes to his guests, former competitive athlete Mario Poppe is all about slowing down and promoting a healthy lifestyle. Anyone who wants to follow his example will find a warm welcome at Carpe Diem and can enjoy the finer points of the slow life.

Entschleunigend ist das Attribut, dass einen Aufenthalt im Carpe Diem wohl am besten beschreibt. Zur Ruhe kommen, sich einfach mal um nichts kümmern müssen, außer um sich selbst – das wird einem in diesem Haus mit mediterranem Flair im Ostseeküstenort Prerow wahrlich leicht gemacht. Sehr persönlich und mit ganz viel Leidenschaft wird dieses kleine Hotel vom Ehepaar Poppe geführt. Für die heilenden Anwendungen von Betreiber und Osteopath Mario Poppe kommen die Gäste aus ganz Deutschland ins Carpe Diem, aber natürlich auch, um die regelmäßig stattfindenden Gourmet- oder Gesundheitswochen in Anspruch zu nehmen. Das Haus ist mit seinem meditativen Ambiente ein friedlicher Ort, an dem man sich fallen lassen kann, egal ob im Wellnessbereich, beim Yoga oder auf einer Sonnenliege im weitläufigen Garten. So wie im ganzen Haus, begegnen den Gästen auch im Außenbereich Kunstwerke, die zum ungestörten Betrachten einladen.

Die Passion der Gastgeber zeigt sich ebenfalls kulinarisch, denn das reichhaltige vegetarisch-vegane Biofrühstücksbuffet mit hausgemachten Aufstrichen und selbstgebackenem Vollkornbrot ist alles andere als Standard. Nachmittags und abends darf man sich ebenso vollwertig und lecker verwöhnen lassen ... gerne auch bei einem Glas hausgemachter Holunderblütenlimonade.

Wen es in die nähere Umgebung zieht, der kann die wildromantische Halbinsel Darß mit ihren kilometerlangen Stränden und tiefen Wäldern auf langen erholsamen Spaziergängen erkunden.

Der einstige Leistungssportler Mario Poppe setzt heute für seine Gäste auf Entschleunigung und eine gesunde Lebensweise. Wer ihm das gleichtun möchte, ist im Carpe Diem herzlich willkommen und kann sich an der Kunst der Langsamkeit erfreuen.

ROOMS: 11
SPECIALTIES: SAUNA, STEAM BATH, GYM, MASSAGES, YOGA, FASTING, NATURAL BEACH, IN-HOUSE NATUROPATHIC PRACTICE, OSTEOPATHY

BIOHOTEL CARPE DIEM
GRÜNE STR. 31 B
18375 OSTSEEBAD PREROW
GERMANY (DEUTSCHLAND)
WWW.CARPE-DIEM-PREROW.DE
+49 382 337 080

ZIMMER: 11
BESONDERHEITEN: SAUNA, DAMPFBAD, FITNESSRAUM, MASSAGEN, YOGA, FASTEN, NATURSTRAND, HAUSEIGENE NATURHEILPRAXIS, OSTEOPATHIE

INGREDIENTS
SERVES 6

Gravy
1 red beet
1 leek
1 parsnip
3 carrots
2 onions
1 garlic clove
Sunflower oil
7 oz/200 g tomato paste
1 qt/1 l grape juice
2 bay leaves
3 allspice berries
5 juniper berries
Salt, pepper, freshly chopped thyme

Nut cutlet
10 oz/300 g carrots
1⅓ cup/200 g red onions
1 leek
1 parsnip
1 red banana pepper
Sunflower oil
14 oz/400 g nuts (hazelnuts, Brazil nuts, walnuts or cashews), half finely ground and half medium-coarsely ground
1 tbsp each tomato paste, mustard, psyllium husks, nutritional yeast flakes
Freshly chopped garden herbs
Salt, pepper
Chives, stems and blossoms

Beet-horseradish carpaccio
2 medium-sized red beets
½ organic apple, seeds removed, finely grated
2 tsp freshly grated horseradish
Juice of 1 orange
2 tbsp sesame oil
Salt, pepper, cumin, date sugar
2 handfuls of purslane

Quinoa
1 cup/200 g quinoa
Salt

VEGAN NUT CUTLETS
WITH BEET-HORSERADISH CARPACCIO AND QUINOA

METHOD

Gravy: Wash and cut the unpeeled vegetables into pieces approximately 1 inch/ 2 cm in size. Heat a little oil in a pot and brown the vegetables on high heat. Add the tomato paste and fry for 5 to 8 minutes, stirring constantly. Deglaze the pan with the grape juice, then add the bay leaf, allspice, and juniper berries. Simmer on medium heat for around 1 hour until thickened. Then strain the gravy through a sieve and season with salt, pepper, and thyme.

Nut cutlets: Preheat the oven to 375°F/200°C (do not use convection heat).
Place six stainless steel ring molds on a baking sheet lined with parchment paper. Wash, trim and peel the vegetables and chop into a fine dice. Heat a little oil in a pan and sear the vegetable cubes. Mix in the nuts, tomato paste, mustard, psyllium husks, nutritional yeast, and herbs and season to taste with salt and pepper. Fill the ring molds, pressing down lightly, and bake for around 30 minutes until golden brown. Remove from the oven, cool, and release from the ring molds.

Beet-horseradish carpaccio: Wash the beets and cook in water until done. Then thinly slice the beets. Mix together the apple, horseradish, orange juice, and sesame oil. Season the dressing with salt, pepper, cumin, and date sugar. Wash the purslane and shake dry. Toss the beet slices with the dressing and arrange with the purslane on six plates.

Quinoa: Place the quinoa in a pot with 1¾ cups/400 ml of water and a little salt and bring to a boil. Reduce the heat to low and simmer for 10 to 15 minutes until the water is absorbed. Ladle a little gravy on six plates and place a cutlet on top. Place a ring mold next to each cutlet and fill with quinoa. Garnish with the chive stems and blossoms and serve with the beet carpaccio.

VEGANER NUSSBRATEN
MIT ROTE-BETE-MEERRETTICH-CARPACCIO

ZUTATEN
FÜR 6 PERSONEN

Braten-Jus
1 Rote Bete
1 Stange Lauch
1 Pastinake
3 Möhren
2 Zwiebeln
1 Knoblauchzehe
Sonnenblumenöl
200 g Tomatenmark
1 l Traubensaft
2 Lorbeerblätter
3 Pimentkörner
5 Wacholderbeeren
Salz, Pfeffer, frisch gehackter Thymian

Nussbraten
300 g Möhren
200 g rote Zwiebeln
1 Stange Lauch
1 Pastinake
1 rote Spitzpaprika

Sonnenblumenöl
400 g Nusskerne (Hasel-, Para-, Walnuss- oder Cashewkerne), je zur Hälfte fein und mittelgrob gemahlen
je 1 EL Tomatenmark, Senf, Flohsamenschalen,
   Vollwerthefeflocken
frisch gehackte Gartenkräuter
Salz, Pfeffer
Schnittlauchhalme und -blüten

Rote-Bete-Meerrettich-Carpaccio
2 mittelgroße Rote Beten
½ Bio-Apfel, entkernt und fein gerieben
2 TL frisch geriebener Meerrettich
Saft von 1 Orange
2 EL Sesamöl
Salz, Pfeffer, Kreuzkümmel, Dattelsüße
2 Handvoll Gartenpostelein (Portulak)

Quinoa
200 g Quinoa
Salz

ZUBEREITUNG

Für den Jus die Gemüse waschen und mit Schale in etwa 2 cm große Stücke schneiden. Etwas Öl in einem Topf erhitzen und die Gemüsestücke darin bei starker Hitze braun anbraten. Das Tomatenmark zugeben und unter Rühren 5–8 Minuten mitbraten. Mit Traubensaft ablöschen, Lorbeer, Piment und Wacholderbeeren zufügen und alles bei mittlerer Hitze etwa 1 Stunde einkochen lassen. Den Jus danach durch ein Sieb abgießen und mit Salz, Pfeffer und Thymian abschmecken.

Für den Nussbraten den Backofen auf 200 °C (Ober-/Unterhitze) vorheizen, sechs Edelstahlringe auf ein mit Backpapier belegtes Backblech setzen. Die Gemüse waschen und putzen bzw. schälen und in feine Würfel schneiden. Etwas Öl in einer Pfanne erhitzen und die Gemüsewürfel darin anbraten. Nüsse, Tomatenmark, Senf, Flohsamenschalen, Hefeflocken und Kräuter untermischen und die Masse mit Salz und Pfeffer abschmecken. In die Ringe füllen, leicht andrücken und im Ofen in etwa 30 Minuten goldbraun backen. Herausnehmen, abkühlen lassen und aus den Ringen lösen.

Für das Carpaccio die Roten Beten waschen und in Wasser gar kochen. Danach in sehr feine Scheiben schneiden. Apfel, Meerrettich, Orangensaft und Sesamöl verrühren. Das Dressing mit Salz, Pfeffer, Kreuzkümmel und Dattelsüße würzen. Den Postelein waschen und trocken schütteln. Rote-Bete-Scheiben und Dressing mischen und mit dem Gartenpostelein auf sechs Tellern anrichten.

Die Quinoa in einem Topf mit 400 ml Wasser und etwas Salz aufkochen. Dann bei schwacher Hitze 10–15 Minuten ausquellen lassen. Etwas Jus auf sechs Teller geben und einen Nussbraten darauflegen. Die Quinoa in einem weiteren Ring danebensetzen. Mit Schnittlauchhalmen und -blüten dekorieren und mit dem Rote-Bete-Carpaccio servieren.

ALMODÓVAR HOTEL

BERLIN, BERLIN

Friedrichshain is a study in contrasts—squatters and organic lifestyles, graffiti and Nobel architecture, riots and artist studios. Berlin's wild, colorful eastern district is home to people who like to do things just a bit differently than everyone else. Which makes it the perfect place for the Almodóvar organic hotel. Built in 2012, the establishment was designed as an ecological and purely vegetarian hotel from the very beginning.

The Almodóvar does not view vegetarianism and "organics" as passing trends but rather embraces them as its underlying philosophy, reflected in all aspects of the establishment. The furniture in the rooms is made entirely from sustainably grown wood, while the textiles and toiletries are certified organic. The hotel's culinary offerings are vegetarian/vegan. Breakfast options include homemade spreads, bread and cake, as well as vegan cheese and meat alternatives, including chorizo and Currywurst (sausage in a curry-tomato sauce and a specialty of Berlin). Of course, everything comes from monitored organic farms. The Bistro Bardot serves snacks and soups during the day and turns into a relaxed restaurant in the evening, drawing epicures from all over the city.

Guests seeking to escape the hectic world of the big city will find peace and quiet with a round of yoga in their rooms—the standard amenities include a yoga mat. The rooms were designed to ensure enough space so that you don't bump into anything while performing a sun salutation. Alternatively, you can indulge yourself for a few hours in the hotel's Roof Top City Spa. Relax in the sauna and let your gaze sweep over the glittering lights of the city—up here, you can almost touch the sky.

Friedrichshain ist ein Bezirk der Gegensätze – Hausbesetzer und Bioszene, Graffitis und Nobelneubauten, Krawalle und Kunstateliers –, Berlins wilder, bunter Osten und Heimat all jener, die so manches anders machen, als alle anderen. Insofern der richtige Ort für das Almodóvar Biohotel. Das 2012 erbaute Haus wurde von Anfang an als ökologisches und rein vegetarisches Hotel geplant.

Im Almodóvar sind Vegetarismus und Bio keine aufgesetzten Trends, sondern gelebte Philosophie, die sich in allen Aspekten des Hauses widerspiegelt. Die Möbel auf den Zimmern wurden zu einhundert Prozent aus nachhaltigen Hölzern gefertigt, die Textilien und Kosmetika sind biozertifiziert. Kulinarisch ist das Hotel vegetarisch-vegan ausgerichtet. Zum Frühstück gibt es neben hausgemachten Pasten, Brot und Kuchen auch vegane Käse- und Fleischalternativen, wie etwa Chorizo und – schließlich ist man hier in Berlin – vegane Currywurst, natürlich alles aus kontrolliert biologischem Anbau. Das Bistro Bardot, in dem tagsüber Snacks und Suppen angeboten werden, verwandelt sich abends in ein entspanntes Restaurant, das Genießer aus allen Teilen der Stadt anzieht.

Wer in der Hektik der Metropole nach Ruhe sucht, findet diese bei einer Runde Yoga im eigenen Zimmer – die Matten gehören zur Standardausstattung. Und bei der Konzeption wurde natürlich darauf geachtet, dass genug Platz ist, um beim Sonnengruß nicht irgendwo anzustoßen. Oder man gönnt sich ein paar Stunden im Roof Top City Spa auf dem Dach des Hotels. In der Sauna entspannen und den Blick über die glitzernden Lichter der Stadt schweifen lassen – hier ist man dem „Himmel über Berlin" ganz nah!

ROOMS: 60
SPECIALTIES: SAUNA, MASSAGES (E.G. SHIATSU), LOCATED IN A TRENDY NEIGHBORHOOD, ORGANIC DELI

ALMODÓVAR HOTEL
BOXHAGENER STRASSE 83
10245 BERLIN
GERMANY (DEUTSCHLAND)
WWW.ALMODOVARHOTEL.DE
+49 30 692 097 080

ZIMMER: 60
BESONDERHEITEN: SAUNA, MASSAGEN (U.A. SHIATSU), LAGE IM SZENEBEZIRK, BIODELI

The Almodóvar's well thought out concept is apparent in many other details. After all, sustainability runs through everything, even behind the scenes. The hotel orders its office supplies from a sustainable mail order company, heats its spaces with a heat pump and district heating and purchases its electricity entirely from renewable sources. It doesn't get any greener than this.

Dass im Almodóvar alles hervorragend durchdacht ist, zeigt sich in vielen weiteren Details, denn der Nachhaltigkeitsgedanke zieht sich auch durch die Bereiche, die Gäste nicht sehen können. So bestellt das Hotel seine Büromaterialien bei einem nachhaltigen Versandhandel, heizt mit Wärmepumpe und Fernwärme und bezieht seinen Strom zu einhundert Prozent aus erneuerbaren Energien. Grüner geht es wirklich nicht.

A DIFFERENT KIND OF LASAGNA
RAW-FOODS LASAGNE DI ZUCCHINA

INGREDIENTS
SERVES 4

Pesto
1 cup/250 ml sunflower oil
4½ oz/125 g sun-dried tomatoes
3 oz/80 g cashews
4 tsp/10 g pine nuts
1–2 garlic cloves
¼ bunch basil
Salt, pepper

Cashew mayonnaise
½ cup/150 ml olive oil
3.5 oz/100 g cashews (soaked in
  water for 4–5 hours)
1½ tbsp/25 ml cider vinegar
1½ tbsp/15 g mustard seeds
1 tsp agave syrup
Salt

Lasagna
1 zucchini, sliced lengthwise
  into very thin strips
1 tbsp lemon thyme leaves
  or other herbs
1 tbsp sage oil (see tip)
4 tsp/10 g pine nuts, roughly
  pounded with a mortar & pestle

METHOD

Pesto: Place all ingredients with ¼ cup/50 ml water in a blender and puree until smooth. Season the pesto with salt and freshly ground pepper to taste. Wash the blender.

Cashew mayonnaise: Place all ingredients in the blender and pulse until smooth. Season with salt.

Lasagna: Brush half the zucchini strips with a thin layer of pesto and the other half with a thin layer of cashew mayonnaise. Arrange the strips in alternating layers to form precisely aligned stacks. Then cut the stacks into portions, 1.5 to 2 inches (4 to 5 cm) thick. Place 3 pieces on each plate, sprinkle with thyme and sage oil, and garnish with pine nuts.

Tip: To make sage oil, marinate 1 handful of sage leaves in sunflower oil for several hours to flavor the oil. Remove the leaves before using.

A DIFFERENT KIND OF LASAGNE

RAW-FOODS LASAGNE DI ZUCCHINA

INGREDIENTS
SERVES 4

Pesto
1 cup/250 ml sunflower oil
4½ oz/125 g sun-dried tomatoes
3 oz/80 g cashews
4 tsp/10 g pine nuts
1–2 garlic cloves
¼ bunch basil
Salt, pepper

Cashew mayonnaise
½ cup/150 ml olive oil
3.5 oz/100 g cashews (soaked in
  water for 4–5 hours)
1½ tbsp/25 ml cider vinegar
1½ tbsp/15 g mustard seeds
1 tsp agave syrup
Salt

Lasagna
1 zucchini, sliced lengthwise
  into very thin strips
1 tbsp lemon thyme leaves
  or other herbs
1 tbsp sage oil (see tip)
4 tsp/10 g pine nuts, roughly
  pounded with a mortar & pestle

METHOD

Pesto: Place all ingredients with
¼ cup/50 ml water in a blender and
puree until smooth. Season the
pesto with salt and freshly ground
pepper to taste. Wash the blender.

Cashew mayonnaise: Place all ingredients in the blender and pulse until
smooth. Season with salt.

Lasagna: Brush half the zucchini
strips with a thin layer of pesto and
the other half with a thin layer of
cashew mayonnaise. Arrange the strips
in alternating layers to form precisely
aligned stacks. Then cut the stacks
into portions, 1.5 to 2 inches (4 to 5 cm)
thick. Place 3 pieces on each plate,
sprinkle with thyme and sage oil, and
garnish with pine nuts.

Tip: To make sage oil, marinate
1 handful of sage leaves in sunflower
oil for several hours to flavor the oil.
Remove the leaves before using.

LASAGNE MAL ANDERS
ROHKÖSTLICHE LASAGNE
DI ZUCCHINA

ZUTATEN
FÜR 4 PERSONEN

Pesto
250 ml Sonnenblumenöl
125 g getrocknete Tomaten
80 g Cashewkerne
10 g Zedernnüsse
1–2 Knoblauchzehen
¼ Bund Basilikum
Salz, Pfeffer

Cashewmayonnaise
150 ml Olivenöl
100 g Cashewkerne
  (4–5 Stunden in Wasser
  eingeweicht)
25 ml Apfelessig
15 g Senfsaat
1 TL Agavendicksaft
Salz

Lasagne
1 Zucchino, längs in sehr
  dünne Scheiben geschnitten
1 EL Zitronenthymianblättchen
  oder andere Kräuter
1 EL Salbeiöl (siehe Tipp)
10 g Zedernnüsse,
  grob zerstoßen

ZUBEREITUNG
Für das Pesto alle Zutaten mit
50 ml Wasser in einem Standmixer
zu einem cremigen Pesto pürieren.
Das Pesto mit Salz und frisch
gemahlenem Pfeffer abschmecken.
Den Mixer reinigen.
Für die Mayonnaise alle Zutaten in
den Mixer füllen und zu einer cremigen
Mayonnaise verquirlen. Mit Salz
abschmecken.
Für die Lasagne die Hälfte der
Zucchinischeiben dünn mit Pesto
bestreichen, die andere Hälfte dünn
mit Cashewmayonnaise. Die Scheiben
abwechselnd zu exakten Stapeln
aufeinanderschichten. Die Stapel
dann mit einem scharfen Messer in
4–5 cm breite Portionsstücke schneiden.
Jeweils 3 Stücke auf einem Teller
anrichten, mit Thymian bestreuen,
mit Salbeiöl beträufeln und mit
den Nussstückchen garnieren.

Tipp: Für das Salbeiöl 1 Handvoll
Salbeiblätter einige Stunden in
Sonnenblumenöl legen und das Öl
so aromatisieren. Die Blätter danach
herausnehmen.

ESSENTIS ECOHOTEL

BERLIN, BERLIN

Berlin is a world metropolis with an attitude toward life entirely its own. People from all over the globe are drawn to this city, where they can experience right up close the special, colorful atmosphere that combines a spirit of optimism and personal freedom with avant-garde art and culture. A wide range of lifestyles—some loud and often shrill—come together in the German capital.

The entirely vegan essentis Ecohotel is proof that life here can also be quiet and meditative. This jewel of a hotel in the big city symbolizes a completely different, much more relaxed world.

Set in an idyllic location on the banks of the Spree, only half an hour from downtown Berlin, essentis is like a calming island amid the hustle and bustle of the metropolis, surrounded by water, forest, a people's park, and the enchanting boulevards of East Berlin.

These green surroundings make the Biohotel one of the first of its kind in Europe. In this modern and bright retreat, the staff offers a wide range of holistic workshops and events with a focus on health, mindfulness, and culture. From morning meditation and yoga practices to trips to the sauna, with a cooldown in the Spree afterwards, to participating in one of the many seminars and festivals with themes such as transformation, healing, and spirituality—the hotel presents its guests a number of programs to help them develop body and soul.

The first organically certified hotel in Berlin ambitiously follows its vision to become a center of holistic consciousness and is open to new ideas. Guests will also encounter this vison in the hotel's restaurant, Amaranth, which is resolutely vegan and naturally serves only organically grown, healthy, and creative food. The hotel's name, "essentis," is also its motto—derived from the word "essential" as a way to focus on the most important things in life and to connect to one's source. All of which you can do with great success at the essentis Biohotel.

Berlin ist eine Weltmetropole mit unverwechselbarem Lebensgefühl. Menschen aus der ganzen Welt zieht es hierher, um die spezielle bunte Mischung aus Aufbruchstimmung, persönlicher Freiheit, avantgardistischer Kunst und Kultur hautnah zu erleben. Unterschiedlichste Lebensstile – mal laut und oft auch schrill – kommen in der Hauptstadt zusammen.

Dass es auch leise und meditativ zugehen kann, beweist das komplett vegane essentis Biohotel. Dieses Kleinod in der Großstadt symbolisiert eine ganz andere, viel gelassenere Welt.

Idyllisch an der Spree gelegen, nur eine halbe Stunde von der Berliner City entfernt, ist das essentis wie eine beruhigende Insel in der Hektik der Metropole, umgeben von Wasser, Wald, Volkspark und den bezaubernden Ostberliner Alleen.

In jener grünen Umgebung ist das Biohotel eines der ersten seiner Art in Europa. Das Team offeriert an diesem modernen und hellen Rückzugsort eine Vielzahl von ganzheitlichen Workshops und Events zum Thema Gesundheit, Bewusstsein und Kultur. Vom morgendlichen Meditations- und Yogaangebot über den Besuch der Sauna mit anschließender Abkühlung in der Spree bis hin zur Teilnahme an einem der vielfältigen Seminare und Festivals zu Themen wie Transformation, Heilung und Spiritualität – dem Gast wird einiges zur Entfaltung von Körper und Geist geboten.

Das erste biozertifizierte vegane Hotel Berlins verfolgt seine Vision als Zentrum für ganzheitliches Bewusstsein mit großen Ambitionen und ist offen für die Umsetzung neuer Ideen. Das bemerken die Besucher auch im hoteleigenen Restaurant Amaranth, welches konsequent vegan ausgerichtet ist und natürlich nur biologisch erzeugte und gesund-kreative Lebensmittel serviert. Der Name des Hotels ist gleichzeitig das Motto – er wurde abgeleitet von „essenziell", sich auf das Wesentliche konzentrieren und sich mit seiner Quelle zu verbinden. Das essentis Biohotel ist so ein Ort, an dem einem genau das gelingen kann.

ROOMS: 60
SPECIALTIES: SAUNA AREA WITH DIRECT ACCESS TO THE SPREE, YOGA, MEDITATION, ENERGIZED WATER, SOLAR POWERED CLEAN ENERGY, EV CHARGING STATION, PERMACULTURE GARDEN, COOKING CLASSES, LIBRARY

ESSENTIS ECOHOTEL
WEISKOPFFSTRASSE 16/17
12459 BERLIN
GERMANY (DEUTSCHLAND)
WWW.ESSENTIS.DE
+49 30 530 0500

ZIMMER: 60
BESONDERHEITEN: SAUNABEREICH MIT DIREKTEM ZUGANG ZUR SPREE, YOGA, MEDITATION, ENERGETISIERTES WASSER, SAUBERE ENERGIE DURCH SOLARANLAGE, E-AUTO-LADE-STATION, KOCHKURSE, BIBLIOTHEK

HOTEL
GUTSHAUS STELLSHAGEN

STELLSHAGEN, MECKLENBURG-VORPOMMERN

Gutshaus Stellshagen stands on a small hill, surrounded by ancient trees, fields, and meadows as far as the eye can see. A fresh breeze carries the aroma of the nearby Baltic Sea. You can breathe deeply here and enjoy the warmth and security of the stately, landmarked manor, which was renovated according to building biological principles, with the addition of outbuildings for guest rooms, conference rooms, and a naturopathic practice.

Everything in the hotel is aimed at ecological sustainability, from the power supply to the room furnishings to the vegetarian meals, which are always served buffet-style. Sometimes the cuisine evokes the local Mecklenburg region, sometimes Italy, and occasionally even India. The hotel's own organic farm supplies fresh herbs and vegetables, and an in-house bakery provides the tasty cakes. The kitchen staff immediately harvests and processes whatever produce is currently ripe in the vegetable garden, which is why meal preparation requires a great deal of creativity and spontaneity. The Tao health center right next to the manor offers many beauty and wellness treatments, yoga and meditation, massages in traditions from Ayurveda to TCM, along with seminars and dance and concert evenings—a versatile and diverse program is scheduled daily. The best way to wait out stormy weather during the coldest part of the year is to enjoy a cup of tea in the winter garden and let your gaze wander over the landscape as compensation for many a raging storm. On sunnier days, the region demands to be explored—on foot, bicycle, or the back of a horse.

Das Gutshaus Stellshagen befindet sich auf einem kleinen Hügel, umgeben von alten Bäumen, Feldern und Wiesen, so weit das Auge reicht. Eine frische Brise trägt das Aroma der nahen Ostsee herüber. Hier darf man durchatmen, und die geborgene Atmosphäre des stattlichen, denkmalgeschützten Herrenhauses genießen, das im Laufe der Jahre baubiologisch renoviert und um Nebengebäude für Gästezimmer, Tagungsräume und eine Naturheilpraxis erweitert wurde.

Alles hier ist auf ökologische Nachhaltigkeit ausgerichtet: von der Energieversorgung über die Zimmerausstattung bis hin zu den vegetarischen Mahlzeiten, die stets in Büffetform angeboten werden – mal mecklenburgisch, mal italienisch und auch mal indisch. Frisches Gemüse und Kräuter kommen aus der eigenen Biolandwirtschaft, der köstliche Kuchen aus der hausinternen Biobackstube. Was im Gemüsegarten reif ist, wird sofort geerntet und verarbeitet, daher werden Kreativität und Spontanität in der Küche großgeschrieben.

Im Tao-Gesundheitszentrum gleich neben dem Gutshaus werden zahlreiche Beauty- und Wellnessbehandlungen, Yoga und Meditation, Massagen von Ayurveda bis TCM sowie Seminare und Tanz- und Konzertabende angeboten – das tägliche Programm ist vielseitig und abwechslungsreich. Und kaum irgendwo sonst lässt sich das stürmische Wetter zur kalten Jahreszeit besser aushalten als im Wintergarten bei einer Tasse Tee – der weite Blick über die Landschaft entschädigt für so manche schlechte Witterung. An sonnigeren Tagen lädt die Gegend zur Erkundung per pedes, mit dem Fahrrad oder hoch zu Ross ein.

ROOMS: 57
SPECIALTIES: YOGA, MEDITATION, QI GONG, VARIOUS SEMINARS AND LECTURES, IN-HOUSE HEALTH CENTER

HOTEL GUTSHAUS STELLSHAGEN
LINDENSTR. 1
23948 STELLSHAGEN
GERMANY (DEUTSCHLAND)
WWW.GUTSHAUS-STELLSHAGEN.DE
+49 38825 440

ZIMMER: 57
BESONDERHEITEN: YOGA, MEDITATION, QIGONG, GROSSES PROGRAMM AN SEMINAREN UND VORTRÄGEN, HAUSEIGENES GESUNDHEITSZENTRUM

TOFU PATTIES
WITH HERBS AND MILLET GRITS

TOFUBRATLINGE
MIT KRÄUTERN UND HIRSEGRIESS

INGREDIENTS
SERVES 4

10 oz/300 g tofu (plain)
¼ cup/50 g red bell pepper
⅓ cup/50 g onions
3 tbsp/50 g prepared mustard
2 eggs (or vegan alternative)
½ cup/100 g millet grits
1 tsp freshly chopped marjoram
1 tsp freshly chopped thyme
Salt, pepper
3 tbsp olive oil

ZUTATEN
FÜR 4 PERSONEN

300 g Tofu (natur)
50 g rote Paprikaschote
50 g Zwiebeln
50 g Senf
2 Eier (oder vegane Alternative)
100 g Hirsegrieß
1 TL frisch gehackter Majoran
1 TL frisch gehackter Thymian
Salz, Pfeffer
3 EL Olivenöl

METHOD

Finely grate the tofu. Wash the bell pepper and remove the seeds. Peel the onions. Chop the pepper and onion into a fine dice.

Mix together the tofu, diced bell pepper and onion, mustard, eggs, 7 tbsp/80 g of the millet grits, marjoram, thyme, 1 tsp of salt, and pepper. Allow the tofu mixture to rest for around 30 minutes.

Wet your hands and form the tofu mixture into patties. Dredge the patties in the remaining grits. Heat the oil in a pan and fry the patties for 4 minutes per side. Remove from the pan and serve immediately.

Tip: Arrange the patties on spinach sauce.

ZUBEREITUNG

Den Tofu fein reiben. Die Paprika waschen und die Kerne entfernen, die Zwiebeln schälen. Dann beides in feine Würfel schneiden.

Tofu, Paprika- und Zwiebelwürfelchen, Senf, Eier, 80 g Hirsegrieß, Majoran, Thymian, 1 TL Salz und Pfeffer vermischen. Die Tofumasse etwa 30 Minuten ruhen lassen. Danach aus der Tofumasse mit angefeuchteten Händen Bratlinge formen. Die Bratlinge im restlichen Grieß wenden. Das Öl in einer Pfanne erhitzen und die Bratlinge darin von jeder Seite etwa 4 Minuten braten. Herausnehmen und sofort servieren.

Tipp: Die Bratlinge auf Spinatsauce anrichten.

HOTEL GUTSHAUS PARIN

PARIN, MECKLENBURG-VORPOMMERN

Mecklenburg-Western Pomerania is nature's wonderland. Few other regions in Germany have such an impressive biodiversity. Intact habitats, fragrant fields and meadows, ancient trees, tranquil villages where the hustle and bustle of the big city are virtually unknown—and in the middle of it all: the Hotel Gutshaus Parin with its two pink circus caravans. To experience it all in person, head for Parin, which may sound a bit like Paris but has precious little to do with the French metropolis.

At the far end of the village you will find the Hotel Gutshaus Parin, where bucolic charm meets elegant ambience and provides an unlimited, relaxing view of a beautiful landscape—so you not only rest your eyes but your spirit as well. Those two pink caravans that house a sauna and a relaxation room, a marvelous, natural swimming pond and a small beach with wicker beach chairs also belong to the estate.

Health-conscious gourmets can expect to find a bountiful organic, vegetarian buffet in the old-fashioned basement vault of the entirely organic hotel housed in a restored manor, which also has a rustic wine bar. In fine weather, coffee and cake lovers can celebrate their passion on the spacious terrace next to the hotel pond.

What guests might not notice at first glance is owner Gertrud Cordes's praiseworthy and notable commitment to the environment and sustainability. If you like to take zero-emission vacations, you've come to the right place. Gutshaus Parin harbors many entirely positive surprises.

Naturparadies Mecklenburg-Vorpommern: Eine größere Artenvielfalt weist kaum ein anderes Bundesland vor. Intakte Lebensräume, duftende Wiesen und Felder, Baumveteranen, beschauliche Dörfer, in denen Hektik ein Fremdwort ist – und mittendrin das Hotel Gutshaus Parin mit seinen zwei rosaroten Zirkuswagen. Wer das selbst erleben will, sollte sich einmal auf den Weg nach Parin machen, das zwar fast wie Paris klingt, aber mit der Metropole herzlich wenig zu tun hat.

Ganz am Ende des Dorfes findet man das Gelände des Gutshauses Parin, wo ländlicher Charme auf elegantes Ambiente trifft und sich ein unbegrenzter erholsamer Blick in die wunderschöne Landschaft bietet — hier kommen nicht nur die Augen, sondern auch der Geist zur Ruhe. Die besagten rosaroten Zirkuswagen beherbergen zudem eine Sauna und einen Ruheraum. Ein herrlicher Naturbadeteich nebst kleinem Strand mit Strandkörben gehört ebenso zum Anwesen.

Im urigen Kellergewölbe des vollständig baubiologisch restaurierten Hotels mit rustikaler Weinstube erwartet den gesundheitsbewussten Genießer ein umfangreiches vegetarisches Biobüffet. Bei schönem Wetter kann man Kaffee- und Kuchenfreuden auf der weitläufigen Terrasse am Gutshausteich zelebrieren.

Was der Gast vermutlich nicht gleich sieht, ist das lobens- und erwähnenswerte Engagement der Gastgeberin Gertrud Cordes in Sachen Umwelt und Nachhaltigkeit – wer CO₂-neutral Urlaub machen möchte, ist hier genau richtig. Das Gutshaus Parin überrascht in vielerlei Hinsicht und zwar ausschließlich positiv.

ROOMS: 30
SPECIALTIES: SAUNA, ECOLOGICAL SWIMMING POND (27 YARDS), YOGA, MEDITATION, TAI CHI, QI GONG, COOKING CLASSES

HOTEL GUTSHAUS PARIN
WIRTSCHAFTSHOF 1
23948 PARIN
GERMANY (DEUTSCHLAND)
WWW.GUTSHAUS-PARIN.DE
+49 3881 756 890

ZIMMER: 30
BESONDERHEITEN: SAUNA, NATURBADETEICH (25 METER), YOGA, MEDITATION, TAI-CHI, QIGONG, KOCHKURSE

NATURKOSTHOTEL HARZ

BAD GRUND, LOWER SAXONY

Rugged cliffs, dark forests, mystical moors, valleys, and lakes—the Harz is the magical heart of Germany. Legends abound in the mountains. Like the one about the witches who traditionally celebrate Walpurgis Night on the Brocken, and the nature spirits who cloak the mountain peaks in dense mist. Bad Grund, the oldest mountain town in the Upper Harz, is known for the saga of Hübich, the benevolent dwarf king who ruled here and protected man and beast against impending disaster with the magical powers of his beard. Hübich would likely have approved of the vegan hotel situated here, which serves primarily raw foods.

While the breakfast buffet does include a number of hot items, a three-course menu made up entirely of raw foods awaits the guests every evening. And many of the ingredients are produced right here in the Harz. The Naturkosthotel's kitchen staff are well versed in the wild herbs that grow in the region and use them in their cooking. That means that the occasional local moss variety may end up in your green smoothie along with spinach and nettles. If you'd like to learn more about the delicious herbs on your plate, you can go on a wild herb walk. The establishment is also known for its guided fasts; guests relax in the wellness zone, with its sauna and large swimming pool.

However, man and beast are not the only things near and dear to the Naturkosthotel Harz—thanks to the hotel's own dual heat and power generator as well as solar panels on the roof, it bears the certified seal of "Climate Protection Hotel."

Schroffe Felsen, dunkle Wälder, geheimnisvolle Hochmoore, Täler und Seen – der Harz ist das magisch anmutende Herz Deutschlands. Zahlreiche Mythen ranken sich um das Gebirge. Etwa, dass die Hexen ihre Walpurgisnacht traditionell auf dem Brocken feiern und die Bergkuppen von Naturgeistern in dichten Nebel gehüllt werden. In Bad Grund, der ältesten der Oberharzer Bergstädte, herrscht der Sage nach Zwergenkönig Hübich mit gütiger Hand. Er beschützt mit der magischen Kraft seines Bartes Mensch und Tier vor drohendem Unheil. Es findet sicher Hübichs Zustimmung, dass dort ein rein veganes Hotel mit Schwerpunkt auf Rohkost beheimatet ist.

Gibt es morgens noch warme Speisen am Buffet, wartet jeden Abend ein komplett rohköstliches Drei-Gänge-Menü auf die Gäste. Und viele der Zutaten stellt der Harz selbst bereit: Im Naturkosthotel sind alle Wildkräuter der Umgebung bekannt und werden in der Küche verwendet – so kann es sein, dass neben Spinat und Brennnesseln auch mal heimische Moose im Grünen Smoothie landen. Wer etwas mehr über die köstlichen Kräuter lernen möchte, kann an einer Wildkräuterwanderung teilnehmen. Auch für seine betreuten Fastenkuren ist das Haus bekannt; Entspannung finden die Gäste im Wellnessbereich mit Sauna und großem Schwimmbecken.

Doch nicht nur Mensch und Tier liegen dem Naturkosthotel Harz am Herzen – dank eigenem Blockheizkraftwerk und Solarzellen auf dem Dach trägt es das zertifizierte Siegel „Klimaschutzhotel".

ROOMS: 21
SPECIALTIES: INDOOR SWIMMING POOL, SAUNA, INFRARED CABIN, YOGA, MEDITATION, RUNNING WORKOUT, MOUNTAINBIKE TOURS, GUIDED FASTING AND HERB WALKS

NATURKOST-HOTEL HARZ
VON-EICHENDORFF-STR. 18
37539 BAD GRUND
GERMANY (DEUTSCHLAND)
WWW.NATURKOST-HOTEL.DE
+49 5327 2072

ZIMMER: 21
BESONDERHEITEN: HALLENBAD, SAUNA, INFRAROTKABINE, YOGA, MEDITATION, LAUFTRAINING, MOUNTAINBIKE-TOUREN, GEFÜHRTE FASTEN- UND KRÄUTERWANDERUNGEN

If you're looking to shed a few pounds, detox your body, or change your diet—you can do all these things with help from the Naturkosthotel Harz's team of experts. They offer special programs such as detox cures, therapeutic fasting weeks, and respiratory therapy in mine tunnels (Heilstollen) to reboot your body. The atmosphere in Bad Grund's mine tunnel is 99-percent dust-free with 100 percent humidity. Each treament is supplemented and rounded out by a vegan raw foods diet that is tailored to each guest's special needs.

Ein paar Pfunde loswerden, Entschlacken oder die Ernährung umstellen – all das kann man mithilfe des Expertenteams im Naturkosthotel Harz schaffen. Für den körperlichen Neustart gibt es spezielle Angebote wie Detoxkuren, Heilfastenwochen oder die Heilstollentherapie. Im Heilstollen von Bad Grund herrscht 99-prozentige Staubfreiheit und 100-prozentige Luftfeuchtigkeit. Jede Therapie wird durch eine speziell abgestimmte vegane Rohkosternährung ergänzt und abgerundet.

RAW FOODS PIZZA
A LA ITALIA

ROHKOSTPIZZA
NACH ITALIENISCHER ART

INGREDIENTS

SERVES 4

Pizza crust

7 oz/200 g buckwheat groats,
  sprouted soaked for at least 5 hours
5 oz/150 g sunflower seeds, sprouted
2 tbsp olive oil, plus more
  for rolling out the dough
½ tsp sea salt
5 oz/150 g golden flaxseeds

Tomato sauce

2 tomatoes, sliced
2½ oz/75 g sun-dried tomatoes
1 tbsp olive oil
2 dates, pitted
6 basil leaves
1 sprig rosemary, needles only
1 tbsp fresh oregano or 1 tsp. dried
1 tbsp lemon juice
1 pinch chili powder

Cashew cheese

4 oz/120 g cashews
½ zucchini, cut into pieces
3 tbsp nutritional yeast
1 tbsp lemon juice
Sea salt

Toppings

3.5 oz/100 g mushrooms, sliced
1 tbsp Tamari soy sauce
1 tbsp olive oil
5 cherry tomatoes, sliced
½ red bell peppers, cut into pieces
1 medium-sized red or
  white onion, diced
1 bunch dandelion greens or arugula
10 olives, pitted
½ avocado, sliced

ZUTATEN
FÜR 4 PERSONEN

Pizzaboden

200 g Buchweizen, gekeimt oder
  mindestens 5 Stunden eingeweicht
150 g Sonnenblumenkerne, gekeimt
2 EL Olivenöl, plus mehr zum Ausrollen
½ TL Meersalz
150 g Goldleinsamen

Tomatensauce

2 Tomaten, in Scheiben geschnitten
75 g getrocknete Tomaten
1 EL Olivenöl
2 Datteln, entsteint
6 Blätter Basilikum
1 Zweig Rosmarin, Nadeln abgezupft
1 EL frischer Oregano oder
  1 TL getrockneter
1 EL Zitronensaft
1 Msp. Chilipulver

Cashewkäse

120 g Cashewkerne
½ Zucchino, in Stücke geschnitten
3 EL Würzhefeflocken
1 EL Zitronensaft
Meersalz

Belag

100 g Champignons,
  in Scheiben geschnitten
1 EL Tamari-Sojasauce
1 EL Olivenöl
5 Cocktailtomaten,
  in Scheiben geschnitten
½ rote Paprikaschote,
  in Stücke geschnitten
1 mittelgroße rote oder weiße Zwiebel,
  in Würfel geschnitten
1 Bund Löwenzahn oder Rucola
10 Oliven, entkernt
½ Avocado, in Scheiben geschnitten

METHOD

Pizza crust: Combine the buckwheat groats, sunflower seeds, oil, and salt in a food processor to form a dough. Place the dough in a bowl. Grind the flaxseeds into a powder and add to the dough. Add a little water and knead well. Line the work surface with parchment paper, sprinkle with water, and place a non-stick baking sheet on top. Coat the sheet and rolling pin with a little oil, then roll out the dough on the sheet to a thickness of ⅛ inch/5 mm. (The oil keeps the dough from sticking and helps it to release from the baking sheet later on.) Let the pizza crust dry for 2 hours at 100°F/40°C. Remove the baking sheet and allow the crust to continue drying on a rack for another 2 hours. The crust should remain soft enough to be cut with a knife and fork.

Tomato sauce: Place all ingredients in a blender with a little water and puree.

Cashew cheese: Place all ingredients with 2 tablespoons/30 ml water in a blender and puree until smooth.

Toppings: Marinate the mushrooms in tamari and olive oil. Brush the pizza crust with the tomato sauce and distribute the cashew cheese over it. Top with cherry tomatoes, bell pepper, onion, dandelion greens, mushrooms, olives, and avocado. Serve immediately.

Tip: If you'd like to serve the pizza warm, heat the topped pizza (without avocado slices) in a dehydrator for 1 to 2 hours at 100°F/40°C. Garnish with avocado.

ZUBEREITUNG

Für den Boden Buchweizen, Sonnenblumenkerne, Öl und Salz in der Küchenmaschine zu einem Teig vermischen. Den Teig in eine Schüssel füllen. Den Leinsamen mahlen und zugeben. Etwas Wasser zugießen und alles gut verkneten. Küchenpapier auf die Arbeitsfläche legen, befeuchten und eine Dörrfolie darauflegen. Folie und Nudelholz mit etwas Öl bestreichen, dann den Teig 5 mm dick auf der Folie ausrollen. (Durch das Öl klebt der Teig nicht fest und lässt sich später leicht von der Folie lösen.) Den Boden im Backofen oder Dörrautomaten bei 40 °C etwa 2 Stunden trocknen lassen. Die Dörrfolie entfernen und den Boden auf einem Gitter noch etwa 2 Stunden weitertrocknen lassen. Der Boden soll so weich bleiben, dass er sich gut mit Messer und Gabel zerteilen lässt.

Für die Tomatensauce alle Zutaten und etwas Wasser im Mixer pürieren.

Die Champignons in einer Marinade aus Olivenöl und Tamari einlegen.

Für den Cashewkäse alle Zutaten mit 30 ml Wasser im Mixer cremig pürieren.

Den Pizzaboden mit der Tomatensauce bestreichen und den Cashewkäse darauf verteilen. Mit Cocktailtomaten, Paprika, Zwiebel, Löwenzahn, Champignons, Oliven und Avocado belegen. Sofort servieren.

Tipp: Möchten Sie die Pizza warm servieren, die belegte Pizza 1–2 Stunden bei 40 °C im Dörrautomaten erwärmen. Erst danach mit den Avocadoscheiben belegen.

RELEXA HOTEL MÜNCHEN

MUNICH, BAVARIA

When on a business trip, vegans often have an especially hard time finding a suitable hotel. Usually, the only items on the breakfast buffet that they can enjoy are a plain roll, spread with jam and washed down with black coffee. The relexa hotel in the heart of Munich proves that it doesn't always have to be this way. In a city famous for its Leberkäse meatloaf and leg of pork, the staff of this business hotel has dedicated itself to making sure that their vegetarian and vegan guests enjoy a downright pleasant stay, rich in variety. Not only does the breakfast buffet offer a profusion of selections, but the room furnishings are entirely vegan—from the blankets and the pillow cases to the furniture.

The hotel also features a Ladies' Executive Floor, tailored specifically to the needs of female guests. Its brightly lit hallways lead to cheerfully furnished rooms, where the minibar is filled with fresh fruits and mineral water instead of beer and peanuts. The relexa is ideally situated for a stroll through the Bavarian capital, should there be time for this between business appointments. The establishment's location near the main train station means that you can quickly reach the Stachus square, Marienplatz, or the Gärtnerplatz Quarter on foot. The city's more than thirty vegan and vegetarian cafés and restaurants along the way invite you to come inside and fortify yourself for the next leg of your walk.

Those who are in a rush in the morning do not have to leave the hotel hungry—from 6:30 on, the staff departs from the usual way of things and serves a quick, healthy business breakfast at the lobby bar.

Wer als Veganer geschäftlich unterwegs ist, hat es oftmals besonders schwer, das passende Hotel zu finden. Meist bleibt einem beim Frühstücksbuffet nur ein blankes Brötchen mit Marmelade, das man mit schwarzem Kaffee herunterspülen muss. Dass es auch anders geht, zeigt das relexa hotel im Herzen von München. Ausgerechnet in der Hauptstadt von Leberkas und Schweinshaxen hat es sich das Team dieses Businesshotels zur Aufgabe gemacht, den Aufenthalt von vegetarisch oder vegan lebenden Gästen ausgesprochen angenehm und abwechslungsreich zu gestalten. Nicht nur das Frühstücksbuffet bietet reichlich Auswahl, auch die Zimmereinrichtung ist komplett vegan – von den Bettdecken über die Kissenbezüge bis hin zu den Möbeln.

Eine weitere Besonderheit des Hotels ist die speziell auf weibliche Gäste zugeschnittene Ladies Executive Floor. Auf dieser Etage führen hell erleuchtete Flure zu den freundlich eingerichteten Zimmern, in denen anstelle von Bier und Erdnüssen frische Früchte und Mineralwasser in der Minibar warten. Sollte zwischen den Geschäftsterminen Zeit für einen Spaziergang durch die bayerische Landeshauptstadt sein, so bietet das relexa hierfür eine Toplage. Nahe des Hauptbahnhofs gelegen, ist man schnell zu Fuß am Stachus, Marienplatz oder im Gärtnerplatzviertel. Zwischendurch laden die über dreißig vegan-vegetarischen Cafés und Restaurants der Stadt zu einem Besuch und zur Stärkung für die nächste Etappe ein.

Wer es am Morgen eilig hat, muss keineswegs hungrig das Haus verlassen – das Hotelteam serviert schon ab 6.30 Uhr schnell und unkonventionell ein gesundes Businessfrühstück an der Lobbybar.

ROOMS: 121
SPECIALTIES: CENTRAL LOCATION, LADIES EXECUTIVE FLOOR (ROOMS FOR WOMEN ONLY WITH ADDITIONAL SERVICE, E.G. YOGA MATS, MAGAZINES, VALET PARKING), VEGAN ROOM FACILITIES (E.G. BLANKETS WITHOUT DOWN FEATHERS, CARPETS WITHOUT WOOL)

RELEXA HOTEL MÜNCHEN
SCHWANTHALERSTR. 58-60
80336 MÜNCHEN
GERMANY (DEUTSCHLAND)
WWW.RELEXA-HOTEL-MUENCHEN.DE
+49 89 996 5060

ZIMMER: 121
BESONDERHEITEN: ZENTRALE LAGE, LADIES EXECUTIVE FLOOR (ZIMMER EXKLUSIV FÜR FRAUEN MIT ZUSÄTZLICHEN SERVICES; U.A. YOGAMATTE, ZEITSCHRIFTEN, VALET PARKING), VEGANE ZIMMERAUSSTATTUNG (U.A. DECKEN OHNE DAUNEN, TEPPICHE OHNE WOLLE)

BERGHÜS SCHRATT

OBERSTAUFEN-STEIBIS, BAVARIA

Enjoy your vegan/vegetarian vacation in the mountains. The magnificent Allgäu Alps, with their striking crests, wide valleys, and vast plateaus, form a picture-perfect backdrop right at the doorstep of the organic vegetarian Berghüs Schratt hotel. From here, you can make your way directly to the Nagelfluhkette Nature Park. A large network of hiking trails, mountain railways, ski lifts, waterfalls, and even refreshment stops are only a few minutes walk away. The area offers unlimited outdoor activities in both summer and winter—from the summer toboggan run to the ski lift just around the corner. This alpine region turns into a perfect winter wonderland from Christmas to April.

With the guest card you'll automatically gain free mountain rail rides and entrance to a wide range of nearby attractions at no extra charge. In the morning, therefore, you should fortify yourself with the hotel's bountiful, organic vegetarian breakfast buffet before embarking on any outing.

"Organic" in this hotel means organic by conviction. The kitchen staff have been preparing refined vegetarian and vegan dishes from fresh ingredients for more than 30 years now, using regional products and native herbs. The certified organic hotel is a true pioneer in this regard. Everything is made from scratch, and the varied menu is constantly reinventing itself with creative meals that satisfy even the most sophisticated tastes.

Guests look forward with special delight to the four-course dinner menu, served in a cozy ambience, when they return to Berghüs Schratt, happy and satisfied, after a marvelous day in the mountains.

Vegetarisch und vegan Ihren Urlaub im Bergdorf genießen. Direkt vor der Haustür des vegetarischen Biohotels Berghüs Schratt liegen die prächtigen Allgäuer Alpen mit ihren markanten Bergrücken, Tälern, und vorgelagerten Hochebenen – eine echte Postkartenkulisse! Von hier aus geht es direkt in den Naturpark Nagelfluhkette. Zu Fuß erreicht man in nur wenigen Minuten ein großes Wanderwegenetz, Bergbahnen, Skilifte, Wasserfälle und auch Einkehrmöglichkeiten. Outdoor-Aktivitäten sind im Sommer wie im Winter kaum Grenzen gesetzt: von der Sommerrodelbahn bis zum Skilift um die Ecke. Das perfekte weiße Wintermärchen erlebt man in dieser Alpenregion von Weihnachten bis April.

Mit der Gästekarte erhält man freie Fahrt bei Bergbahnen und freien Eintritt für zahlreiche Attraktionen der Region – daher sollte man sich morgens am besten beim reichhaltigen vegetarischen Biofrühstücksbuffet des Hotels für alle Ausflüge stärken.

„Bio" heißt hier tatsächlich Bio aus Überzeugung, schon seit über 30 Jahren werden vegetarische und vegane Gerichte frisch und mit Raffinesse zubereitet und möglichst regionale Produkte mit heimischen Kräutern verarbeitet – das zertifizierte Biohotel ist ein echter Pionier. Hausgemacht – die abwechslungsreiche Küche erfindet sich immer wieder neu und bleibt kreativ für gehobene Ansprüche.

Da freut man sich als Gast besonders auf das abendliche Vier-Gänge-Menü in gemütlicher Atmosphäre, wenn man nach einem großartigen Tag in den Bergen glücklich und zufrieden wieder einkehrt ins Berghüs Schratt.

ROOMS: 16
SPECIALTIES: CENTRAL LOCATION IN A NATURE PARK, SAUNA, INFRARED CABIN, MASSAGES, SERVICES FOR FREE (E.G. MOUNTAIN RAILWAY, WATERPARK, SKI PASS, CLIMBING PARK, MUSEUM)

BERGHÜS SCHRATT VEGETARISCHES BIOHOTEL SÄGMÜHLE 19 87534 OBERSTAUFEN/ALLGÄU GERMANY (DEUTSCHLAND) WWW.BIOHOTEL-SCHRATT.DE +49 8386 980 10

ZIMMER: 16
BESONDERHEITEN: ZENTRALE LAGE IM NATURPARK, SAUNA, INFRAROT-KABINE, MASSAGE, KOSTENFREIE LEISTUNGEN (U.A. BERGBAHNEN, ERLEBNISBAD, SKIPASS, KLETTER-GARTEN, MUSEEN)

MAS LA JAÏNA

BARGEMON, PROVENCE-ALPES-CÔTE D'AZUR

Mas la Jaïna is an unusual hotel and B&B. After all, what other hotel can claim to have its very own small farm? Although the donkeys, llamas, dogs, cats, and chickens that live here will never end up on the dinner table, the fruit, vegetables, aromatic and medicinal herbs that grow in the hotel garden and greenhouse are ready to be turned into delicious meals. "Charming" is a fitting attribute to describe this lovingly designed and furnished house in Provence, which was built by the innkeepers, Ingrid and Johan with the help of friends and family, in typical Provençal style. It is rooted in a secluded, green valley among the region's most beautiful mountain towns—Bargemon, Claviers, and Callas.

Most of the building materials came from ruins or very old farmsteads in the vicinity, which is why you get the feeling that you're living in a restored estate with a colorful past. All the themed rooms are decorated with objects from humanitarian projects. The hotel uses part of its earnings to further support these projects.

As an additional special feature, the climate throughout the establishment is controlled by a modern, geothermal installation. Geothermal energy is used to heat the hotel in winter and cool it in summer.

After enjoying the now famous breakfast with artistically decorated and homemade as well as regional treats, such as fruit salads, organic cheeses, and inventive jams (e.g. green olive with rosemary), guests can refresh themselves in the large organic swimming pool situated in the garden, whose clean spring water is filtered exclusively with plants and UV light. Sustainability and the charm of old traditions blend seamlessly together with amazing success. Although the hotel offers many pleasant amenities, such as an indoor swimming pool, sauna, and fitness studio, a trip to the vibrant town of Bargemon, with its pretty, narrow alleys, is not to be missed.

Mas la Jaïna ist ein ungewöhnliches Hotel und B&B, denn welches Hotel kann schon seinen eigenen kleinen Bauernhof vorzeigen? Die hier wohnenden Esel, Lamas, Hunde, Katzen und Hühner werden selbstverständlich nicht gegessen, dafür stehen allerdings die Früchte, das Gemüse, die Würz- und Heilkräuter aus dem eigenen Garten und Gewächshaus bereit. „Charmant" ist das passende Attribut für dieses liebevoll gestaltete und eingerichtete Haus in der Provence, welches im typisch provenzalischen Stil von den Gastgebern Ingrid und Johan mithilfe von Freunden und Familie erbaut wurde und in einem grünen Tal zwischen den schönsten Bergstädten dieser Region – Bargemon, Claviers und Callas – geschützt verwurzelt ist.

Die meisten verwendeten Baumaterialien stammen aus Ruinen oder sehr alten Gehöften der Umgebung, weshalb man durchaus das Gefühl bekommt, auf einem restaurierten Landsitz mit bewegter Geschichte zu verweilen. Alle Räume wurden thematisch mit Objekten dekoriert, die aus humanitären Projekten stammen. Mit einem Teil der Einkünfte unterstützt das Hotel diese Projekte darüber hinaus weiter.

Eine zusätzliche Besonderheit ist die moderne geothermische Installation, die das ganze Haus klimatisiert: Erdwärme wird genutzt, um im Winter zu heizen oder im Sommer zu kühlen. Und im Garten sorgt ein großer Bioswimmingpool für Erfrischung, dessen sauberes Quellwasser ausschließlich mit Pflanzen und UV-Licht gefiltert wird.

Das kunstvoll arrangierte Frühstück ist ein Erlebnis für sich. Die hausgemachten und regionalen Köstlichkeiten wie Fruchtsalate, Biokäsesorten und originelle Marmeladen (z.B. grüne Olive mit Rosmarin) sind bei den Gästen mittlerweile berühmt. Modernste Technologie, Nachhaltigkeit und der Charme des Alten greifen erstaunlich nahtlos ineinander. Trotz der vielen Annehmlichkeiten des Hauses, wie Indoorswimmingpool, Sauna und Fitnessraum, sollte man auf keinen Fall einen Besuch der lebendigen Stadt Bargemon mit ihren hübschen engen Gassen auslassen.

ROOMS: 2 ROOMS, 2 SUITES, 2 APARTMENTS
SPECIALTIES: NATURAL SWIMMING POND, INDOOR POOL, JACUZZI, GYM, INFRARED CABIN, GARDENING CLASSES, COOKING CLASSES, WINE TASTING, EV CHARGING STATION

MAS LA JAÏNA
LES ESPOUROUNES
83830 BARGEMON
FRANCE (FRANKREICH)
WWW.MASLAJAINA.COM
+33 688 997 993

ZIMMER: 2 ZIMMER, 2 SUITEN, 2 APPARTEMENTS
BESONDERHEITEN: NATURBADETEICH, INNENPOOL, JACUZZI, FITNESSRAUM, INFRAROTKABINE, GARTENKURSE, KOCHKURSE, WEINPROBEN, E-TANKSTELLE

INGREDIENTS
SERVES 4

Walnut Pesto
3 cups/70 g fresh basil leaves
1 cup/110 g walnuts
¼ cup/35 g pine nuts
¼ cup/15 g chopped fresh parsley (optional)
3 tbsp organic extra-virgin olive oil
Juice of 1 lime
1 tbsp white miso (or ½ tsp sea salt)
3 garlic cloves, chopped
12 fresh sage leaves
3 fresh mint leaves

Mushrooms
12 medium white mushrooms, stems removed
¼ cup/60 ml organic soy sauce
4 tbsp organic extra-virgin olive oil
2 garlic cloves, finely chopped
1 tsp herbed seasoning salt,
  such as Herbamare
6½ cups/200 g spring mix
12 cherry tomatoes

ZUTATEN
FÜR 4 PERSONEN

Walnusspesto
70 g Basilikumblätter
110 g Walnusskerne
35 g Pinienkerne
15 g Petersilie, gehackt (nach Belieben)
3 EL natives Bio-Olivenöl extra
Saft von 1 Limette
1 EL weiße Miso-Paste (oder ½ TL Meersalz)
3 Knoblauchzehen, gehackt
12 Salbeiblätter
3 Minzeblätter

Pilze
12 mittelgroße Champignons, Stiele entfernt
60 ml Bio-Sojasauce
4 EL natives Bio-Olivenöl extra
2 Knoblauchzehen, fein gehackt
1 TL Kräutersalz (z. B. von Herbamare)
200 g Salatmischung
12 Kirschtomaten

STUFFED MUSHROOMS
WITH WALNUT-PESTO FILLING

GEBACKENE PILZE
MIT WALNUSSPESTO-FÜLLUNG

METHOD

Walnut pesto: Place all the ingredients in a blender or food processor and process until combined but not completely smooth.

Mushrooms: Combine the mushrooms, soy sauce, oil, garlic, and salt in a large bowl. Stir to coat the mushrooms and let sit for at least 30 minutes or up to 2 hours, stirring occasionally. Remove the mushrooms, gently squeezing them to rid them of excess marinade. (The marinade can be saved to use for other recipes.) Preheat the oven to 160°F/70°C. Stuff the mushrooms with the pesto and place on a baking sheet. Bake for 30 minutes to 1 hour.

Spread the spring mix on four plates and arrange the stuffed mushrooms on top. Garnish with the tomatoes and serve.

Tip: The mushrooms can be made a day ahead of time and refrigerated. Dehydrate them in the oven just before serving.

ZUBEREITUNG

Für das Pesto alle Zutaten im Mixer oder in der Küchenmaschine zu einer groben Paste mixen, jedoch nicht cremig pürieren.

Für die Pilze die Champignons mit Sojasauce, Öl, Knoblauch und Kräutersalz in einer großen Schüssel mischen, bis sie rundum überzogen sind. Die Pilze dann 1–2 Stunden durchziehen lassen, dabei gelegentlich durchrühren. Die Champignons danach aus der Marinade nehmen und leicht ausdrücken, damit die Marinade abtropft. (Die Marinade kann noch anderweitig verwendet werden).

Den Backofen auf 70 °C vorheizen, ein Backblech mit Backpapier belegen. Die Pilze mit dem Pesto füllen, auf das Blech legen und im Ofen 30–60 Minuten backen.

Den Salat auf vier Tellern ausbreiten und die gefüllten Pilze darauf anrichten. Mit den Tomaten garnieren und servieren.

Tipp: Die Pilze können Sie schon am Vortag zubereiten und im Kühlschrank lagern. Vor dem Servieren dann nochmals im Ofen erwärmen.

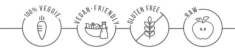

LE LOGIS DES QUATRE PUITS

NEUVICQ, NOUVELLE-AQUITAINE

When one thinks of Bordeaux, one will inevitably picture the wine that famously comes from the eponymous region in southwestern France. Just a short hour's drive from the World Heritage Site of Bordeaux, Le Logis des Quatre Puits, in the department of Charente Maritime, has been lovingly restored. The owners Keith Robinson and John Botteley have been vegetarians for more than 35 years and were theater actors and directors in their previous lives. Today, the manor is a charming home away from home for guests who would like to use it as a base for exploring the wine region and for relaxing holidays with family and friends. Parts of the country estate date back to the 16th century, and the hotel is surrounded by 84 acres (34 hectares) of idyllic forest and meadowland.

Whether you prefer to simply sleep here or take advantage of the full vacation package, Keith and John are happy to accommodate their guests' every taste and feed them delicious vegetarian and vegan meals.

One of the hotel's special features is a large, futuristic geodesic dome, a special structure made of steel bars in triangular patterns. The innkeepers hold yoga retreats and other events in the dome's unusual ambience. The varied landscape of the surrounding area, on the other hand, is more rustic than futuristic. The lovely Beau Vallon lake, which has a marvelous sandy beach, is only a few minutes away, while the Atlantic coast and picture-perfect little towns like Saint-Émilion (also UNESCO-classified) are within easy reach. Those who enjoy a fine vintage can learn first-hand how wine and cognac are grown and produced—wine tasting permitted!

Denkt man an Bordeaux, kommt einem wohl unweigerlich der entsprechende Wein in den Sinn, und der kommt bekanntlich aus der gleichnamigen Region im Südwesten Frankreichs. Nur eine Autostunde von der Weltkulturerbestadt Bordeaux entfernt, wurde das Herrenhaus Le Logis des Quatre Puits im Département Charente Maritime liebevoll restauriert. Die Gastgeber Keith Robinson und John Botteley sind seit über 35 Jahren Vegetarier und in ihrem „früheren Leben" Theaterschauspieler und Regisseure. Heute ist das Herrenhaus ein charmantes Zuhause auf Zeit für Gäste, die von hier aus die Weinregion erkunden wollen und entspannte Ferien mit Familie und Freunden verbringen möchten. Das teilweise im 16. Jahrhundert erbaute Landgut ist umgeben von 34 Hektar Grundstück, bestehend aus idyllischem Weideland und Wald. Egal ob reine Übernachtungsgäste oder Urlauber, die das Yoga-Retreatangebot nutzen möchten – Keith und John freuen sich über jeden Besuch und versorgen diesen mit vorzüglichen vegetarisch-veganen Mahlzeiten.

Ein besonderes Highlight des Hauses ist die futuristisch anmutende, große geodätische Kuppel, eine spezielle Konstruktion aus dreieckigen Stahlteilen. Hier finden unter anderem Yoga-Retreats in ungewöhnlichem Ambiente statt. Weniger futuristisch, dafür eher rustikal-ländlich ist es in der abwechslungsreichen Umgebung. Nur wenige Minuten entfernt findet man den schönen Badesee Beau-Vallon mit einem herrlichen Sandstrand, doch auch die Atlantikküste und bildhübsche Städtchen wie Saint-Émilion, ebenfalls UNESCO-klassifiziert, sind nicht weit weg. Freunde des gepflegten Tropfens können sich vor Ort anschauen, wie Wein und Cognac angebaut und hergestellt werden – Probieren natürlich erlaubt!

ROOMS: 5 ROOMS, 3 COTTAGES
SPECIALTIES: SALTWATER POOL, YOGA, SPORT FACILITIES (E.G. TABLE TENNIS, POOL TABLE, BIKE RENTAL, SOCCER FIELD, BADMINTON), COUNTRYSIDE WALKS

LE LOGIS DES QUATRE PUITS
17270 NEUVICQ
FRANCE (FRANKREICH)
WWW.LESQUATREPUITS.COM
+33 546 043 269

ZIMMER: 5 ZIMMER, 3 COTTAGES
BESONDERHEITEN: SALZWASSER-POOL, YOGA, SPORTANGEBOTE (U.A. TISCHTENNIS, BILLARDTISCH, FAHRRADVERLEIH, FUSSBALLFELD, BADMINTON), WANDERWEGE

LA MAISON DU VERT

TICHEVILLE, BASSE NORMANDIE

Visit La Maison du Vert, "the green house," in Normandy, and you will immediately understand how the place got its name. It's true that this prize-winning vegetarian and vegan hotel does not sport a green façade—it's a red brick structure—but all around it the landscape radiates green. The gorgeous, vast landscaped garden stretching out behind the house resembles a park, with its countless numbers of flowers, trees, and bushes. You will find many cozy spots in this green idyll to sit down and enjoy dinner outdoors, accompanied by a glass of fine organic wine.

The fruit and vegetable garden at the back of the hotel supplies the daily ingredients for freshly prepared dishes and wonderful homemade sorbets. It is also not unusual to encounter the odd turkey or duck—a wide range of animals share this lovely home with its owners and guests. Children are also heartily welcome, and they're allowed to help out at feeding time.

The garden offers a spectacular view of the Touques Valley and the nearby village. Picturesque coastal towns, such as Honfleur, Deauville, and Trouville-sur-Mer, along with wide, sandy beaches, are only an hour's drive away. The region is also known for its magnificent castles and gardens. The locals and tourists from all over the world all flock to La Maison du Vert for the gourmet vegetarian and vegan menu served in the hotel restaurant. After all the Viva! animal protection organization named the wonderful establishment the best hotel for vegetarians and vegans for a very good reason.

Wer La Maison du Vert, „Das grüne Haus", in der Normandie besucht, versteht die Namensgebung sofort. Zugegeben, dieses preisgekrönte vegetarisch-vegane Hotel hat keine grüne Fassade – es wurde aus roten Backsteinen erbaut – doch rundherum grünt es um die Wette. Der riesige, wunderschöne Landschaftsgarten, der sich hinter dem Haus erstreckt, erinnert an einen Park, mit seinen zahllosen Blumen, Bäumen und Sträuchern. In dieser grünen Idylle lassen sich auch viele lauschige Sitzgelegenheiten für das Abendessen im Freien bei einem guten Glas Biowein finden.

Die Zutaten aus dem Obst- und Gemüsegarten gleich hinterm Haus sorgen für tagesfrische Gerichte auf dem Teller und herrliches hausgemachtes Fruchteis. Es ist auch nicht ungewöhnlich, wenn sich mal ein Truthahn oder eine Ente dazugesellt – eine ganze Reihe von Tieren teilt sich dieses wunderbare Zuhause mit seinen Betreibern und Gästen. Kinder sind ebenfalls herzlich willkommen und dürfen natürlich beim Füttern helfen.

Vom Garten aus hat man einen spektakulären Blick über das Touques-Tal und das nächste Dorf. Nur eine Autostunde entfernt liegen pittoreske Küstenorte wie Honfleur, Deauville und Trouville-sur-Mer, inklusive breiter Sandstrände. Bekannt ist die Region auch für seine herrschaftlichen Schlösser und Gärten. Das La Maison du Vert selbst ist vor allem für seine vegetarisch-veganen Gourmetmenüs im hauseigenen Restaurant beliebt, sowohl bei Einheimischen als auch bei Touristen aus aller Welt. Das wunderbare Haus wurde schließlich nicht ohne Grund als bestes Hotel für Vegetarier und Veganer von der Tierschutzorganisation Viva! ausgezeichnet.

ROOMS: 3 ROOMS, 1 COTTAGE
SPECIALTIES: ANIMAL SANCTUARY, LUSH GARDEN FOR RELAXATION AND DINING, CYCLING, HIKING

LA MAISON DU VERT
LE BOURG
61120 TICHEVILLE
FRANCE (FRANKREICH)
WWW.MAISONDUVERT.COM
+33 233 369 584

ZIMMER: 3 ZIMMER, 1 GÄSTEHAUS
BESONDERHEITEN: KLEINER HOF FÜR GERETTETE TIERE, GROSSER BEPFLANZTER GARTEN ZUR ENTSPANNUNG UND ZUM SPEISEN, FAHRRADFAHREN, WANDERN

SOAMI RETREAT RESORT

MILLSTATT, CARINTHIA

Health, clarity, purity of nature, and balance—these are the principles of the SOAMI Retreat Resort. You will find them all over the hotel, from the architecture to the vegan cuisine. Built according to feng shui principles, the establishment harmoniously nestles up against the side of a mountain. When you arrive at SOAMI, the first thing to capture your attention is the breathtaking view of Austria's Carinthian mountains.

The light-filled rooms and seminar spaces exude minimalism, clarity, and elegance, and the natural materials used, such as bamboo and wood along with a great deal of glass, create a pleasant, almost living, breathing atmosphere. In this wholesome place with absolutely the best air and water quality as well as pristine nature as far as the eye can see, the yoga retreat not only provides a beautiful vacation experience—it is also a journey to your own center, a mindful transformation. If you've been yearning to destress, deacidify your body, relax, and enjoy good air and a view of the mountains, you will love the holistic detox weeks at the SOAMI Retreat Resort—and you'll return home feeling energized.

The close relationship between yoga and nourishment is a cornerstone of the hotel's philosophy. After all, a diet tailored to an individual's specific needs, along with an effective yoga practice, is essential in order to live a full and vigorous life. The SOAMI's vital cuisine, made from high quality ingredients, is therefore aimed at gently unburdening the entire organism. Incidentally, SOAMI—a Sanskrit word from an Indian mantra—means to "be in harmony." The perfect name for this place of rest and rejuvenation!

Gesundheit, Klarheit, Naturbelassenheit und Balance – das sind die Prinzipien des SOAMI Retreat Resort. Diese finden sich überall im Haus wieder, von der Architektur bis zur veganen Küche. Das nach den Grundlagen des Feng-Shui gebaute Haus schmiegt sich harmonisch an den Berghang. Kommt man im SOAMI an, fesselt zuallererst die atemberaubende Aussicht auf die Kärntner Bergwelt.

Die lichtdurchfluteten Zimmer und Seminarräume sind geprägt von Minimalismus, Klarheit und Noblesse, und die verwendeten Naturmaterialien wie Bambus und Holz sowie ganz viel Glas vermitteln ein angenehmes, fast atmendes Raumklima. An diesem heilsamen Ort mit allerhöchster Luft- und Wasserqualität und unberührter Natur so weit das Auge reicht, vermittelt ein Yoga-Retreat nicht einfach nur ein schönes Urlaubserlebnis – es ist vielmehr eine Reise zur eigenen Mitte, eine achtsame Transformation. Wer Sehnsucht nach körperlicher Entlastung, Entsäuerung, Entspannung, guter Luft und Bergen hat, wird die ganzheitlichen Detoxwochen im SOAMI Retreat Resort lieben – und voller Energie heimkehren.

Die enge Verbindung von Yoga und Ernährung ist ein Eckpfeiler der Philosophie des Hauses, denn gesunde typgerechte Ernährung ist eine wichtige Voraussetzung für ein kraftvolles, erfülltes Leben, genauso wie eine wirkungsvolle Yogapraxis. Die hochwertige und vitale SOAMI-Küche ist daher auf die sanfte Entlastung des gesamten Organismus abgestimmt. SOAMI – ein Sanskrit-Begriff aus einem indischen Mantra – bedeutet übrigens „in Einklang sein". Ein wahrlich passender Name für diesen Ort der Erholung!

ROOMS: 17
SPECIALTIES: YOGA, DETOX RETREATS, NUTRITION CONSULTATION, ZEN ROOMS, POOL (NO CHLORINE), CONSERVATION OF RESOURCES (E.G. SOLAR COLLECTORS, TOILETS WITH RAINWATER)

SOAMI RETREAT RESORT
OBERMILLSTATT 196
9872 MILLSTATT
AUSTRIA (ÖSTERREICH)
WWW.SOAMI.AT
+43 (0)476 6230 00

ZIMMER: 17
BESONDERHEITEN: YOGA, DETOX-PROGRAMM, ERNÄHRUNGS-BERATUNG, ZENZIMMER, POOL (OHNE CHLOR), RESSOURCEN-SCHONUNG (U.A. SOLARENERGIE, TOILETTEN MIT REGENWASSER)

Every guest of the SOAMI Retreat Resort can request a personal dietary consultation, where they learn to eat
a healthy diet in keeping with their own special needs and to select foods that do the body good over those that disrupt
the body's equilibrium. The SOAMI book, which contains 200 of the hotel's most popular recipes and many interesting tips
on nutrition, yoga, meditation, and personal development, also helps you incorporate what you've learned and experienced
into your everyday life so that you stay healthy and in balance.

Im SOAMI Retreat Resort erhält jeder Gast auf Wunsch eine individuelle Ernährungsberatung, bei der er lernt,
sich typgerecht gesund zu ernähren und die Nahrungsmittel auszuwählen, die dem eigenen Körper guttun, statt solchen,
die ihn aus der Balance bringen. Das SOAMI-Buch mit 200 der beliebtesten hauseigenen Rezepte und viel Wissenswertem
über Ernährung, Yoga, Meditation und Persönlichkeitsentwicklung hilft zusätzlich, das Erlebte und Erlernte in den Alltag
einfließen zu lassen und so dauerhaft gesund und im Gleichgewicht zu bleiben.

SOAMI BALANCE PLATE
WITH RED RICE AND SWEET POTATO TEMPEH BURGER

SOAMI BALANCE-TELLER
MIT ROTEM REIS UND SÜSSKARTOFFEL-TEMPEH-BURGER

INGREDIENTS
SERVES 4

Red rice
1 cup/185 g red rice
1 pinch salt
1 tbsp soy sauce (tamari)
1 tsp toasted sesame oil

Gomasio
10 tbsp/100 g unhulled sesame seeds
1 tsp sea salt

Sweet potato tempeh burger
1 tbsp coconut oil
10 oz/200 g tempeh, sliced
1 tbsp ginger, minced
1 garlic clove (optional), minced
3 tsp soy sauce (tamari)
1 tsp maple syrup
1 tbsp arrowroot
2 medium-sized sweet potatoes,
   sliced ¼ inch/0.5 cm thick

Chard
1 pinch salt
4 large chard leaves

Serve with
Avocado, flesh formed into small balls
Pickled ginger
Wasabi
Teriyaki sauce

ZUTATEN
FÜR 4 PERSONEN

Roter Reis
1 Tasse roter Reis
1 Prise Salz
1 EL Sojasauce (Tamari)
1 TL geröstetes Sesamöl

Gomasio
100 g ungeschälte Sesamsamen
1 TL Meersalz

Süßkartoffel-Tempeh-Burger
1 EL Kokosöl
200 g Tempeh, in Scheiben geschnitten
1 EL Ingwer fein gehackt
1 Knoblauchzehe (nach Belieben),
  fein gehackt
3 EL Sojasauce (Tamari)
1 TL Ahornsirup
1 EL Pfeilwurzelmehl
2 mittelgroße Süßkartoffeln,
  in 5 mm dicke Scheiben geschnitten

Mangold
1 Prise Salz
4 große Mangoldblätter

Zum Servieren
Avocado, zu Kugeln ausgestochen
Ingwerpickels
Wasabi
Teriyakisauce

METHOD

Red rice: Place the rice in a sieve and rinse under running water until the water runs clear. Drain off excess water and bring to a boil in a pot with 2 cups/470 ml water. Add salt, cover, and simmer the rice for 50 minutes on medium heat. Stir in tamari and sesame oil.

Gomasio: Rinse the sesame seeds and toast in a pan on low heat. Place in a mortar. Then toast the salt as well until it turns light gray. Add to the sesame seeds and grind everything with a pestle.

Sweet potato tempeh burger: Heat the oil in a pan and sear the tempeh. Add the ginger and garlic (if using), soy sauce, maple syrup, and 2⅛ cups/500 ml water. Cover and simmer for 25 minutes on medium heat.
Whisk the arrowroot with 3 tablespoons cold water, add to the pan and stir until tempeh slices are completely coated. Braise the sweet potato slices in a little water for 8 minutes on medium heat. Preheat the oven to 375°F/200°C. Assemble the burgers from the sweet potato and tempeh slices and bake in the oven for 15 minutes.

Chard: Bring 4¼ cups/1 l water to a boil in a pot and add salt. Blanch the chard leaves for 2 minutes. Remove the chard, plunge into ice water, and spread out onto four plates.

Arrange the rice on the chard and sprinkle with gomasio. Place the burgers on the side and serve with avocado balls, pickled ginger, wasabi and teriyaki sauce.

ZUBEREITUNG

Den Reis in einem Sieb unter fließendem Wasser abspülen, bis das Wasser klar abläuft. Abtropfen lassen, dann mit 2 Tassen Wasser in einem Topf aufkochen. Salzen und den Reis zugedeckt bei mittlerer Hitze 50 Minuten ausquellen lassen. Tamari und Sesamöl einrühren.

Für das Gomasio den Sesam waschen und in einer Pfanne bei schwacher Hitze rösten. In einen Mörser geben. Das Salz ebenfalls anrösten, bis es sich leicht grau verfärbt. Zum Sesam geben und alles zerstoßen.

Für die Burger das Öl in einer Pfanne erhitzen und den Tempeh darin anbraten. Ingwer, nach Belieben Knoblauch, Sojasauce, Ahornsirup und 500 ml Wasser zugeben. Alles zugedeckt bei mittlerer Hitze 25 Minuten köcheln lassen. Das Pfeilwurzelmehl mit 3 EL kaltem Wasser verquirlen und die Masse damit binden. Süßkartoffelscheiben in wenig Wasser bei mittlerer Hitze 8 Minuten garen. Den Ofen auf 200 °C vorheizen. Aus den Süßkartoffel- und Tempehscheiben vier Burger zusammensetzen und im Ofen 15 Minuten backen.

Für den Mangold 1 l Wasser in einem Topf aufkochen und salzen. Die Mangoldblätter darin 2 Minuten blanchieren. Herausnehmen, eiskalt abschrecken und auf vier Tellern ausbreiten.

Den Reis darauf anrichten und mit Gomasio bestreuen. Die Burger danebensetzen und mit Avokadokugeln, Ingwerpickels, Wasabi und Teriyakisauce servieren.

Q! RESORT KITZBÜHEL

KITZBÜHEL, TYROL

Perhaps it is the small and unusual touches that make a stay at the Q! Resort Health & Spa so special—from a special power corner filled with superfoods and vitamin compounds at the breakfast buffet to fruit and mineral water stations to the option of selecting an herbal pillow from the pillow menu in the evenings to ensure a restful sleep. Guests at this stylish family-run health oasis will also appreciate the spacious and comfortable rooms, the 7,535-square-foot (700-square-meter) spa area, a natural bathing pond with a stunning view of the mountains, and an extensive exercise and vitality program that changes daily.

The certified organic hotel is also home to a restaurant that lives up to its name, "Happy Kuh" (The Happy Cow), and serves inventive vegetarian and vegan meals. The culinary concept's guiding principle is for guests to savor food without weighing down the body. This is evident in the sumptuous breakfast buffet, with its "power station" and abundant vegan options, as well as the four-course dinner menu that features elaborate creations made primarily from regional products. For individuals who want to have an enjoyable experience fasting without feeling hungry, the range of special alkaline fasting options at the Q! Resort Health & Spa offers a gentle way for guests to detoxify their bodies by consuming healthy alkaline meals. With all the numerous amenities and the pleasant atmosphere at the resort, you will find it easy to leave everyday life behind, relax, and revitalize yourself with positive energy.

Have we already mentioned that one of the most famous ski areas in Europe is right outside your door?

Es sind vielleicht auch die kleinen und ungewöhnlichen Extras, die den Aufenthalt im Q! Resort Health & Spa so besonders machen – von der Kraftecke mit Superfoods und Vitaminpräparaten beim Frühstücksbuffet über Obst- und Heilwasserstationen bis hin zum Angebot, sich abends ein Kräuterkissen aus dem Kissenmenü für einen erholsamen Schlaf auszusuchen. Aber natürlich schätzt man als Gast in der familiengeführten stylishen Gesundheitsoase auch die gemütlich-großzügigen Zimmer, den 700 Quadratmeter umfassenden Spa-Bereich, den Naturbadeteich vor atemberaubender Bergkulisse und das äußerst umfangreiche, täglich wechselnde Sport- und Vitalprogramm.

Das biozertifizierte Hotel beherbergt auch ein Restaurant, das ganz nach dem Credo „Happy Kuh" agiert und sehr einfallsreiche vegetarische und vegane Menüs anbietet. Genießen, ohne den Körper zu belasten, ist die Prämisse des Küchenkonzepts, sowohl beim reichhaltigen Frühstücksbuffet mit Kraftstelle und ungewöhnlich reichhaltigem veganem Angebot als auch beim abendlichen Vier-Gänge-Menü mit kunstvollen Kreationen aus überwiegend regionalen Produkten. Für Menschen, die genussbetont fasten wollen, ohne zu hungern, sind die speziellen Basenfastenangebote des Q! Resort Health & Spa eine sanfte Methode, mit gesunden basischen Mahlzeiten zu entgiften. Den Alltag komplett hinter sich lassen, zur Ruhe kommen und positive Lebensenergie tanken, das fällt einem in der angenehmen Atmosphäre des gesamten Hauses und bei den zahlreichen Annehmlichkeiten nicht schwer.

Erwähnten wir bereits, dass sich eines der berühmtesten Skigebiete Europas gleich vor der Haustür befindet?

ROOMS: 77
SPECIALTIES: BASE FASTING WEEKS, SELECTION OF 6 DIFFERENT HERBAL PILLOWS, YOGA, MEDITATION, PILATES, GYM, SAUNA, STEAM BATH, INFRARED ROOM, PRIVATE SPA, ECOLOGICAL SWIMMING POND

Q! RESORT KITZBÜHEL
BAHNHOFPLATZ 1
6370 KITZBÜHEL
AUSTRIA (ÖSTERREICH)
WWW.QRESORT.AT
+43 5356 62136

ZIMMER: 77
BESONDERHEITEN: BASENFASTEN-WOCHEN, AUSWAHL AUS 6 VERSCHIEDENEN KRÄUTERKISSEN, YOGA, MEDITATION, PILATES, FITNESSRAUM, SAUNA, DAMPFBAD, ZIRBEN-INFRAROTRAUM, PRIVATE SPA, NATURBADETEICH

NATURHOTEL LECHLIFE

WÄNGLE, TYROL

Germany's most successful vegan cookbook authors shouldn't be the only ones who return year after year to enjoy a relaxing stay at the Naturhotel LechLife in Tyrol. Indeed, other vegan gourmands should also be able to get their money's worth. The hotel gives entirely new meaning to the expression "vegan-friendly," since well prepared, healthful vegan dishes are simply par for the course with the establishment's kitchen staff.

The strict standards of extraordinary cuisine and passion for experimentation can be tasted in every bite you enjoy in the restaurant, while taking in the impressive, panoramic view. The wide range of rare, nearly forgotten vegetable, fruit and grain varieties, super foods, along with antioxidant-rich local delicacies and seasonal specialties, turn a meal at the Naturhotel LechLife into an extraordinary experience. LechLife even offers vegan beverages, from sodas to wine, vegan skincare products in the rooms, and a vegan challenge week.

This VeganWelcome-certified hotel can even organize a fully vegan stay without prior notice, since the Kühbachers, who run the establishment, also follow a vegan lifestyle. Wellness seminars, cleansing and detox weeks, yoga, and relaxation programs as well as cooking courses round out the Naturhotel LechLife's extensive range of wellness services. A Biozoom scanner even allows guests to measure the positive effects of their stay on their health right on the premises. Incidentally, guests who enjoy an active lifestyle will find the hotel's quite, sunny location to be an excellent base for exploring the many nearby hiking and biking trails or enjoying a day of alpine or cross-country skiing. The surrounding nature is the perfect hideaway to find your inner balance, and it lives up to the hotel's motto: "Respect Life—Respect Yourself!" The perfect vacation for everyone—and not just vegan celebrities.

Wenn Deutschlands erfolgreichste vegane Kochbuchautoren immer wieder gerne zur Erholung ins Naturhotel LechLife nach Tirol reist, sollten wohl auch andere Fans der veganen Ernährung voll auf ihre Kosten kommen. Tatsächlich bekommt der Ausdruck „vegan-friendly" hier eine ganz neue Bedeutung, denn wirklich gut gemachte, gesunde vegane Gerichte gehören für das Küchenteam des Hotels einfach ganz selbstverständlich dazu.

Den hohen Anspruch an eine außergewöhnliche Küche und leidenschaftliche Experimentierfreude schmeckt man bei jedem Bissen heraus, den man im Panoramarestaurant mit beeindruckendem Ausblick genießt. Die Vielfalt seltener, fast vergessener Gemüse-, Obst- und Getreidesorten, Superfoods und antioxidative Lebensmittel sowie heimische Schmankerl und saisonale Spezialitäten machen das Essen im Naturhotel LechLife zu etwas Besonderem. Selbst vegane Getränke von Limonaden bis Wein, vegane Pflegeprodukte auf den Zimmern und eine vegane Challenge-Woche stellt LechLife zur Verfügung.

Der gesamte Aufenthalt kann in diesem von VeganWelcome zertifizierten Hotel immer auch ohne Vorankündigung vegan gestaltet werden, denn das Betreiberehepaar Kühbacher hat den veganen Lifestyle auch für sich selbst entdeckt. Gesundheitsseminare, Entschlackungs- und Detoxwochen, Yoga- und Entspannungsangebote sowie Kochkurse runden das große Gesundheitsangebot im Naturhotel LechLife ab. Die positiven gesundheitlichen Auswirkungen des Aufenthalts lassen sich übrigens noch vor Ort mit einem Biozoom-Messgerät überprüfen. Und die ruhige, sonnige Lage ist, nebenbei bemerkt, auch für Aktivurlauber ein hervorragender Ausgangspunkt zu den zahlreichen Wander- und Radwegen, Skipisten und Langlaufloipen. Die umliegende Natur ist der perfekte Rückzugsort, um wieder die eigene Mitte zu finden, ganz nach dem Motto des Hauses: „Respect Life – Respect Yourself!" So erholen sich nicht nur Veganpromis gerne.

ROOMS: 39
SPECIALTIES: SELECTION OF 5 DIFFERENT HERBAL PILLOWS, SAUNA, STEAM BATH, INFRARED CABIN, MASSAGES, SWIMMING POOL, EV CHARGING STATION

NATURHOTEL LECHLIFE
HOLZ 1A
6610 WÄNGLE
AUSTRIA (ÖSTERREICH)
WWW.LECHLIFE.AT
+43 5672 642 34

ZIMMER: 39
BESONDERHEITEN: AUSWAHL AUS 5 VERSCHIEDENEN KRÄUTERKISSEN, SAUNA, DAMPFBAD, INFRAROT-KABINE, MASSAGEN, SCHWIMMBAD, E-AUTO-LADESTATION

CLUB SANDWICH
WITH SPELT SEITAN AND WASABI MAYO

CLUBSANDWICH
MIT DINKEL-SEITAN UND WASABI-MAYO

INGREDIENTS
SERVES 1

Spelt seitan
6 lb/3 kg spelt flour
3 qt/3 l vegetable broth
1 qt/1 l soy sauce
5 each bay leaves, cloves,
  and juniper berries
2–3 chili peppers
5 garlic cloves
Salt, pepper

Wasabi mayonnaise
1 tbsp mustard
Salt
1¼ cups/300 ml soy drink, unflavored
2½ cups/600 ml canola oil
Wasabi paste

METHOD

Spelt seitan: Mix the flour with 2 qt/2 l water in a blender or food processor and knead to form a dough. Fill one bowl with warm water (95 to 98°F/35 to 37°C) and another one with cold water. Rinse the dough first in the warm water, kneading it constantly. Then knead the dough in the cold water. Knead the dough again in a fresh change of warm water, then switch to the cold water. Repeat, switching between the warm and cold water, until the water is clear. Divide the seitan into pieces (7 oz/200 g each). Combine the vegetable broth, soy sauce, spices, chilies, garlic, salt, and pepper in a pot and bring to a boil. Place the seitan pieces in the pot liquor and simmer for 2 hours. Turn off the stove and let the seitan steep in the pot liquor for another 2 hours. Then cut one piece of seitan into two slices (approximately ⅓-inch/1-cm thick) for the sandwich. Place the rest of the seitan along with the pot liquor in a container with a tight-fitting lid and refrigerate.

Wasabi mayonnaise: Blend the mustard, salt, and soy drink with an immersion blender. Gradually add the oil and blend until a mayonnaise forms. Remove 3½ tablespoons/ 50 g of the mayonnaise and season to taste with wasabi paste. Place the rest in a screw-top jar and refrigerate.

Sandwich
Smoked salt
Smoked ground paprika
2 tbsp olive oil
2 eggplant slices
3 slices of whole grain bread
1 tomato, sliced
2 leaves of Lollo Rosso and Lollo Bionda
  lettuce (red and green loose-leaf lettuce)
6 slices cucumber

ZUTATEN
FÜR 1 PERSON

Dinkel-Seitan
3 kg Dinkelmehl
3 l Gemüsebrühe
1 l Sojasauce
je 5 Lorbeerblätter, Gewürznelken
  und Wacholderbeeren
2–3 Chilischoten
5 Knoblauchzehen
Salz, Pfeffer

Wasabi-Mayonnaise
1 EL Senf
Salz
300 ml Sojadrink natur
600 ml Rapsöl
Wasabipaste

Sandwich
geräuchertes Salz
geräuchertes Paprikapulver
2 EL Olivenöl
2 Auberginenscheiben
3 Scheiben Vollkorntoast
1 Tomate, in Scheiben geschnitten
2 Blätter Lollo Rosso und Lollo Bionda
6 Scheiben Salatgurke

Sandwich: Preheat the oven to 350°F/180°C. Combine the salt, paprika, and 1 tablespoon oil. Brush the mixture on the eggplant slices, coating both sides, and roast in the oven for 10 minutes. Heat 1 tablespoon oil in a pan and sear the seitan slices. Toast the bread slices until crispy. Spread wasabi mayonnaise on all pieces of toast. Layer lettuce, cucumber, tomato, and seitan on two slices of toast. Place the third slice on top. Tack the eggplant slices onto the sandwich with two wooden skewers.

Tip: Once prepared, the seitan and mayonnaise will keep in the refrigerator for 3 to 4 weeks. You can therefore make a sandwich anytime you wish.

ZUBEREITUNG

Für den Seitan das Mehl mit 2 l Wasser in einer Küchenmaschine zu einem Teig verkneten. Eine Schüssel mit warmem Wasser (35–37 °C) und eine mit kaltem Wasser bereitstellen. Den Teig zuerst im warmen Wasser auswaschen, dabei beständig kneten. Dann den Teig im kalten Wasser durchkneten. Das warme Wasser wechseln, den Teig wieder darin kneten und das kalte Wasser wechseln. So im Wechsel fortfahren, bis das Wasser klar bleibt. Den Seitan in Stücke (à 200 g) teilen. Gemüsebrühe, Sojasauce, Gewürze, Chilis, Knoblauch Salz und Pfeffer in einem Topf aufkochen. Die Seitan-Stücke in den Sud geben und 2 Stunden köcheln lassen. Den Herd ausschalten und den Seitan noch 2 Stunden im Sud ziehen lassen. Danach für das Sandwich ein Seitan-Stück in zwei Scheiben (etwa 1 cm dick) schneiden. Den Rest mit Sud in eine gut schließende Dose füllen und kühlen. Für die Mayonnaise Senf, Salz und Sojadrink mit dem Pürierstab verquirlen. Das Öl nach und nach untermixen, bis eine Mayonnaise entsteht. 50 g abnehmen und mit Wasabipaste nach Geschmack verrühren. Den Rest in ein Schraubglas füllen und kühlen.
Für das Sandwich den Backofen auf 180 °C vorheizen. Salz, Paprikapulver und 1 EL Öl verrühren. Die Auberginenscheiben auf beiden Seiten damit bestreichen und im Ofen 10 Minuten rösten. In einer Pfanne 1 EL Öl erhitzen und die Seitan-Scheiben darin anbraten. Die Toastscheiben knusprig rösten. Alle Toasts mit der Wasabi-Mayo bestreichen. Zwei Scheiben mit Salat, Gurken, Tomaten und Seitan belegen. Übereinanderstapeln und mit der dritten Toastscheibe (Mayo nach unten) abdecken. Die Auberginen mit 2 Holzspießen in das Sandwich stecken.

Tipp: Einmal zubereitet sind Seitan und Mayonnaise im Kühlschrank 3–4 Wochen haltbar. So können Sie sich ganz spontan ein Sandwich bauen.

BÖDELE ALPENHOTEL
SCHWARZENBERG, VORARLBERG

The Bödele Alpenhotel is situated at an elevation of 1,140 meters in the heart of the Austrian alps. Along with its impressive panoramic views of the Bregenz Forest Mountains, this alpine hotel also has a history steeped in tradition. It all began in 1888, when a doctor from nearby Dornbirn opened an alpine inn for guests seeking rest and relaxation. After a series of managers over the years, including the famous alpine ski champion Marc Girardelli, the hotel was taken over by its current owners in 2006, who turned it into a contemporary, stylish refuge. However, all owners had one important goal in common: to create a retreat that emphasizes health and relaxation surrounded by nature.

The wellness hotel follows the guiding principle that guests should leave a restaurant healthier than when they arrived. Its restaurant therefore serves fewer alcoholic drinks and addictive foods and more wholesome, organic meals made from vegetarian and vegan ingredients. The result is sustainable gastronomy that benefits people and the environment. The menu offers vintage nonalcoholic wines, caffeine-free coffees made from roasted lupine beans, and dishes that represent the finest examples of the culinary arts, from delectable salads to reinterpreted Mediterranean classics to exotic curries. The hotel's wholesome, healthful cuisine tempts the palate—complete with a magnificent view. Many vacation and leisure activities can be found nearby: the Bödele ski resort, an excellent choice for families with children, cross-country skiing across alpine meadows, toboggan runs, hiking and mountain biking trails, with Lake Constance a short distance away—and the list goes on. In winter, the region boasts excellent snow conditions; in summer, the hotel makes the perfect base camp for leisure activities in the fresh alpine air. The Bödele's owners were always driven by the ideals of health, nature and relaxation, and these goals have not changed in over a century.

Inmitten der österreichischen Alpen auf 1140 Metern Höhe liegt das Bödele Alpenhotel. Nicht nur ein Ort mit eindrucksvollem Rundblick auf die Berge des Bregenzerwaldes, sondern auch mit einer traditionsreichen Geschichte. Diese begann 1888, als ein Stadtarzt aus dem nahegelegenen Dornbirn hier einen Alpgasthof für Erholung suchende Gäste in Betrieb nahm. Später wurde das Hotel unter anderem vom berühmten Skisportler Marc Girardelli geführt, bevor es 2006 an die heutigen Besitzer übergeben wurde, die das Haus in ein zeitgemäßes, stilvolles Refugium verwandelten. Eines war allen Betreibern gleichermaßen wichtig: einen Rückzugsort für Gesundheit und Erholung zu schaffen, in dem Natur erlebt werden kann.

Der Gast soll ein Restaurant gesunder verlassen als er es betritt. Das ist das Credo im Bödele Alpenhotel. Weniger Genuss- und Suchtmittel, dafür mehr biologische, vollwertige, vegane und vegetarische Ernährung – nachhaltige Gastronomie für Mensch und Schöpfung. Erlesene alkoholfreie Weine, koffeinfreie Kaffeesorten von der Süßlupine und Gerichte auf höchstem kulinarischem Niveau werden angeboten, von feinen Salatplatten über neu interpretierte Klassiker der mediterranen Küche bis hin zu exotischen Currys. Hier kann man den Gaumen gesund verwöhnen lassen – der herrliche Ausblick ist inklusive.

In direkter Umgebung bieten sich zahllose Urlaubs- und Freizeitmöglichkeiten: das Skigebiet Bödele, auch bestens geeignet für Familien mit Kindern, Langlaufloipen durch unberührte Almlandschaften, Rodelstrecken, Wander- und Mountainbikewege, der nahegelegene Bodensee – diese Liste ließe sich endlos fortführen. Beste Schneeverhältnisse im Winter, der perfekte Start für Freizeitaktivitäten an der frischen Luft im Sommer. Gesundheit, Natur und Erholung waren stets die Motive der Betreiber vom Bödele – daran

---

ROOMS: 11 SPACIOUS SUITES
SPECIALTIES: HEALTH WEEK PROGRAM, WINTER AND SUMMER OUTDOOR ACTIVITIES (E.G. SKIING, CROSS-COUNTRY SKIING, SLEDDING, MOUNTAIN BIKING, HIKING)

BÖDELE ALPENHOTEL
BÖDELE 473
6850 SCHWARZENBERG
AUSTRIA (ÖSTERREICH)
WWW.BOEDELE.AT
+43 660 444 7777

ZIMMER: 11 GROSSZÜGIGE SUITEN
BESONDERHEITEN: GESUNDHEITS-WOCHEN, WINTER- UND SOMMER-FREIZEITANGEBOTE (U.A. SKIFAHREN, LANGLAUFEN, RODELN, MOUNTAIN-BIKE FAHREN, WANDERN)

DAS GRÜNE HOTEL ZUR POST
SALZBURG, SALZBURG

When I think of Salzburg, Mozart comes to mind—along with Mozartkugeln. While these traditional chocolates also have a green center, the Green Hotel zur Post undoubtedly lies at the heart of this tradition-rich Austrian city. Sustainability is a top priority of the family-run establishment. Every detail in this hospitable hotel was chosen especially for its environmental friendliness, from the rooftop photovoltaic system to energy-efficient LED light bulbs, organic cotton towels and electric car charging stations out front to the hearty organic breakfast buffet with vegan and gluten-free selections. Guests who like to travel with a clear environmental conscience can rest assured that they will leave behind a clearly visible ecological footprint.

After enjoying a hearty breakfast of homemade jams, freshly baked bread, coffee, and fruit, you may feel like heading into town. If so, a short walk from the hotel will take you straight to the center of the Old Town. And guests who aren't sure what sights to visit first can get excellent advice from the husband-and-wife team who run the hotel. The Maiers and their team know the city inside and out—after all, the hotel has been in their family since 1949. They will be happy to provide directions for finding the greenest route through the city on the Salzach River, including insider tips on the establishments that offer the best vegetarian and vegan cuisine.

Denk ich an Salzburg, denk ich an Mozart – und an Mozartkugeln. Zwar hat die traditionelle Pralinenleckerei auch einen grünen Kern, doch die grüne Seele der österreichischen Traditionsstadt ist sicher Das Grüne Hotel zur Post. In dem Familienbetrieb wird Nachhaltigkeit großgeschrieben – kein Detail in dem freundlichen Hotelbetrieb, das nicht auf seine Umweltverträglichkeit abgeklopft wurde. Von der Photovoltaikanlage auf dem Dach über stromsparende LED-Lampen, Handtüchern aus Biobaumwolle und Stromtankstellen vor dem Haus bis hin zum reichhaltigen Biofrühstücksbuffet mit veganen und glutenfreien Angeboten. Ein besseres Umweltgewissen kann man beim Reisen kaum haben – der ökologische Fußabdruck, oder besser Matratzenabdruck, kann sich sehen lassen.

Wenn man sich nach dem Genuss des reichhaltigen Frühstücks mit hausgemachten Aufstrichen, frischem Brot, Kaffee und Obst bereit für einen Ausflug in die Stadt fühlt, gelangt man nach einem kurzen Spaziergang mitten ins Zentrum der historischen Altstadt. Und wenn man als Gast nicht weiß, was man als Erstes ansehen soll, so hat das Betreiberehepaar Maier, ebenso wie ihr ganzes Team, die besten Tipps parat. Sie kennen die Stadt in- und auswendig – das Hotel befindet sich bereits seit 1949 in Familienbesitz. Gerne geben sie Auskunft über die grünste Route durch diese Stadt an der Salzach, inklusive Insidertipps für die besten vegetarisch-veganen Schlemmeradressen.

ROOMS: 42
SPECIALTIES: 10 % PRICE REDUCTION WHEN ARRIVING BY E-CAR, BIKE OR TRAIN, CONSERVATION OF RESOURCES (E.G. PHOTOVOLTAICS, EV CHARGING STATION), CENTRAL LOCATION, SAUNA

DAS GRÜNE BIO HOTEL ZUR POST
MAXGLANER HAUPTSTRASSE 45
5020 SALZBURG
AUSTRIA (ÖSTERREICH)
WWW.HOTELZURPOST.INFO
+43 662 832 3390

ZIMMER: 42
BESONDERHEITEN: 10 % RABATT BEI ANREISE MIT ELEKTROAUTO, FAHRRAD ODER ZUG, RESSOURCENSCHONUNG (U.A. PHOTOVOLTAIK, E-AUTO-LADESTATION), ZENTRALE LAGE, SAUNA

CARROT NUT BUTTER
SPICY VEGAN SPREAD

MÖHREN-NUSS-AUFSTRICH
WÜRZIGER, VEGANER BROTAUFSTRICH

INGREDIENTS

SERVES 4

1 tbsp olive oil
7 oz/200 g carrots, cubed
3.5 tbsp/50 ml vegetable broth
1 garlic clove
Salt
Pepper or cayenne
1 pinch cumin
1 splash lemon juice
2 tbsp ground nuts
1 tsp fresh chopped herbs

ZUTATEN

FÜR 4 PERSONEN

1 EL Olivenöl
200 g Möhren, in Würfel geschnitten
50 ml Gemüsebrühe
1 Knoblauchzehe
Salz
Pfeffer oder Cayennepfeffer
1 Msp. Kreuzkümmel
1 Spritzer Zitronensaft
2 EL gemahlene Nüsse
1 TL frisch gehackte Kräuter

METHOD

Heat the olive oil in a pan and briefly sweat the carrot cubes. Add the vegetable broth and braise the carrots for about 5 minutes until tender.

Meanwhile, peel the garlic clove, put it through a press, and season with salt, pepper, cumin, and lemon juice.

Drain the carrots. Place the vegetables, garlic spice paste, and nuts in a blender and puree until smooth; you can also use an immersion blender. Mix in the herbs and serve.

ZUBEREITUNG

Das Olivenöl in einer Pfanne erhitzen und die Möhrenwürfel kurz darin andünsten. Die Gemüsebrühe dazugießen und die Möhren in etwa 5 Minuten weich dünsten.

Inzwischen den Knoblauch schälen, durch die Presse drücken und mit Salz, Pfeffer, Kreuzkümmel und Zitronensaft vermischen.

Die Möhren abgießen. Das Gemüse dann mit der Knoblauch-Gewürz-Paste und den Nüssen im Standmixer oder mit dem Pürierstab cremig pürieren. Die Kräuter unterrühren und den Aufstrich servieren.

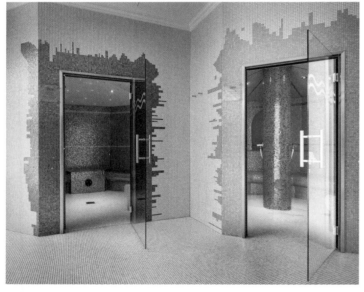

DAS ALPENHAUS GASTEINERTAL

BAD HOFGASTEIN, SALZBURG

Guests know that they can look forward to carving out some time for themselves at Das Alpenhaus Gasteinertal, a four-star sport, spa, and health hotel. The Gastein valley area is referred to as the "valley of health" thanks to its optimal altitude, hot springs, and a wide range of recreational and wellness activities. It is no coincidence that this valley is also home to the hotel. It truly is the perfect place if you want to get away from it all, relax, and recharge your batteries.

The hotel's 21,500 square feet (2000 square meter) wellness area is the ideal place for guests to start relaxing. The ALPEN.VEDA.SPA offers an indoor swimming pool with panoramic views, whirlpools, a variety of saunas, and a wide range of treatments and activities. Yet that's not all, because the holiday resort embraces a holistic approach to wellness. Developed specifically with this strategy in mind, the ALPEN.KRAFT.SELFNESS program combines healthy exercise and nutrition, the experience of nature, relaxation, enjoyment, and mindfulness. The goal of the program is to help guests leave everyday stresses and worries behind and enhance awareness and mindfulness—in essence, to encourage guests to finally take time for themselves. Guests will find food that is both healthy and delicious at the stylish Alpenhaus restaurant, which serves an array of Austrian and Gastein specialties, healthy wellness cuisine, and vegetarian and vegan creations. Head chef Franz Huick refers to his concept as VEGAN ALPENHAUS.CUISINE. The hotel's guiding principle is "Preserving tradition while moving with the spirit of the times," a motto that applies both to the restaurant as well as the entire hotel. Regional authenticity re-interpreted in a contemporary and uncomplicated fashion—that is the Alpine lifestyle, and it corresponds perfectly with the hotel's focus on health and wellness.

Endlich „Zeit fürs Ich" – diese erwartet den Gast garantiert im Viersterne-Sport-, Spa- und Gesundheitshotel Das Alpenhaus Gasteinertal. Es liegt wohl nicht ganz zufällig im Tal der Gesundheit – so wird das Gebiet wegen seiner optimalen Höhenlage, seiner Thermalquellen und natürlich auch wegen seiner Erholungs- und Gesundheitsangebote bezeichnet. Ein wahrlich guter Ort, um anzukommen, abzuschalten und Kraft zu tanken.

Die Erholung darf gerne im 2000 Quadratmeter großen Wellnessbereich des Hauses beginnen. Das ALPEN.VEDA.SPA bietet ein Panoramahallenbad, Whirlpools, eine Saunalandschaft sowie ein großes Behandlungs- und Aktivangebot. Damit aber nicht genug, denn das Auszeitresort verfolgt einen ganzheitlichen Wellnessansatz. Eigens dafür wurde das ALPEN.KRAFT.SELFNESS Programm entwickelt, das gesunde Bewegung und Ernährung, Naturerleben, Entspannung, Genuss und Achtsamkeit zusammenbringt. Das Ziel: Ballast abwerfen, Bewusstsein und Achtsamkeit schärfen – endlich Zeit fürs Ich eben. Für gesunde Ernährung und Genuss sorgt das stilvolle Alpenhaus.Restaurant. Österreichische und Gasteiner Spezialitäten, gesunde Genussküche und Kreationen aus der veganen Küche – VEGANE ALPENHAUS.KULINARIK nennt Küchenchef Franz Huick sein Konzept. Der Leitsatz des Hauses, „Die Tradition bewahren und den Zeitgeist hereinlassen", gilt hier übrigens für die Küche und das ganze Haus gleichermaßen. Regionale Authentizität, zeitgemäß und unkompliziert neu interpretiert – das ist alpiner Lifestyle, und der passt gut zu Gesundheit und Wellness.

ROOMS: 89
SPECIALTIES: MASSAGES, BEAUTY TREATMENTS, GYM, INDOOR SWIMMING POOL, SAUNA, YOGA, WINTER AND SUMMER OUTDOOR ACTIVITIES (E.G. SKIING, GOLF, HIKING)

DAS ALPENHAUS GASTEINERTAL
KURGARTENSTRASSE 26
5630 BAD HOFGASTEIN
AUSTRIA (ÖSTERREICH)
WWW.ALPENHAUS-GASTEIN.AT
+43 6432 6356

ZIMMER: 89
BESONDERHEITEN: MASSAGEN, BEAUTY-BEHANDLUNGEN, FITNESSRAUM, HALLENBAD, SAUNA, YOGA, WINTER- UND SOMMERFREIZEITANGEBOTE (U.A. SKIFAHREN, GOLF, WANDERN)

CELLOPHANE NOODLE SALAD
WITH TOFU AND TANDOORI SEASONING

GLASNUDELSALAT
MIT TOFU UND TANDOORI

INGREDIENTS
SERVES 6

10 oz/300 g tofu (plain), sliced
¼ cup/60 ml soy sauce
1 tbsp/20 g freshly grated ginger
1 lb/600 g cellophane noodles
Sesame oil
5 oz/160 g mixed sprouts
Salt, pepper
Sesame seeds
2 tbsp/40 g tandoori paste
4 oz/100 g seasonal lettuce leaves
Oil for pan- and deep-frying

ZUTATEN
FÜR 6 PERSONEN

300 g Tofu (natur),
  in Scheiben geschnitten
60 ml Sojasauce
20 g frisch geriebener Ingwer
600 g Glasnudeln
Sesamöl
160 g gemischte Sprossen
Salz, Pfeffer
Sesamsamen
40 g Tandoori-Würzpaste
100 g Salatblätter nach Saison
Öl zum Braten und Frittieren

METHOD

In a bowl, mix the tofu slices with soy sauce and grated ginger and let marinate.

Meanwhile, pour hot water over the cellophane noodles in a large bowl and allow to steep for several minutes according to the package instructions. Then drain the noodles, and set some of them aside for deep-frying.

Briefly sear the tofu in sesame oil. Sweat the sprouts and cellophane noodles in sesame oil. Season with salt and pepper, then mix in the sesame seeds and tandoori paste. Arrange the cellophane noodle salad and tofu in individual portions on salad plates.

Heat a good amount of oil in a pot. Deep-fry the remaining noodles until crisp, drain, and arrange on the salad as garnish.

ZUBEREITUNG

Die Tofuscheiben in einer Schüssel mit Sojasauce und geriebenem Ingwer mischen und marinieren.

Inzwischen die Glasnudeln in einer großen Schüssel mit heißem Wasser übergießen und nach Packungsangabe einige Minuten ziehen lassen. Dann abgießen, abtropfen lassen und einen Teil davon zum Frittieren beiseitelegen.

Den Tofu kurz in Sesamöl anbraten. Sprossen und Glasnudeln in Sesamöl anschwitzen. Mit Salz und Pfeffer würzen, Sesamsamen und Tandooripaste untermischen. Glasnudelsalat und Tofu portionsweise auf den Salatblättern anrichten.

Reichlich Frittieröl in einem Topf erhitzen. Die übrigen Glasnudeln darin knusprig frittieren, abtropfen lassen und den Salat damit dekorieren.

DAS ALPENHAUS KAPRUN

KAPRUN, SALZBURG

Alpenhaus Kaprun is situated at an elevation of 2,579 feet (786 meters) in the heart of Kaprun, Austria, nestled between the Kitzsteinhorn glacier in the Pinzgau mountains in the state of Salzburg and the picturesque Lake Zell. The hotel is run under the motto, "living close to the mountains." Guests of this four-star establishment immediately feel close to nature here, and the spectacular panoramic view of the mountains is a definite plus point. Authentic alpine lifestyle, warm hospitality and a wide range of activities and wellness programs combine to create a thoroughly pleasant vacation. At the Alpenhaus, traditional, natural alpine charm is closely tied to the region and its modern yet authentic, down-to-earth flair.

Kaprun is an attractive vacation destination all year round. In winter, the focus is on skiing, and the glacier slopes are open from October to May. In summer, Lake Zell, bicycle paths, hiking trails, and the Hohe Tauern National Park are waiting to be discovered. Alpenhaus Kaprun is the perfect base camp for all summer and winter tourists as well as anyone who simply wants to take things easy and enjoy wholesome food, yoga, and a sauna. Guests relax in the spacious ALPEN.VEDA.SPA wellness area, while the hotel's bar and restaurant serve culinary delights. One special draw for vegans is the innovative range of plant-based crossover meals, which guarantee new gastronomic experiences and combine both traditional and creative recipes.

Zwischen dem Gletscher Kitzsteinhorn, der Bergwelt des Salzburger Pinzgaus und dem malerischen Zeller See befindet sich im Zentrum von Kaprun auf 786 Metern Höhe Das Alpenhaus Kaprun. „Leben nahe den Bergen", lautet das Motto des Hotels. In diesem Viersternehaus spürt man als Gast sofort eine gewisse Naturverbundenheit, und das spektakuläre Bergpanorama ist selbstverständlich auch nicht zu verachten. Einem gelungenen Urlaub auf höchstem Niveau steht dank einer Mischung aus authentischem alpinen Lifestyle, herzlicher Gastfreundlichkeit und vielfältigen Aktivitäts- und Wellnessangeboten nichts im Weg. Der ursprüngliche und traditionelle Charme der Alpen ist im Alpenhaus eng verbunden mit der Region und einem modernen, aber authentisch-bodenständigen Flair.

Die österreichische Ferienregion Zell am See-Kaprun ist wahrlich eine ganzjährig attraktive Urlaubsdestination. Im Winter steht natürlich alles im Zeichen des Skisports, mit Gletscherskipisten, die von Oktober bis Mai befahren werden können. Im Sommer warten der Zeller See, Fahrradrouten, Wanderwege und der Nationalpark Hohe Tauern darauf, entdeckt zu werden. Das Alpenhaus Kaprun ist das perfekte Basislager für alle Sommer- und Winterurlauber, aber auch für jene, die sich einfach bei gesundem Essen, Yoga und in der Sauna erholen wollen. Relaxt wird im großzügigen Wellnessbereich ALPEN.VEDA.SPA, während das Restaurant und die Bar des Alpenhauses für kulinarische Genüsse sorgen. Ein besonderer Anziehungspunkt für vegane Gäste: das innovative Angebot einer pflanzenbasierten Crossover-Küche, die neue Geschmackserlebnisse garantiert und elegant traditionelle und kreative Rezepte vereint.

ROOMS: 122
SPECIALTIES: MASSAGES, BEAUTY TREATMENTS, GYM, OUTDOOR POOL (SUMMER), INDOOR SWIMMING POOL, SAUNA, YOGA, WINTER AND SUMMER OUTDOOR ACTIVITIES (E.G. GLACIER SKIING UNTIL JULY, CROSS-COUNTRY SKIING, HIKING)

DAS ALPENHAUS KAPRUN
SCHLOSSSTRASSE 2
5710 KAPRUN
AUSTRIA (ÖSTERREICH)
WWW.ALPENHAUS-KAPRUN.AT
+43 6547 7647

ZIMMER: 122
BESONDERHEITEN: MASSAGEN, BEAUTY-BEHANDLUNGEN, FITNESS-RAUM, AUSSENPOOL (SOMMER), HALLENBAD, SAUNA, YOGA, WINTER- UND SOMMERFREIZEITANGEBOTE (U.A. GLETSCHERSKIFAHREN BIS JULI, LANGLAUFEN, WANDERN)

HOTEL SWISS

KREUZLINGEN, CANTON OF THURGAU

The Swiss Hotel has many attractive features to recommend it, but the biggest highlight of this elegant establishment near Lake Constance may well be its food. Every Friday evening, the hotel's restaurant, the Roter Schwan, serves top-notch, gourmet vegan meals that are not only healthy but also incredibly refined, creative, and delicious. Little wonder, since top chef Raphael Lüthy, who is well known even outside Switzerland, presides over the kitchen. Not only his unforgettable dinner creations but also his vegan cooking classes, seminars, and individual dietary recommendations never fail to delight his guests. Not a few of them are amazed to discover how varied and tasty a healthy vegan meal can be.

You can now reproduce as many as 300 of his dishes in the comfort of your own home, as he has written a cookbook titled *Vegan Gesund* (Healthy Vegan), a veritable standard work of vegan cuisine. Nevertheless, his food tastes simply twice as good when sampled in the extraordinary ambience of the Hotel Swiss. Vegan and non-vegan guests will enjoy the bountiful breakfast in this completely vegan four-star hotel with equal enthusiasm.

The urban business hotel is situated right in the heart of Kreuzlingen in one of Switzerland's most beautiful regions. Many historical and cultural treasures are to be found in the surrounding area, with its varied landscape, including the lovely city of Konstanz on the lake that bears its name, the picturesque Meersburg, and the Napoleon Museum in Arenenberg Castle.

Das größte Highlight des Hotel Swiss dürfte wohl seine Küche sein – auch wenn das elegante Hotel unweit des Bodensees auch sonst zu überzeugen weiß. Im hauseigenen Restaurant Roter Schwan wird jeden Freitagabend eine vegane Gourmetküche auf Topniveau serviert, die nicht nur gesund, sondern auch noch unglaublich raffiniert, kreativ und köstlich ist. Kein Wunder, denn den Kochlöffel schwingt hier der über die Grenzen der Schweiz hinaus bekannte Spitzenkoch Raphael Lüthy. Nicht nur seine unvergesslichen Dinnerkreationen, auch seine veganen Kochkurse, Seminare und individuellen Ernährungsempfehlungen werden von den Gästen begeistert angenommen – nicht Wenige sind erstaunt, wie abwechslungsreich und schmackhaft eine gesunde vegane Küche sein kann.

Gleich 300 seiner Gerichte können inzwischen sogar selber zu Hause nachgekocht werden, denn er hat mit dem Kochbuch *Vegan Gesund* ein echtes Standardwerk der veganen Küche geschrieben. Trotzdem: im außergewöhnlichen Ambiente des Hotel Swiss schmeckt es einfach noch mal doppelt so gut. Das komplett vegane Viersternehotel begeistert mit seinem reichhaltigen Frühstück Veganer wie Nichtveganer gleichermaßen.

Das Business- und Stadthotel liegt in einer der schönsten Regionen der Schweiz, mitten im Zentrum von Kreuzlingen. Zur abwechslungsreichen Umgebung gehören zahlreiche historische und kulturelle Highlights wie die wunderschöne Bodenseestadt Konstanz, das pittoreske Meersburg oder auch das Napoleonmuseum Schloss Arenenberg.

ROOMS: 15 ROOMS, 1 SUITE
SPECIALTIES: COOKING CLASSES, MANY POINTS OF INTEREST (E.G. FLOWER ISLAND MAINAU, LAKE CONSTANCE)

HOTEL SWISS
HAUPTSTRASSE 72
8280 KREUZLINGEN
SWITZERLAND (SCHWEIZ)
WWW.HOTELSWISS.INFO
+41 716 778 040

ZIMMER: 15 ZIMMER, 1 SUITE
BESONDERHEITEN: KOCHKURSE, VIELE SEHENSWÜRDIGKEITEN (U.A. BLUMENINSEL MAINAU, BODENSEE)

HOTEL BALANCE

LES GRANGES, CANTON OF VALAIS

The old plank floor and the stairs creak comfortably when you walk through the hundred-year-old house, with its slightly slanting walls and ceilings, on your way to the cozy rooms furnished with antique peasant furniture. Guests seeking rest and relaxation have been coming to the Hotel Balance since 1893—its perfect and quiet location on the outskirts of town, with a view of the imposing, snow-covered, 4,000-meter peaks, is impossible to resist.

The environmentally conscious and child-friendly, organic hotel in Switzerland's Canton Valais is the first Swiss hotel to receive the highest distinction of a leading Swiss seal of quality for sustainability management: five ibexes for its thoroughly sustainable concept. This also means that the hotel's macrobiotic kitchen prepares only organic food, and its programs include lectures on healthy diets and herb walks.

The Eberle family turned the Hotel Balance into a place to experience healthy meals along with a whole lot more: Yoga, meditation, and Qi Gong classes in the meditation and seminar room help guests find their inner balance. Cleansing Ayurvedic massages, a jump into the refreshing organic pool, or a good book by the fireside in the cozy library all contribute to this goal. Guests can even take in deep lungfuls of the clear mountain air during barefoot walks over dewy meadows or through the nearby forest.

Der alte Dielenboden und die Treppen knarzen schön heimelig, wenn man durch das über einhundert Jahre alte Haus mit seinen bisweilen leicht schiefen Wänden und Decken zu den gemütlichen, mit alten Bauernmöbeln eingerichteten Zimmern geht. Seit 1893 reisen Erholung-suchende ins Hotel Balance – die perfekte und ruhige Lage am Ortsrand mit Blick auf die imposanten schneebedeckten Viertausender überzeugt einfach.

Das umwelt- und kinderfreundliche Biohotel im schweize-rischen Kanton Wallis wurde für sein durch und durch nachhaltiges Konzept als erstes Hotel in der Schweiz mit der Höchstnote von fünf Steinböcken eines führenden Schweizer Gütesiegels für Nachhaltigkeitsmanagement ausgezeichnet. Dazu gehört auch, dass in der makrobio-tischen Küche selbstverständlich nur mit Biolebensmitteln gekocht wird und Ernährungsvorträge und Kräuterwande-rungen zum Angebot zählen.

Das Ehepaar Eberle hat mit dem Hotel Balance einen Ort geschaffen, an dem gesunde Ernährung gelebt wird, und noch viel mehr: Im Meditations- und Kursraum helfen Angebote wie Yoga, Meditation oder Qigong dabei, die innere Balance zu finden. Dazu tragen ebenfalls reinigende Ayurveda-Massagen, ein Sprung in den erfrischenden Biopool oder ein gutes Buch vor dem Kaminfeuer in der gemütlichen Bibliothek bei. Und auch Barfußspaziergänge über feuchte Wiesen oder durch den nahen Wald lassen den Gast in der klaren Bergluft ganz tief durchatmen.

ROOMS: 23 ROOMS, 5 APARTMENTS
SPECIALTIES: SHIATSU TREATMENTS, SAUNA, MASSAGES, POOL (NO CHLORINE), YOGA, MEDITATION, LIBRARY, WINTER AND SUMMER OUTDOOR ACTIVITIES

HOTEL BALANCE
1922 LES GRANGES
SWITZERLAND (SCHWEIZ)
WWW.VEGETARISCHES-HOTEL.CH
+41 277 611 522

ZIMMER: 23 ZIMMER, 5 APPARTEMENTS
BESONDERHEITEN: SHIATSU-BEHANDLUNGEN, SAUNA, MASSAGEN, POOL (OHNE CHLOR), YOGA, MEDITATION, BIBLIOTHEK, WINTER- UND SOMMERFREIZEITANGEBOTE

HOTEL SASS DA GRÜM
„ORT DER KRAFT"

SAN NAZZARO-VAIRANO, CANTON OF TICINO

Leave your daily cares behind—isn't that what every vacation is supposed to offer? Few places in Europe are better suited to doing this than Sass da Grüm in Ticino, Switzerland. At this hotel, they take the idea of "getting rid of your baggage" at face value: as soon as you arrive, the freight elevator relieves you of your luggage, while you hike for 20 to 30 minutes through the chestnut forest until you reach the high plateau above Lago Maggiori. With every step you take, your everyday worries fall away, and your energy begins to flow. After all, the pyramid-shaped plateau is a recognized place of power. In few other places do the natural surroundings provide such a wholesome combination of energizing elements.

Everything in this hotel, framed by tall chestnut trees, is aimed at helping guests relax and find their true selves, so that they can leave this place refreshed and with renewed strength. The unobstructed view of the lake's glistening water allows you to breathe more freely. Televisions and WiFi are banished from the bright rooms furnished with natural materials, and you will not find any industrially processed food anywhere in the establishment's organic, vegetarian kitchen. Which is likely one reason why most guests book a stay with all meals included. Everything at Sass da Grüm is homemade, and 70 varieties of wild herbs grown in the kitchen garden refine the hotel's meals. A yoga trail (the Sentiero dello Yoga), hikes with panoramic views, massages, and a varied weekly program give every guest the opportunity to customize their vacations to their own preferences. It's hardly surprising that many visitors keep finding their way back to the plateau high above Lago Maggiore.

Die Lasten des Alltags hinter sich lassen – wer wünscht sich das nicht in seinem Urlaub? Kaum ein anderer Ort in Europa ist wohl hierfür besser geeignet, als das Sass da Grüm im Schweizerischen Tessin. Hier wird die Sache mit dem „Ballast hinter sich lassen" wörtlich genommen, denn gleich nach der Ankunft kümmert sich der Lastenaufzug um das mitgebrachte Gepäck, während man selbst in 20 bis 30 Minuten im schattigen Kastanienwald zum Plateau über dem Lago Maggiore hochwandert. Mit jedem Schritt lässt man den Alltag weiter hinter sich, und die Kräfte beginnen zu strömen. Denn das pyramidenförmige Plateau ist ein anerkannter Ort der Kraft, an wenigen anderen Plätzen bietet die Natur eine solch heilsame Kombination aus energiespendenden Faktoren.

Alles in diesem von hohen Kastanienbäumen umgebenen Haus ist darauf ausgerichtet, dass die Gäste hier zur Ruhe und zu sich selbst kommen, um diesen Ort frisch und gestärkt wieder verlassen zu können. Der freie Blick über das glitzernde Wasser des Sees lässt einen gleich freier atmen, die hellen, mit natürlichen Materialien ausgestatteten Zimmer verzichten bewusst auf Fernseher oder WLAN, und industriell verarbeitete Lebensmittel sucht man in der vegetarischen Bioküche des Hauses vergebens. Wahrscheinlich einer der Gründe, warum die meisten Gäste hier gleich Vollpension buchen. Im Sass da Grüm ist alles hausgemacht, die Hotelküche wird mit 70 Wildkräutern aus dem eigenen Garten verfeinert. Ein Yoga-Parcours, der Sentiero dello Yoga, Panoramawanderungen, Massagen und ein abwechslungsreiches Wochenprogramm bieten jedem Gast die Möglichkeit, den eigenen Urlaub individuell zusammenzustellen. Kein Wunder also, dass viele Besucher immer wieder den Weg auf das Plateau über dem Lago Maggiore finden.

ROOMS: 19
SPECIALTIES: YOGA, MEDITATION, TAI CHI, MASSAGES (E.G. SHIATSU, LOMI LOMI, HOT STONE), VARIOUS HEALTH WEEK PROGRAMS AVAILABLE

HOTEL SASS DA GRÜM
VIA CAMPEA 27
6575 SAN NAZZARO-VAIRANO
SWITZERLAND (SCHWEIZ)
WWW.SASSDAGRUEM.CH
+41 917 852 171

ZIMMER: 19
BESONDERHEITEN: YOGA, MEDITATION, TAI-CHI, MASSAGEN (U.A. SHIATSU, LOMI LOMI, HOT STONE), GROSSES ANGEBOT AN GESUNDHEITSWOCHEN

THE NEW VEGGIE GOURMET
DER NEUE VEGGIE-GENUSS

How things have changed. It wasn't all that long ago that people poked fun at vegetarians or even pitied them—and vegans had it worst of all. But now it has become positively hip to follow a healthy and plant-based diet. Just few years ago, it was still fairly difficult to order a dish in a restaurant that didn't contain animal ingredients, and yet today this is no longer a problem, especially in large cities. Places like Berlin, London, and New York even offer a wealth of strictly vegan restaurants to choose from. Moreover, we are seeing enormous improvements not only in the quantity of these choices but also in their quality. The options range from vegan street food to fine dining establishments. The patrons of these restaurants are no longer exclusively vegan; most of them simply watch what they put in their bodies and are open to trying out new, refined plant-based cuisines. And why shouldn't they? This kind of food is generally healthier, lighter, and less harmful to the environment. The fact that it also tastes good is reason enough for increasing numbers of people to dine on vegetarian or vegan meals more and more often.

Doing so in no way means depriving yourself. To the contrary. Eating vegan and vegetarian meals opens the door to an exciting, culinary journey of discovery—one that is colorful, delicious, varied, and usually also does the body good. The variety and quality of the ingredients used, along with the opportunity to experience entirely new tastes, usually win over even the staunchest skeptics. Vegetarian and vegan cooks are innovative and self-assured, and they do not try to simply imitate familiar meat dishes but bring entirely new creations to the table. Indeed, because vegetables are the main event, both professional and home cooks alike greatly value the use of locally grown ingredients—and you can taste the difference. VeggieHotels establishments and VeganWelcome hotels frequently use one hundred percent organic ingredients, not only because most people find that they taste better but also because they are not contaminated with pesticides and other chemicals. Pure, preferably unprocessed foods give the body the best energy without any unwanted side effects. The chefs also generally emphasize the use of locally grown produce—in season, whenever possible. Not only does this approach make sense from an ecological standpoint, but it also supports local and regional farms. Many VeggieHotels even have their own gardens, which deliver freshly harvested fruit, vegetables, and herbs to the table.

Wie sich das Bild doch gewandelt hat: Vor nicht allzu langer Zeit wurden Vegetarier, und erst recht Veganer von ihren Mitmenschen belächelt oder gar bedauert. Mittlerweile ist es geradezu „hip", sich gesund und pflanzenbasiert zu ernähren. War es vor wenigen Jahren noch ziemlich schwierig, in Restaurants ein Gericht ohne tierische Zutaten zu bekommen, ist das heute besonders in Großstädten völlig problemlos möglich. In Metropolen wie Berlin, London oder New York muss man sich sogar zwischen zahlreichen rein veganen Restaurants entscheiden. Doch nicht nur quantitativ ist eine enorme Verbesserung festzustellen, auch qualitativ hat sich einiges getan. Die Bandbreite reicht von veganem Streetfood bis hin zu Fine-Dining-Etablissements. Die Gästeschar besteht in solchen Restaurants längst nicht mehr nur aus Veganern, die meisten ernähren sich einfach bewusst und sind offen für eine neue, raffinierte pflanzenbasierte Küche. Warum auch nicht? Sie ist in der Regel gesünder, leichter und belastet weniger. Wenn obendrein noch der Geschmack stimmt, gibt es für immer mehr Menschen jede Menge gute Gründe, häufiger vegetarisch oder vegan zu essen.

Und das bedeutet keinesfalls Verzicht, im Gegenteil, vegan oder vegetarisch zu essen öffnet die Tore zu einer spannenden kulinarischen Entdeckungsreise – und die ist bunt, lecker, abwechslungsreich und meistens auch noch ziemlich wohltuend. Die Vielfalt und Qualität der verwendeten Lebensmittel sowie bisher ungeahnte Geschmackserlebnisse überzeugen auch die größten Skeptiker. Es ist eine innovative, selbstbewusste Art des Kochens, die sich nicht darin erschöpft, altbekannte Fleischgerichte zu imitieren, sondern ganz neue Kreationen auf den Teller bringt. Gerade weil das Gemüse hier zumeist der Hauptdarsteller ist, legen Profi- und Hobbyköche viel Wert auf eine hohe Qualität der Zutaten – man schmeckt den Unterschied. Die Restaurants der VeggieHotels und VeganWelcome-Häuser nutzen nicht selten zu einhundert Prozent Biolebensmittel. Nicht nur weil diese den meisten Menschen besser schmecken, sondern auch weil sie nicht mit Pestiziden und anderen Chemikalien belastet sind. Reine, möglichst unverarbeitete Lebensmittel bringen dem Körper die beste Energie, ohne unerwünschte Nebenwirkungen. Außerdem wird in diesen Küchen in der Regel großer Wert darauf gelegt, dass die Nahrungsmittel aus der Region stammen und möglichst gerade Saison haben. Das ist nicht nur aus ökologischer Sicht sinnvoll, sondern unterstützt auch die lokale und regionale Wirtschaft.

There is absolutely no reason not to follow a plant-based diet—and many reasons why you should! One thing is certain: a vegetarian or vegan diet in no way means giving up everything that tastes good. And you can even recreate these wonderful tastes at home. This book offers a number of tasty dishes from the kitchens of the VeggieHotels and VeganWelcome establishments showcased within its pages. We absolutely recommend giving them a try!

Zahlreiche VeggieHotels haben sogar einen eigenen Garten, aus dem Gemüse, Obst und Kräuter erntefrisch auf den Teller kommen.

Es spricht einfach nichts dagegen, sich pflanzenbasiert zu ernähren – aber eine ganze Menge dafür! Eines ist ganz sicher: Der Genuss bleibt keinesfalls auf der Strecke, auch zu Hause nicht! Dieses Buch bietet einige köstliche Gerichte aus den Küchen der hier vorgestellten VeggieHotels und VeganWelcome-Häuser, und die sind natürlich absolute Genussempfehlungen zum Nachkochen!

HOTEL BALATURA

TRIBALJ, PRIMORJE-GORSKI KOTAR

Situated only six kilometers from the Mediterranean and yet surrounded by mountains and forests, the small Balatura literary hotel receives guests from all over the world who come here seeking peace and quiet or to indulge their passion for art and culture. The three-hundred-year-old estate encompasses large and small stone houses that were lavishly renovated using regional materials. The results are rooms furnished to create a romantic ambience and meet individual tastes—from the Lemon Room and the Violet Room to the Lavender Room in shades of yellow, violet, and lilac—where guests can completely relax under historic, whitewashed beams. The inn's literary theme repeats over and over in the long bookshelves and cozy corners that invite you to curl up with a good book.

Over time, Balatura has become a cultural fixture in the region, hosting regular readings, concerts, and workshop on a wide range of topics. As a result, you can listen to contemporary authors, take piano lessons, or even find out which wine is best paired with which reading material. And should you have a mind to go on an outing, the owners are happy to provide insider tips on lesser known beaches or the best hiking trails through the surrounding karst mountains.

When the Godecs and their children emigrated from Cologne to Croatia 17 years ago, the couple never suspected where the journey would take them. But they knew exactly what they were looking for: a place surrounded by nature where they could combine work and family life, indulge their passions, and leave the hectic world of the big city behind. In the Hotel Balatura, they found all they could wish for, and they are happy to share this dream with every guest they welcome into their home.

Nur sechs Kilometer vom Mittelmeer entfernt und doch umgeben von Bergen und Wäldern, empfängt das kleine Literaturhotel Balatura Ruhesuchende sowie Kunst- und Kulturbegeisterte aus aller Welt. Das dreihundert Jahre alte Anwesen umfasst große und kleine Steinhäuser und wurde mit regionalen Materialien aufwendig saniert. Dabei entstanden romantisch eingerichtete und individuell gestaltete Zimmer – vom gelben Zitronenzimmer über das violette Veilchen- bis hin zum zartlilanen Lavendelzimmer – in denen man sich unter historischen, weiß gekalkten Deckenbalken so richtig entspannen kann. Der literarische Schwerpunkt des Hauses begegnet dem Gast immer wieder in langen Bücherregalen oder gemütlichen Ecken, die dazu einladen, sich zum Lesen niederzulassen.

Mit der Zeit ist das Balatura zur festen kulturellen Größe in der Region geworden, es finden regelmäßig Lesungen, Konzerte und Workshops zu verschiedensten Themen statt – so kann man zeitgenössischen Autoren lauschen, Klavierstunden nehmen oder auch herausfinden, welcher Wein am besten zu welcher Lektüre passt. Und sollte einem der Sinn nach einem Ausflug stehen, geben die Betreiber gerne Insidertipps zu weniger bekannten Stränden oder den besten Wanderrouten durch die umliegenden Karstberge.

Als das Ehepaar Godec mit seinen Kindern vor 17 Jahren von Köln nach Kroatien auswanderte, ahnten beide nicht, wohin sie die Reise führen würde. Aber sie wussten genau, wonach sie suchten: Nach einem Platz inmitten der Natur, an dem sie Arbeit und Familie kombinieren, ihren Leidenschaften frönen und die Hektik der Großstadt hinter sich lassen können. Mit dem Hotel Balatura haben sie sich ihren Wunsch erfüllt und teilen diesen Traum gerne mit allen, die sie als ihre Gäste begrüßen dürfen.

ROOMS: 10
SPECIALTIES: LITERATURE READINGS, MUSIC WORKSHOPS, YOGA, CYCLING, HIKING

HOTEL BALATURA
MALI SUŠIK 2
HR 51243 TRIBALJ
CROATIA (KROATIEN)
WWW.HOTEL-BALATURA.HR
+385 514 553 40

ZIMMER: 10
BESONDERHEITEN: LESUNGEN, MUSIKWORKSHOPS, YOGA, FAHRRADFAHREN, WANDERN

MANI-SONNENLINK

MANI, PELOPONNES

Sometimes, when Austrian musician Burgi Bläuel attends one of the popular concerts at Mani-Sonnenlink, or joins in with her own violin, she finds herself reminiscing. Burgi thinks about that summer many years ago, when quite by chance she met Fritz, the man who would become her husband, right here in the south of the Peloponnese. He had come to Greece with a Viennese commune to lead the simple life of an olive farmer, in sync with the rhythms of nature. In those days, when the two single people became a couple, Burgi learned how much joy can be found in the small things in life. She saw how an olive tree, deeply rooted in the Mani Plateau, braves every storm with perseverance and pride—displaying a true ability to make the best of things. That journey changed everything. She and Fritz stayed in Mani—and dedicated themselves to making olive oil, as organic and high-quality as possible.

Today, their prize-winning organic Mani® Olive Oil products are available all over the world.

Mani-Sonnenlink, the comfortable oasis that they built according to feng shui principles, is the first organically certified hotel in Greece, complete with lovingly designed bungalows and apartments. A vacation at Burgi and Fritz's hotel feels like a relaxing get-together with friends, refreshingly uncomplicated, distinctive, informal, and highly personal. Here on the sunny side of the Taygetos Mountains, with a view of the clear, deep blue and turquoise sea, guests can enjoy either company or solitude. They can meditate or listen to music in the small amphitheater, go hiking, swimming, or share a good meal: one hundred percent organic, down to earth, regional, and vegetarian— naturally accompanied by their hosts' own olive products.

Manchmal, wenn die österreichische Musikerin Burgi Bläuel einem der beliebten Konzerte im Mani-Sonnenlink beiwohnt oder selber dazu geigt, erinnert sie sich an einen Sommer vor vielen Jahren, hier im Süden des Peloponnes, als sie ihrem heutigen Mann Fritz begegnete. Er war mit einer Wiener Kommune nach Griechenland gekommen, um das einfache Leben der Olivenbauern im Rhythmus der Natur zu führen. Damals, als es sofort ein „Wir" gab und sie lernte, wie viel Glück in kleinen Dingen steckt. Als sie sah, wie tief verwurzelt hier in der Mani-Region ein Olivenbaum jedem Unwetter trotzt, ausdauernd und stolz – ein echter Lebenskünstler eben. Diese Reise veränderte alles: Sie blieben und gemeinsam verschrieben sie sich dem Olivenöl, dem Bioanbau, der Lebensqualität.

Heute sind die preisgekrönten Mani®-Bio-Olivenprodukte weltweit zu finden.

Ihre nach Feng-Shui-Prinzipien gebaute Wohlfühloase Mani-Sonnenlink mit den liebevoll gestalteten Bungalows und Appartements ist das erste biozertifizierte Hotel Griechenlands. Ein Urlaub bei Burgi und Fritz fühlt sich an wie eine Auszeit mit Freunden – erfrischend unkompliziert, individuell, familiär und sehr persönlich. Hier, auf der Sonnenseite des Taygetos-Gebirges mit Blick auf das klare türkisblaue Meer, können Gäste die Gemeinschaft genauso wie die Zurückgezogenheit genießen. Bei Meditation, Yoga oder gemeinsamer Musik im kleinen Amphitheater, beim Wandern, Baden und natürlich bei gutem Essen: einhundert Prozent biologisch, bodenständig, regional und vegetarisch – und selbstverständlich mit den eigenen Olivenprodukten.

ROOMS: 2 APARTMENTS, 3 BUNGALOWS
SPECIALTIES: GREEK OPEN AIR THEATER, MUSIC EVENTS, SEMINAR GROUPS WELCOME, MASSAGES, YOGA, MEDITATION

MANI-SONNENLINK, BOUTIQUE RESORT
24024 PYRGOS, WEST MANI
GREECE (GRIECHENLAND)
WWW.MANI-SONNENLINK.COM
+30 272 107 8077

ZIMMER: 2 APPARTEMENTS, 3 BUNGALOWS
BESONDERHEITEN: GRIECHISCHES FREILUFTTHEATER, MUSIK-BEGEGNUNGEN, SEMINARGRUPPEN WILLKOMMEN, MASSAGEN, YOGA, MEDITATION

NIŞANYAN HOUSES HOTEL

SELÇUK, IZMIR

When Müjde Tönbekici discovered the as yet unknown little paradise of Şirince 35 years ago, she was so overcome by the village's beauty that she decided to stay forever.

Unsurprisingly, Şirince did not remain a secret for long, since the historic village with its old houses, most of them built more than a century ago, is embedded in a marvelous valley between olive trees, vineyards, and pines. Only ten minutes farther down the road, as you head toward the sea, ruins of the ancient city of Ephesus bear witness to the fact that the most powerful Roman metropolis in Asia Minor once stood here. The World Heritage Site is one of Turkey's most important tourist attractions.

The Nişanyan Houses Hotel stands a short distance above Şirince and offers a lovely view of the village. Yet it is far enough away for you to experience magically quiet nights and wake in the morning to the call of the peacocks who live on the premises.

The establishment is famous not only for its friendly, peaceful atmosphere but also for the excellent gourmet meals that emerge from its kitchen, over which Müjde Tönbekici herself presides. She has presented her culinary arts on international TV programs. "I think that the heart of our hotel is the kitchen and the great herb gardens," she says and delights her guests with Aegean cuisine, prepared from the best ingredients—and she grows the vegetable varieties and herbs and even makes the olive oil herself. Cooking enthusiasts also have the opportunity to take vegan cooking classes at the Nişanyan Houses Hotel.

Initially, the hotel encompassed three historic village houses. Today, it consists of 20 buildings, all of which are different sizes and feature their own unique styles and creative decorations, distributed throughout the extensive property. Müjde remains convinced of one thing: If paradise on earth exists, it would have to be this extraordinary, wildly romantic place!

Als Müjde Tönbekici vor 35 Jahren das damals noch unbekannte kleine Paradies Şirince für sich entdeckte, beschloss sie für immer hier zu bleiben, so überwältigt war sie von der Schönheit des Ortes. Dass Şirince auch von anderen nicht lange unentdeckt blieb, überrascht nicht, denn das historische Dorf mit seinen meist über einhundert Jahre alten Häusern liegt herrlich eingebettet in einem Tal zwischen Olivenbäumen, Weingärten und Pinienbäumen. Und nur zehn Minuten weiter in Richtung Meer zeugen Überreste der antiken Stadt Ephesos davon, dass sich hier die einst mächtigste römische Metropole Kleinasiens befand. Das Weltkulturerbe ist eine der wichtigsten Touristenattraktionen der Türkei.

Das Nişanyan Houses Hotel liegt ein wenig oberhalb von Şirince, mit schönem Blick über das Dorf und weit genug entfernt, um magisch-ruhige Nächte zu erleben, aus denen man am Morgen zu den Rufen der ansässigen Pfaue erwacht. Dass das Hotel nicht nur mit seinem freundlichen, ruhigen Charakter überzeugt, sondern auch mit ausgezeichneter Gourmetküche, dafür sorgt Müjde Tönbekici persönlich. Ihre Kochkünste präsentierte sie bereits in internationalen TV-Sendungen. „Ich glaube, das Herz unseres Hotels ist die Küche und die großartigen Kräutergärten", sagt sie und begeistert ihre Gäste mit einer ägäischen Küche, zubereitet aus besten Zutaten – die verwendeten Gemüsesorten, Kräuter und auch das Olivenöl stammen aus eigenem Anbau. Und wer von der Küche begeistert ist, hat auch die Möglichkeit, an veganen Kochkursen im Nişanyan Houses Hotel teilzunehmen.

Drei historische Dorfhäuser umfasste das Hotel anfänglich. Heute besteht es aus 20 Gebäuden, die sich allesamt in Größe, Stil und kreativer Dekoration unterscheiden und über das großzügige Gelände verteilt stehen. Müjde ist nach wie vor davon überzeugt: Gibt es ein Paradies auf Erden, so muss es dieser außergewöhnliche und wild-romantische Ort sein!

ROOMS: 20 ROOMS & COTTAGES
SPECIALTIES: POOL, TURKISH BATH, COOKING CLASSES, MEDITATION, TAI CHI

NIŞANYAN HOUSES HOTEL
35920 ŞIRINCE KÖYÜ / SELÇUK
TURKEY (TÜRKEI)
WWW.NISANYAN.COM
+90 232 898 3208 |
+90 533 304 09 33

ZIMMER: 20 ZIMMER & COTTAGES
BESONDERHEITEN: POOL, TÜRKISCHES BAD, KOCHKURSE, MEDITATION, TAI-CHI

YEWFIELD
VEGETARIAN GUEST HOUSE

CUMBRIA, NORTH WEST ENGLAND

The Yewfield Vegetarian Guest House is situated in the heart of England's Lake District National Park, around 4 miles (7 kilometers) from the picturesque town of Ambleside. Built in 1859, the gothic manor now houses a vegetarian bed & breakfast with the elegant ambience of a country estate. Its exquisitely furnished rooms combine pretty striped, brocade, and checked fabrics to create an intimate atmosphere of British charm. Guests who prefer to look after their own needs can rent one of the three fully furnished apartments. No matter which form of hospitality you choose, the breathtaking view of the Lake District's mist-cloaked hills is always included. Green mountains and calm waters shape the landscape of what the locals simply call "The Lakes." Little wonder, since the region's roughly one thousand lakes of varying sizes are waiting to be discovered. However, it's also worth your while to look up, for England's only pair of golden eagles circle the sky of the Lake District.

The Yewfield Guest House serves a sumptuous breakfast. In addition to fresh juices, fruits, and smoothies, Innkeeper Derek Hook and his team also offer a typical, vegan English breakfast—with grilled tomatoes, vegan sausages, and scrambled tofu as an alternative to scrambled eggs. Ambleside's vegetarian restaurants beckon in the evening—provided, of course, that the hotel has not organized an in-house concert. This event is not to be missed, since music, especially jazz and classical music, is a cause for great celebration at the Yewfield Guest House. The Steinway piano in the lounge offers the promise of an extraordinary musical experience, and sometimes the guests themselves participate in a concert recording, thanks to the establishment's studio equipment. Bravo! Incidentally, many Hobbit fans are convinced that the Lake District served as the inspiration for the Shire in J.R.R. Tolkien's books, where his characters live a tranquil life.

Rund sieben Kilometer außerhalb der malerischen Kleinstadt Ambleside liegt das Yewfield Vegetarian Guest House mitten im britischen Nationalpark Lake District. Das gotische Herrenhaus aus dem Jahr 1859 beherbergt heute ein vegetarisches Bed & Breakfast im gehobenen Landhausstil. Es verfügt über exquisit eingerichtete Zimmer, in denen sich vertraute Streifen-, Brokat- und Karomuster zur schönsten Form britischer Behaglichkeit zusammenfügen. Wer sich selbst versorgen möchte, der kann auch eines der drei voll ausgestatteten Appartements mieten. So oder so: den atemberaubenden Ausblick auf die nebelbedeckten Hügel des Lake District bekommt man auf jeden Fall inklusive. Grüne Berge und stille Gewässer prägen die Landschaft, die im Volksmund nur „The Lakes" genannt wird. Kein Wunder, denn rund eintausend Seen unterschiedlicher Größen kann man hier entdecken. Doch auch ein Blick nach oben lohnt sich, am Himmel des Lake District kreist nämlich das einzige Steinadlerpärchen Englands.

Zum Frühstück wird im Yewfield Guest House einiges aufgetafelt. Denn neben frischen Säften, Früchten und Smoothies serviert das Team um Gastgeber Derek Hook auch ein veganes, typisch englisches Frühstück – mit gegrillten Tomaten, veganen Würstchen und Scrambled Tofu als Rührei-Ersatz. Abends locken die vegetarischen Restaurants von Ambleside – natürlich vorausgesetzt, dass kein Hauskonzert ansteht. Dieses sollte man sich schließlich keinesfalls entgehen lassen, denn im Yewfield Guest House wird Musik, bevorzugt Jazz und Klassik, auf hohem Niveau zelebriert. Der Steinway-Flügel im Salon verspricht ein außergewöhnliches Klangerlebnis, und manchmal wird man dank der Studioausrüstung des Hauses selbst Teil eines Konzertmitschnitts. Bravo! Übrigens sind viele Hobbit-Fans überzeugt, dass der Lake District J. R. R. Tolkien als Vorbild für das Auenland diente, in dem die Helden seiner Bücher ein beschauliches Dasein führen.

ROOMS: 18 ROOMS, 3 APARTMENTS
SPECIALTIES: CLASSICAL AND CONTEMPORARY MUSIC CONCERTS, YOGA, MUSIC WORKSHOPS, LIBRARY

YEWFIELD VEGETARIAN GUEST HOUSE HAWKSHEAD HILL LA22 0PR CUMBRIA UNITED KINGDOM (GROSSBRITANNIEN) WWW.YEWFIELD.CO.UK +44 15394 36765

ZIMMER: 18 ZIMMER, 3 APPARTEMENTS
BESONDERHEITEN: KLASSISCHE UND MODERNE KONZERTE, YOGA, MUSIK WORKSHOPS, BIBLIOTHEK

AMBLESIDE MANOR

AMBLESIDE, NORTH WEST ENGLAND

The English town of Ambleside has two VeggieHotels: the Yewfield Vegetarian Guest House and the Ambleside Manor. The latter is a shining example of vegetarian hospitality, which Derek Hook and his sister, Dorothy, opened in 2015. The family also established a completely unique culinary and cultural center here in the heart of the Lake District. In addition to the two vegetarian inns, the siblings opened two movie theaters and two prize-winning restaurants that serve vegetarian Mediterranean food. So, there's quite a lot going on behind Ambleside's historic stone walls!

The elegant temporary home is a perfect architectural match with the Victorian ambience of this small town. Furnished with select antiques, heavy fabrics, reading nooks, and fireplaces, the rooms radiate British charm. The entire family can relax here, and even dogs are welcome. In the mornings, guests fortify themselves with a sumptuous, vegetarian/vegan breakfast buffet before venturing out to explore their surroundings. Ambleside is a popular point of departure for enthusiastic climbers and hikers. After all, Windermere, England's biggest natural lake, lies only a short distance to the south. Or what about a leisurely stroll through the town? Narrow cobble streets take you past historic mills and along the small brook that runs through town. There is even a university campus here. In the evening, people gather at Fellini's to enjoy an elegant, Italian vegetarian meal or to sample pizza and pasta at the vegetarian Zefferelli's restaurant, which is also a cinema and jazz bar. Depending on the day of the week, you can end the evening with a movie or jazz concert.

Neben dem Yewfield Vegetarian Guest House gibt es noch ein zweites VeggieHotel im englischen Ambleside. Mit Ambleside Manor haben Derek Hook und seine Schwester Dorothy 2015 ein weiteres Kleinod vegetarischer Gastlichkeit eröffnet. Darüber hinaus schuf die Familie hier im Zentrum des Lake District ein kulinarisches und kulturelles Angebot, das seinesgleichen sucht und neben den beiden vegetarischen Gästehäusern auch zwei Kinosäle und zwei preisgekrönte Restaurants mit mediterraner vegetarischer Küche umfasst. Hinter den historischen Bruchsteinmauern ist also einiges los!

Das elegante Zuhause auf Zeit passt architektonisch perfekt zum viktorianischen Ambiente der Kleinstadt Ambleside. Die Zimmer strahlen mit erlesenen Antiquitäten, schweren Stoffen, Leseecken und Kaminen britische Gemütlichkeit aus – hier darf sich die ganze Familie entspannen, auch Hunde sind herzlich willkommen. Am Morgen sorgt das üppige vegetarisch-vegane Frühstücksbuffet für Stärkung, bevor es zu Erkundungsausflügen in die Umgebung gehen kann. Ambleside ist ein beliebter Ausgangspunkt für Kletterbegeisterte und Wanderfreunde, schließlich liegt Windermere, der größte natürliche See Englands, nur etwas weiter südlich. Oder wie wäre es mit einem gemütlichen Stadtspaziergang? Auf schmalen Kopfsteinpflasterstraßen geht es vorbei an historischen Mühlen und entlang am schmalen Bach, der den Ort durchzieht. Sogar einen Unicampus gibt es hier. Abends trifft man sich zu gehobener vegetarisch-italienischer Küche im Fellinis oder zu Pizza und Pasta im Veggie-Restaurant Zeffirellis, das gleichzeitig Kino und Jazzbar ist. Je nach Wochentag kann man so den Abend bei einem Film oder einem Jazzkonzert ausklingen lassen.

ROOMS: 16
SPECIALTIES: LIVE JAZZ CONCERTS IN THE IN-HOUSE BAR, HIKING

AMBLESIDE MANOR
ROTHAY ROAD
LA22 0EJ AMBLESIDE
UNITED KINGDOM (GROSSBRITANNIEN)
WWW.AMBLESIDE-MANOR.CO.UK
+44 15394 32062

ZIMMER: 16
BESONDERHEITEN: LIVE JAZZ-KONZERTE IN DER HAUSEIGENEN BAR, HIKING

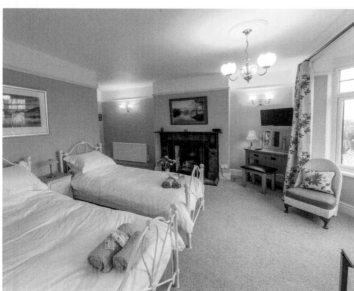

SANDBURNE
VEGETARIAN GUEST HOUSE
KESWICK, NORTH WEST ENGLAND

Up until a few years ago, a man who played a key role in the spread of veganism lived at the Sandburne Vegetarian Guest House in northwestern England. Donald Watson was both a teacher and a passionate vegan, and he also formed the world's first vegan society in 1944. He and his wife Dorothy—also a teacher—coined the expression "vegan" from the idea that for many, being a vegetarian often provided the beginning of the journey with a plant-based diet as the conclusion. So the beginning and end of the word "vegetarian" was used and being a vegan was "born". Sandburne remains in the hands of the Watson family today, having been converted into a welcoming, comfortable bed & breakfast by Anthony, their son-in-law. It provides a delicious, varied breakfast menu for both vegetarians and vegans alike. There are many opportunities to relax in the three sitting rooms or in front of a roaring fire in the winter. The enchantingly pretty 18th-century house is surrounded by a large garden and a varied landscape, where you can escape with a good book borrowed from the hotel's library.

Keswick, the charming yet bustling market town, is visible from the hotel and situated only a short drive or walk away over the nearby fields and pastures. However, the view of the Coledale and Whinlatter fells as well as the Latrigg and Skiddaw mountains is even more impressive. This country idyll is part of the Lake District National Park, awarded UNESCO World Heritage status in 2017, with its magnificent hilly landscape and scattering of lakes. Sandburne is the perfect home base for outings to the picturesque towns and for hiking through the rugged mountains.

Im Sandburne Vegetarian Guest House in Nordwestengland lebte bis vor einigen Jahren ein Mann, der für den Veganismus eine ganz entscheidende Rolle spielte. Donald Watson war nicht nur Lehrer, sondern auch passionierter Veganer, und er gründete 1944 zudem die erste vegane Gesellschaft der Welt, die Vegan Society. Er und seine Frau Dorothy – ebenfalls Lehrerin – prägten auch den Ausdruck „vegan" aus der Idee heraus, dass die Reise eines jeden Vegetariers mit Vegetarismus beginnt und mit einer rein pflanzlichen Ernährung ihr logisches Ende findet. So wurde aus dem Anfang und Ende des Begriffs *vegetarian* die Wortneuschöpfung vegan. Noch heute ist das Haus im Besitz der Familie Watson. Schwiegersohn Anthony betreibt es inzwischen als kleine gemütliche Pension mit köstlichem vegetarischen oder veganen Frühstück und vielen Möglichkeiten zur Entspannung in den drei Salons oder im Winter vor dem knisternden Feuer eines Kamins. Das hübsch-verwunschene Haus aus dem 18. Jahrhundert ist umgeben von einem großen Garten und facettenreicher Landschaft, in die man sich mit einem guten Buch aus der Hausbibliothek zurückziehen kann.

Keswick, das charmante und geschäftige Markstädtchen, ist vom Haus aus zu sehen, und per kurzer Autofahrt oder mit einem Spaziergang über die nahen Wiesen und Felder erreichbar. Noch beeindruckender ist allerdings der Blick auf die Fjell-Landschaften Coledale und Whinlatter sowie die Berge Latrigg und Skiddaw. Diese ländliche Idylle ist Teil des Lake-District-Nationalparks mit seiner eindrucksvollen Hügel- und Seenlandschaft, die 2017 zum UNESCO-Weltkulturerbe erklärt wurde. Als Ausgangspunkt für Ausflüge in pittoreske Ortschaften und Wanderungen durch die raue Bergregion ist Sandburne wie geschaffen.

ROOMS: 2
SPECIALTIES: HIKING, LIBRARY, DISCOUNT ON SHOWS OF THE LOCAL THEATER, LOCAL ADVICE FOR HILL WALKING

SANDBURNE VEGETARIAN GUEST HOUSE CHESTNUT HILL CA12 4LS KESWICK UNITED KINGDOM (GROSSBRITANNIEN) WWW.SANDBURNE.CO.UK +44 17687 73546

ZIMMER: 2
BESONDERHEITEN: WANDERN, BIBLIOTHEK, RABATT AUF DIE VORSTELLUNGEN DES ORTSANSÄSSIGEN THEATERS, RATSCHLÄGE FÜR HÜGEL-WANDERUNGEN

THE PHOENIX RESTAURANT AND B&B

CASTLEMAINE, COUNTY KERRY

If you drive down Ireland's rural route R561 heading for the west coast, perhaps because you wish to check out Inch Beach, you will pass a lovely old brick building on the right, surrounded by green fields, trees, and a mountain range called Sliabh Mis. Slow down and take a good look, and you will see a quaint caravan in the garden. If you catch the right moment, you may even see a satisfied guest emerge from the caravan and walk a few meters farther along to enjoy a vegetarian meal at the prize-winning Phoenix Restaurant.

It would not be a good idea to simply continue on your way. Instead, you will find never dreamed-of delights in the Irish hospitality and homemade bread, the traditional afternoon tea, or pâtés served by restauranteur Lorna. Fortunately, the old house, which has been standing for more than a century, not only houses a popular restaurant but also offers overnight accommodations for a romantic getaway—just in case the culinary treats were not enough and you'd like to stick around a while longer.

A night spent in the restored Gypsy caravan is an experience all on its own—this form of glamorous camping is also known as "glamping" and is enjoying increasing popularity.

A few more rooms can be found in the house, and you are also permitted to pitch a tent in the large garden filled with lush vegetation and paths winding among ponds. Concerts are often held in the evenings, and in the morning a breakfast with porridge, pancakes, and many other delicacies await you when you wake up.

Wer auf der irischen Landstraße R561 Richtung Westküste fährt, um beispielsweise den Inch Beach zu besuchen, passiert auf der rechten Seite ein schönes altes Backsteinhaus, eingerahmt von grünen Feldern, Bäumen und einem Gebirgszug, dem Sliabh Mis. Fährt man langsamer und schaut genauer hin, sieht man im Garten des Hauses einen der urigen Wohnwagen, aus dem vielleicht genau in diesem Augenblick ein zufriedener Gast steigt, um ein paar Meter weiter im preisgekrönten The Phoenix Restaurant vegetarisch zu essen.

Einfach weiterfahren ist also keine gute Idee. Stattdessen sorgen die irische Gastfreundlichkeit und das hausgemachte Brot, der traditionelle Afternoon Tea oder die Pasteten der Besitzerin Lorna für ungeahnte Genüsse. Glücklicherweise beherbergt das über einhundert Jahre alte Haus nicht nur ein beliebtes Restaurant, sondern auch romantische Übernachtungsmöglichkeiten – falls man nach den Gaumenfreuden doch ein wenig länger bleiben möchte.

Eine Nacht im restaurierten Schindelwagen ist schon ein Erlebnis für sich – diese Form des glamourösen Campens wird auch „glamping" genannt und erfreut sich wachsender Beliebtheit.

Im Haus gibt es ein paar weitere Zimmer, und auch Zelten ist im großen und üppig bepflanzten Garten mit Wanderwegen und Teichen erlaubt. Auf dem Abendprogramm stehen häufig Konzerte, und morgens nach dem Aufwachen ist das Frühstück mit Porridge, Pfannkuchen und vielen weiteren Köstlichkeiten bereits angerichtet.

ROOMS: 4 ROOMS, CAMPING POSSIBLE
SPECIALTIES: AYURVEDA, COOKING CLASSES, MEDITATION

THE PHOENIX VEGETARIAN RESTAURANT AND B&B
SHANAHILL EAST
CASTLEMAINE, CO. KERRY
IRELAND (IRLAND)
WWW.THEPHOENIXRESTAURANT.IE
+353 66 976 6284

ZIMMER: 4 ZIMMER, ZELTEN MÖGLICH
BESONDERHEITEN: AYURVEDA, KOCHKURSE, MEDITATION

The Phoenix Restaurant und B&B makes an excellent home base for exploring the surrounding
countryside as well as for long walks, days at the beach and water sports, and a trip
to Castlemaine Harbour, local art and music festivals, or pretty Irish towns such as Killarney,
Dingle, and Tralee. Southwestern Ireland is exactly how you imagined Ireland would be:
green, mountainous, rugged, romantic, and simply gorgeous. Check out Dingle Bay
for breathtaking views of the high cliffs that rise out of the sea.

The Phoenix Restaurant und B&B ist ein hervorragender Ausgangspunkt für Ausflüge
ins Umland – für lange Wanderungen, Strandtage und Wassersport, und den Besuch von
Castlemaine Harbour, lokalen Kunst- und Musikfestivals oder hübschen irischen Städtchen
wie Killarney, Dingle und Tralee. Der Südwesten Irlands ist so, wie man sich Irland vorstellt:
grün, gebirgig, schroff, romantisch und einfach wunderschön. In der Dingle Bay bieten sich
atemberaubende Blicke auf die hohen Klippen, die aus dem Meer ragen.

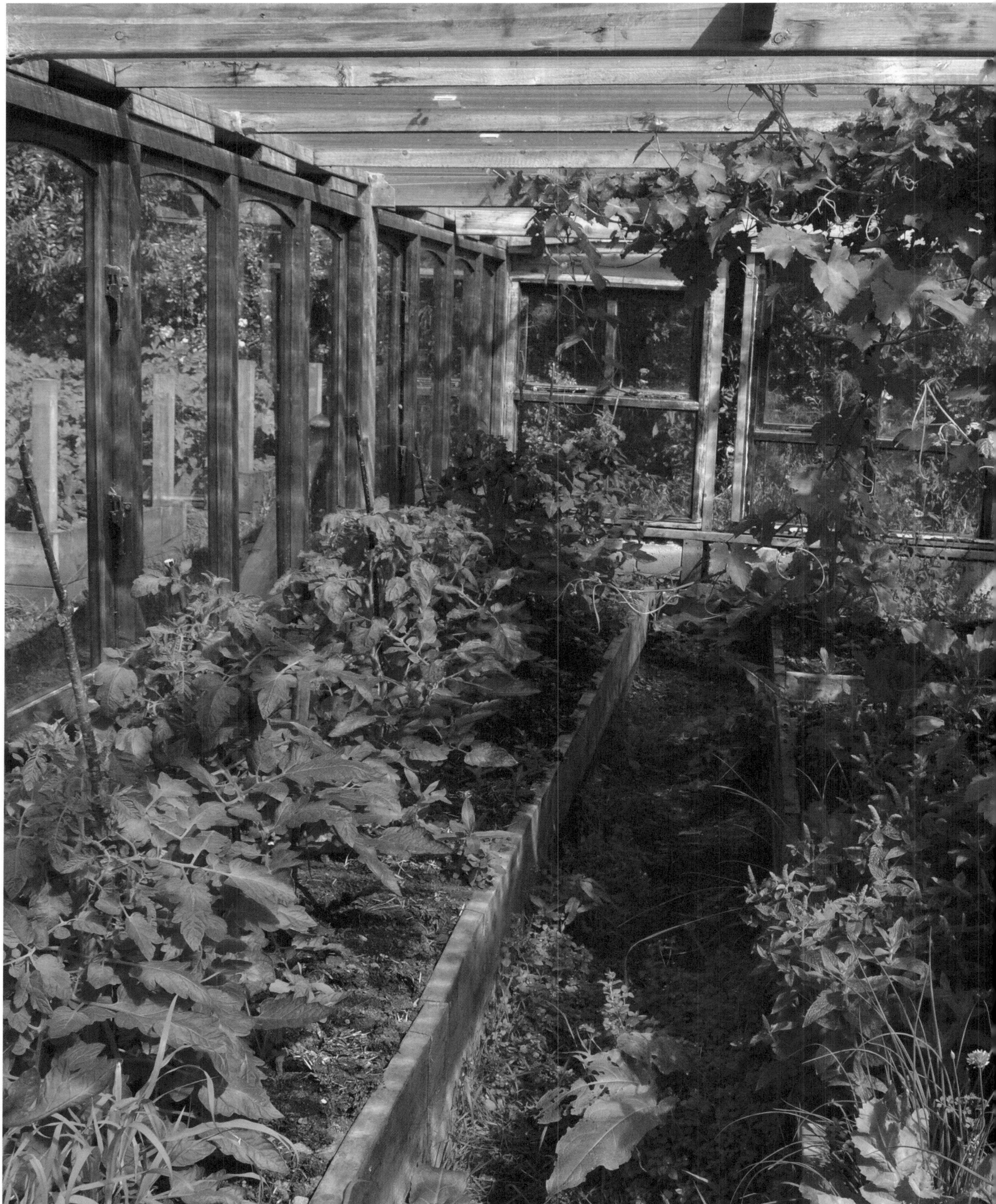

EXOTIC VEGETABLE NOODLE SALAD
WITH RED PEPPER SALSA

EXOTISCHER GEMÜSENUDEL-SALAT
MIT ROTER PAPRIKA-SALSA

INGREDIENTS
SERVES 2

1 large sweet potato, spiralized or
grated into long, thin strips with
a julienne peeler

Dressing
Juice of 1 lemon
Juice of 1 lime
Dash of olive oil
½ tsp toasted sesame oil
½ tsp sea salt
½ tsp cayenne pepper
½ tsp ground turmeric

Salsa
1 cup/140 g pumpkin seeds
1 red bell pepper, stemmed, seeded,
and cut into large pieces
1 medium broccoli head, florets only
1 pear, peeled, cored, and cut into
large pieces
1-inch piece of fresh ginger, chopped
1 garlic clove, chopped
1 cilantro sprig

ZUTATEN
FÜR 2 PERSONEN

1 große Süßkartoffel, in Spiralen oder
  lange, dünne Streifen geschnitten

Dressing
Saft von 1 Zitrone
Saft von 1 Limette
1 Spritzer Olivenöl
½ TL dunkles Sesamöl
½ TL Meersalz
½ TL Cayennepfeffer
½ TL gemahlene Kurkuma

Salsa
140 g Kürbiskerne
1 rote Paprikaschote, entkernt und
  in große Stücke geschnitten
1 mittelgroßer Brokkoli,
  in Röschen geteilt
1 Birne, geschält, entkernt und
  in große Stücke geschnitten
2–3 cm Ingwer, gehackt
1 Knoblauchzehe, gehackt
1 Stängel Koriandergrün

Raw food is essential to any diet. Eating some foods raw allows
for maximum absorption of their nutrients. Here is a very tasty and
fun salad with a zingy broccoli and red pepper salsa. As an added
bonus, it's dairy- and gluten-free.

METHOD
Place the spiralized sweet potato in a large bowl.

Dressing: Whisk all the ingredients together. Pour the dressing over
the sweet potato to begin the softening process.

Salsa: Place the pumpkin seeds in a food processor and pulse
a few times, until finely chopped. Add the bell pepper, broccoli,
pear, ginger, garlic, and cilantro, and pulse until the mixture
is a textured puree.

Transfer to a bowl and, using your fingertips, gently massage all
the ingredients (this breaks down the enzymes of the raw vegetables,
thus making them more digestible).

Tip: This dish can be served right away or stored in the refrigerator
for a few hours. The longer it is kept, the softer and less perky
the vegetables will be.

ZUBEREITUNG
Für den Gemüsenudelsalat die Süßkartoffelspiralen in eine große
Schüssel geben.

Zitrussäfte, beide Öle, Salz, Pfeffer und Kurkuma zu einem Dressing
verquirlen. Das Dressing unter die Süßkartoffel mischen.

Für die Salsa die Kürbiskerne in einer Küchenmaschine in Intervallen
fein hacken. Paprika, Brokkoliröschen, Birne, Ingwer, Knoblauch und
Koriandergrün zugeben und grobstückig pürieren.

Die Salsa zur Süßkartoffel in die Schüssel geben und alles vorsichtig
verkneten. (Das Kneten bricht die Enzyme des rohen Gemüses auf
und macht es leichter verdaulich). Den Salat sofort portionsweise
anrichten und servieren oder einige Stunden kühlen. Je länger
der Salat durchzieht, desto weicher wird das Gemüse.

Tipp: Raw Food gehört auf jeden Speisezettel, denn es garantiert
eine optimale Aufnahme wichtiger Nährstoffe. Dieser sehr leckere
Salat mit Brokkoli und Paprika-Salsa macht das Essen zu einem
Erlebnis. Weiterer Vorteil: Er ist milch- und glutenfrei.

THE JOY OF ENVIRONMENTALLY CONSCIOUS TRAVEL
UMWELTBEWUSSTE URLAUBSFREUDEN

Global mass tourism, with its cheap flights and all-inclusive offers, has a downside—it strains the resources of cities and regions, contaminates ecosystems, and damages unique sites all over our planet. When nature pays a price for the pleasure we take in vacationing, it becomes difficult to reconcile tourism with a sustainable lifestyle. Does this mean that the environmentally conscious must stay at home? Ride a bike instead of flying? Forget about discovering far-away destinations but at best explore one's own backyard?

Not at all, for there's good news. You can indeed discover the world without harming the environment! The magic formula is known as "sustainable tourism," and it essentially means traveling consciously and responsibly, treating locals and their culture with respect, and making sure that neither the environment nor people or animals have to suffer in order for you to have fun.

There are many ways in which you can take a sustainable vacation. When planning how you will arrive and where you will stay, you can choose environmentally and socially compatible alternatives. VeggieHotels establishments and VeganWelcome hotels, in particular, dedicate themselves to protecting the environment and climate. They conserve resources and use green energy sources—their kitchens process primarily regional and seasonal organic products and work closely with mainly local companies and farmers. Many proprietors of VeggieHotels devote a great deal of energy and passion to showing how sustainable tourism can be made attractive. Not least, a vegetarian diet—and especially a vegan one—contributes to a much more beneficial climate balance sheet than does a cuisine that focuses on meat.

If reaching your destination by plane is your only feasible choice, you can compensate for the CO_2 emissions of your flight by investing in the climate protection projects of suitable organizations. And if your length of stay is in reasonable correlation to the distance traveled, you take advantage of local services, and you treat the people, nature, and resources with respect, there is no reason why you can't enjoy a sustainable vacation far from home.

Der weltweite Massentourismus mit Billigfliegern und All-inclusive-Angeboten bringt so einige Schattenseiten mit sich – er belastet Städte und Regionen, aber auch Ökosysteme. Einzigartige Orte unseres Planeten werden durch ihn beschädigt. Wenn Urlaubsfreuden so auf Kosten der Natur gehen, fällt es schwer, Tourismus noch mit einem nachhaltigen Lebensstil zu verbinden. Muss man als umweltbewusster Mensch also zu Hause bleiben? Fahrrad fahren statt fliegen? Nicht mehr in die Ferne, sondern höchstens ins Umland schweifen?

Nein, denn die gute Nachricht ist: Man kann durchaus die Welt entdecken, ohne die Umwelt zu schädigen! Die Zauberformel lautet „Sanfter Tourismus" und bedeutet so viel wie bewusst und verantwortungsvoll zu verreisen, Einheimischen und ihrer Kultur vor Ort respektvoll zu begegnen und darauf zu achten, dass weder Umwelt noch Mensch oder Tier für das eigene Vergnügen leiden müssen.

Es gibt viele Möglichkeiten, sanft Urlaub zu machen – bereits bei der Organisation von Anreise und Unterkunft kann man sich für umweltfreundliche und sozial verträgliche Alternativen entscheiden. Gerade VeggieHotels und viele VeganWelcome-Hotels setzen sich besonders für den Umwelt- und Klimaschutz ein: Ressourcen werden geschont und Ökostrom zur Energiegewinnung genutzt, die hauseigenen Küchen verarbeiten vorwiegend regionale und saisonale Bioprodukte, die Zusammenarbeit mit lokalen Unternehmen und Bauern ist eng. Viele VeggieHotels-Betreiber zeigen mit großem Engagement und Leidenschaft, wie ein nachhaltiger Tourismus attraktiv gestaltet werden kann. Nicht zuletzt weist die vegetarische, und noch mehr die vegane Ernährungsform im Vergleich zu einer fleischlastigen Küche eine viel vorteilhaftere Klimabilanz auf.

Ist die Anreise nur mit dem Flieger machbar, so kann man über Klimaschutzorganisationen die CO_2-Emissionen der eigenen Flugreise ausgleichen und auf diese Weise in Klimaschutzprojekte investieren. Wenn dann noch Entfernung und Aufenthaltsdauer in einem angemessenen Verhältnis zueinander stehen, man vor Ort lokale Dienstleistungen in Anspruch nimmt und respektvoll mit den Menschen, der Natur und den Ressourcen umgeht, steht einer nachhaltigen Fernreise nichts im Wege.

VeggieHotels are the perfect destinations for vacationers who appreciate nature, as these establishments operate in harmony with the environment as a rule and not as the exception. More than a few hotels have received awards for their sustainable management practices, and some even regularly publish sustainability reports.

Conscious and responsible travel does not necessarily mean you have to make sacrifices. Instead, it often makes for a much more intensive vacation experience. In the end, everyone benefits: nature, the climate, the local population and economy, and the travelers themselves. In fact, sustainable vacations are the most fun, wouldn't you say?

VeggieHotels sind perfekte Ziele für Urlauber, denen die Natur am Herzen liegt, denn hier ist ein Handeln in Einklang mit der Umwelt keine Ausnahme, sondern die Regel. Nicht wenige Hotels wurden bereits für ihr nachhaltiges Wirtschaften ausgezeichnet, einige veröffentlichen sogar regelmäßig Nachhaltigkeitsberichte.

Bewusstes und verantwortungsvolles Reisen bedeutet nicht unbedingt Abstriche zu machen, vielmehr bietet es oft sogar ein viel intensiveres Urlaubserlebnis. Am Ende gewinnen alle: Natur, Klima, die Menschen vor Ort, die lokale Wirtschaft und man selbst. Nachhaltige Urlaubsfreuden sind doch die schönsten, oder?

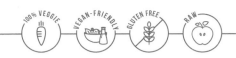

SUGAR RIDGE RETREAT CENTRE

WYEBRIDGE, ONTARIO

Many escapists view the Canadian wilderness as a dream destination. And it is! The expanse of forest, meadows, rolling hills and valleys set the scene for this beautiful retreat center. Tucked into the countryside of Ontario is a peaceful oasis with private cabins, forest in every direction, big open sky and a view of the Wye Marsh conservation area and Georgian Bay – welcome to Sugar Ridge Retreat Centre. The emphasis here is on reflection and "letting go", so the cabins are intentionally simple. No television or phone or noise of traffic but rather comfy beds, snuggly duvets and sounds of forest to retreat from your everyday life, sleep deeply and reconnect to yourself...something that is truly a luxury these days!

Connecting to Nature, relaxing and nurturing your body, mind and soul are the theme of this 150-acre (60-hectare) private property. That means incredible vegan food, fresh air, peace and quiet await you. Every meal is prepared with love using fresh, organic whole foods, local whenever possible. Explore the forest on 16 miles (25 kilometers) of hiking trails or snowshoe or ski in the winter.

Create your own personal retreat with complete silence if you wish or bring a group of friends. Enjoy a bonfire under the stars or curl up with tea and a good book. Writers come here to break through writer's block, artists draw inspiration from the natural world's rich color palette, bird watchers are kept busy and photographers can find a great shot in any direction. Nearly anything seems possible in this special place.

The center offers yoga and meditation programs as well as personal coaching by the owners Liz & Kurt Frost. Both are psychotherapists and yoga teachers.

Just 90 minutes from Toronto and shuttle service from the airport. Your adventure awaits!

Für viele Reisende ist die kanadische Wildnis ein Traumziel. Weitläufige Wälder, Grünflächen, Hügellandschaften und Täler bilden die Kulisse dieses wunderschönen Rückzugsortes. Das Sugar Ridge Retreat empfängt seine Gäste mit einer Oase des Friedens: private Hütten, Wald, wohin das Auge reicht, weiter Himmel und Ausblick auf das Naturschutzgebiet Wye Marsh und die Georgian Bay. Der Ort soll zum Nachdenken und zum „Loslassen" anregen. Daher sind die Hütten einfach eingerichtet: kein Fernseher oder Telefon, kein Lärm oder Verkehr. Vielmehr erwarten die Gäste gemütliche Betten und Stille, die nur durch die beruhigenden Geräusche der Natur unterbrochen wird. All dies ermöglicht Erholung vom Alltag, tiefen Schlaf und Rückbesinnung auf sich selbst ... ein wahrer Luxus heutzutage!

Mit der Natur anknüpfen, Ruhe finden sowie Körper, Geist und Seele nähren. Das bedeutet auf diesem 60 Hektar großen Privatanwesen vor allem: veganes Essen, frische Luft, Ruhe und Frieden. Jedes Gericht wird liebevoll aus frischen und möglichst regionalen Biolebensmitteln zubereitet. Entdecken Sie den Wald auf den 25 km langen Wanderwegen oder im Winter auf Schneeschuhen oder Ski. Schaffen Sie sich Ihren persönlichen Rückzugsort mit vollkommener Stille oder kommen Sie mit Freunden hierher. Genießen Sie ein Lagerfeuer unter freiem Sternenhimmel oder ziehen Sie sich mit Tee und einem guten Buch zurück. Schriftsteller kommen hierher, um Schreibblockaden zu überwinden. Künstler lassen sich vom Farbenreichtum der Natur inspirieren, Vogelkundler sind fasziniert von der Artenvielfalt und Fotografen finden großartige Motive in jeder Himmelsrichtung. Fast alles erscheint hier möglich.

Das Center bietet Yoga- und Meditationsprogramme an, aber auch Personal Coaching durch die Besitzer Liz und Kurt Frost selbst. Beide sind Psychotherapeuten und Yoga-Lehrer. Nur 90 Minuten von Toronto entfernt steht Ihrem Abenteuer nichts im Wege!

ROOMS: 10 CABINS
SPECIALTIES: VARIOUS RETREATS OFFERED THROUGHOUT THE YEAR, ORGANIC GARDEN, OLD FASHIONED MAPLE SYRUP PRODUCTION

SUGAR RIDGE RETREAT CENTRE
5720 FORGETS ROAD
WYEBRIDGE, ONTARIO L0K 2E0
CANADA (KANADA)
WWW.SUGARRIDGE.CA
+1 866 609 1793

ZIMMER: 10 HÜTTEN
BESONDERHEITEN: VERSCHIEDENE RETREATANGEBOTE ÜBER DAS GESAMTE JAHR VERTEILT, BIOGARTEN, EIGENE TRADITIONELLE AHORNSIRUP-PRODUKTION

THE STANFORD INN BY THE SEA

MENDOCINO, CALIFORNIA

The Stanford Inn by the Sea is a hotel like no other. It is the only purely vegan hotel and resort in the United States, and its restaurant, The Ravens (purely vegan, of course), is known throughout the country. Here in Mendocino, California, you still sense some of the hippie charm of a bygone era, since that is what made this small coastal town famous. You may not encounter hippie culture on every street corner anymore—the way you did back in the 1960s—but the region around Mendocino, with its steep coastal cliffs and enchanting bays, is still worth the trip for many reasons. The prospect of eating your way through the Raven's prize-winning menu alone might be enough motivation for many return trips to Mendocino. Renowned chefs from all over the world prepare purely plant-based, gourmet delicacies from ingredients grown in the hotel's own organic garden. It begins at the break of day with a bountiful gourmet breakfast and continues through the multi-course dinner in the evening.

The ecological resort not only provides a heavenly view of its spacious gardens and the majestic Pacific but also elegant rooms with cozy fireplaces and a holistic wellness center that offers a wide range of services, from treatments to yoga to cooking classes.

The Stanford Inn by the Sea also welcomes your four-legged friends and pampers them with homemade sweet potato treats. Fans of outdoor activities will be particularly delighted, as this wildly romantic landscape offers the perfect conditions for excursions, mountain bike tours, and canoe rides.

The Stanford Inn by the Sea ist ein Hotel, das seinesgleichen sucht. Es ist das einzige rein vegane Hotelresort in den USA, und sein – natürlich rein veganes – Restaurant The Ravens ist landesweit bekannt. Hier, im kalifornischen Mendocino, atmet man noch ein wenig den Hippiecharme vergangener Tage, denn dafür war und ist der kleine Ort an der Küste berühmt. Und auch wenn die Hippiekultur heute nicht mehr so deutlich an jeder Ecke zu spüren ist wie in den 1960er-Jahren, die Gegend um Mendocino mit ihrer Steilküste und traumhaften Buchten ist noch immer aus vielen Gründen eine Reise wert. Allein die Aussicht, sich durch die kreativen Menüs des preisgekrönten Restaurants zu schlemmen, könnte Motivation genug sein, immer wieder nach Mendocino zurückzukehren. Renommierte Köche aus der ganzen Welt bereiten mit Zutaten aus dem eigenen Biogarten rein pflanzliche Köstlichkeiten auf höchstem Niveau zu. Das fängt schon zum Tagesstart mit einem vielfältigen Gourmetfrühstück an und reicht bis zum mehrgängigen Dinner am Abend.

Das Eco Resort bietet nicht nur einen Traumblick über seine großzügigen Gärten und den majestätischen Pazifik, sondern ebenso elegante Zimmer mit Kaminfeuer zum Wohlfühlen und ein ganzheitliches Wellnesscenter mit einem großen Angebot, das von Behandlungen über Yoga bis hin zu Kochkursen reicht.

Im The Stanford Inn by the Sea sind Vierbeiner ebenfalls willkommen, gerne werden diese mit hausgemachten Süßkartoffelleckerlis verwöhnt. Liebhaber von Outdoor-Aktivitäten kommen besonders ins Schwärmen, denn in dieser wild-romantischen Landschaft finden sich perfekte Bedingungen für Exkursionen, Mountainbiketouren oder Kanufahrten.

ROOMS: 48
SPECIALTIES: POOL, YOGA, MEDITATION, COOKING CLASSES, HIKING, ART CLASSES, CONSERVATION OF RESOURCES (E.G. EV CHARGING STATION, ALL GREEN CLEANING SUPPLIES, ORGANIC GARDEN)

THE STANFORD INN BY THE SEA
PO BOX 487
95460 MENDOCINO
USA
WWW.STANFORDINN.COM
+1 707 937 5615

ZIMMER: 48
BESONDERHEITEN: POOL, YOGA, MEDITATION, KOCHKURSE, WANDERN, MALKURSE, RESSOURCENSCHONUNG (U.A. E-AUTO-LADESTATION, BIOREINIGUNGSPRODUKTE, BIOGARTEN)

KALE SALAD
WITH AVOCADO-LIME VERJUS DRESSING, TRUMPET ROYALE MUSHROOMS, AND AVOCADO

GRÜNKOHLSALAT
MIT LIMETTEN-VERJUS-DRESSING, PILZ-CEVICHE UND AVOCADO

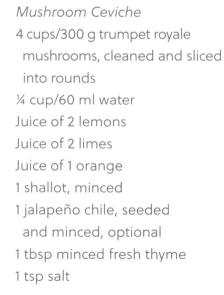

INGREDIENTS
SERVES 4 TO 6

Kale Salad and Dressing
1 bunch kale, stemmed and
   sliced into very thin strips
Salt
2 avocados, halved and pitted
½ cup/15 g tightly packed
   cilantro leaves
Juice of 1 lime
2 tbsp verjus
1 tbsp brown rice vinegar
1 tbsp agave syrup
Pepper
¼ cup/40 g raisins

Mushroom Ceviche
4 cups/300 g trumpet royale
   mushrooms, cleaned and sliced
   into rounds
¼ cup/60 ml water
Juice of 2 lemons
Juice of 2 limes
Juice of 1 orange
1 shallot, minced
1 jalapeño chile, seeded
   and minced, optional
1 tbsp minced fresh thyme
1 tsp salt

1 avocado, halved, pitted,
   and sliced thin
1 red bell pepper, diced

ZUTATEN
FÜR 4–6 PERSONEN

Grünkohlsalat und Dressing
1 Bund Grünkohl, entstielt und
   in sehr dünne Streifen geschnitten
Salz
2 Avocados, halbiert und entkernt
15 g Koriandergrün
Saft von 1 Limette
2 EL Verjus
1 EL brauner Reisessig
1 EL Agavendicksaft
Pfeffer
40 g Rosinen

Pilz-Ceviche
300 g braune Kräuterseitlinge,
   in Scheiben geschnitten
Saft von 2 Zitronen
Saft von 2 Limetten
Saft von 1 Orange
1 Schalotte, fein gehackt
1 Jalapeño-Chilischote, entkernt
   und fein gehackt (nach Belieben)
1 EL frisch gehackter Thymian
1 TL Salz

Zum Servieren
4–6 Servierringe
1 Avocado, halbiert, entkernt
   und in dünne Scheiben geschnitten
1 rote Paprikaschote,
   in kleine Würfel geschnitten

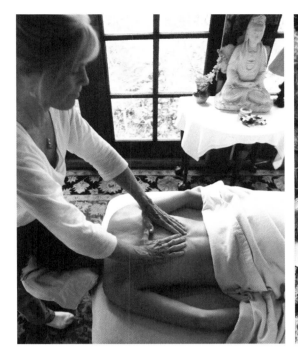

METHOD

Verjus, or verjuice, is a tart grape juice made from unripe grapes. We like to use Navarro Vineyards Verjus. You can substitute romaine lettuce for the kale if you prefer; omit the step of massaging with salt. Trumpet royale mushrooms are in the oyster mushroom family and have a mild flavor and edible stem. If you can't find them, you can use an equal amount of oyster mushrooms or white mushrooms.

Kale salad and dressing: Place the kale in a large bowl and sprinkle with 1 teaspoon salt. Massage the salt into kale leaves until they are well coated. (This process will help break down the cell wall of the kale, making it tender.)

Combine the avocados, cilantro, lime juice, verjus, brown rice vinegar, agave, and salt and pepper to taste in a high-speed blender, and process until smooth.

Combine the raisins and 2 tablespoons of the dressing with the kale and set aside.

Mushroom ceviche: Combine the mushrooms with the water in a skillet and cook over medium heat, stirring occasionally, until the mushrooms are cooked through, about 10 minutes. Drain and transfer to a large bowl.

Add the citrus juices, shallot, jalapeño, thyme, and salt to the mushrooms and mix until well combined. Let sit for at least 3 hours to incorporate the flavors.

For each salad, place a cylinder mold on a salad plate and insert about 3 inches of the massaged and dressed kale, pressing down firmly. Follow with a thin layer of the sautéed mushrooms. Finish with a layer of avocado slices fanned out on top. Remove the mold. Garnish with diced red bell pepper and serve.

ZUBEREITUNG

Für den Salat die Grünkohlstreifen in eine große Schüssel geben und mit 1 TL Salz bestreuen. Das Salz gleichmäßig in den Grünkohl einmassieren (Das öffnet die Zellwände des Kohls und macht ihn zart.)

Für das Dressing Avocados, Koriandergrün, Limettensaft, Verjus, Reisessig und Agavendicksaft im Mixer cremig pürieren.

Mit Salz und Pfeffer abschmecken. Rosinen und 2 EL Dressing unter den Grünkohl mischen.

Für die Pilz-Ceviche Kräuterseitlinge mit 60 ml Wasser in einer Pfanne bei mittlerer Hitze unter gelegentlichem Rühren etwa 10 Minuten garen. Die Pilze in einem Sieb abtropfen lassen und in eine Schüssel geben.

Alle Zitrussäfte, Schalotte, Chili, Thymian und Salz untermischen und die Pilze mindestens 3 Stunden durchziehen lassen.

Pro Portion einen Servierring auf einen Salatteller stellen. Etwa 10 cm hoch Grünkohl hineingeben und nach unten drücken. Eine dünne Lage Pilze daraufschichten und eine Lage Avocadoscheiben fächerförmig darauf anrichten. Die Form abheben, den Salat mit Paprikawürfeln garnieren und servieren.

Tipp: Den Grünkohl können Sie gegen Romana-Salat austauschen, der auch nicht mit Salz geknetet werden muss. Braune Kräuterseitlinge sind mit Champignons verwandt, sie zeichnen sich durch milden Geschmack und essbare Stiele aus. Wenn Sie keine bekommen, verwenden Sie stattdessen Austernpilze oder Champignons. Verjus ist der säuerliche Saft unreifer Weintrauben. Wir verwenden bevorzugt Verjus von Navarro Vineyards.

PARK LANE GUEST HOUSE

AUSTIN, TEXAS

Right downtown in the heart of the historic SoCo district, you will find the greenest little hotel in Austin, Texas. From the lively hustle and bustle of South Congress Avenue, a street lined with food trucks, hip boutiques, galleries, and live music venues, it is just a short walk to the Park Lane Guest House, where guests can immerse themselves in a green oasis of peace and tranquility. Shakti and Devkirn, Park Lane's two likeable owners, describe this special place as an urban eco-oasis. They purchased the property in 1994 and carefully rebuilt it using sustainable materials.

A swimming pool featuring recycled glass tiles is situated where a farm building once stood, and guests can relax in the shade of a 400-year-old live oak tree. The main house was constructed in 1949 from the remains of a nearby fort and an outbuilding was converted into the first guest cottage in 1995—marking the launch of an unusual and enchanting ecological bed and breakfast that was gradually expanded over time with additional cottages. All the cottages are solar-powered and constructed with an abundance of love, creativity, and sustainable materials by Shakti, a retired carpenter. One of Park Lane's options even includes a tiny house, which offers guests everything they need in the smallest of spaces—including an organic mattress. Global travelers Shakti and Devkirn have created an extraordinary and sustainable place of tranquility and relaxation that welcomes guests with incredible warmth and spoils them with delicious and exclusively vegetarian food. It's no surprise that the press and guests are outdoing each other with praise for the Park Lane Guest House.

Das grünste kleine Hotel in Austin, Texas findet man ausgerechnet Downtown im historischen Bezirk SoCo, nahe der belebten South Congress Avenue, wo Foodtrucks, hippe Boutiquen, Galerien und Livemusiklokale aneinander gereiht sind. Vom quirligen Treiben dort braucht es nur einen kurzen Spaziergang, um in eine grüne Oase der Ruhe einzutauchen, dem Park Lane Guest House. „Ökologische Stadtoase" nennen die sympathischen Gastgeberinnen Shakti und Devkirn diesen ganz besonderen Ort, den sie 1994 übernahmen und behutsam mit nachhaltigen Materialien umbauten.

Dort wo früher das erste Gebäude eines Bauernhofs stand, badet man heute in einem Swimmingpool aus recycelten Glasfliesen und entspannt im Schatten einer 400 Jahre alten Eiche. Das heutige Haupthaus wurde 1949 aus Resten eines nahegelegenen Forts errichtet, und das Außengebäude 1995 zum ersten Gästecottage umfunktioniert – der Startschuss für ein ungewöhnliches und bezauberndes Eco Bed & Breakfast, das nach und nach um weitere Cottages erweitert wurde. Alles mit viel Liebe, Kreativität und nachhaltigen Materialien von Betreiberin Shakti – im früheren Leben Schreinerin – gebaut und mit Solarstrom versorgt. Sogar ein Tiny House bietet hier auf kleinstem Raum alles, was man braucht, inklusive Biomatratze. Die Weltenbummlerinnen Shakti und Devkirn haben einen ungewöhnlichen und nachhaltigen Ort der Ruhe und Erholung geschaffen, der seine Gäste mit ganz viel Herzlichkeit empfängt und an dem man mit köstlichem, ausschließlich vegetarischem Essen verwöhnt wird. Kein Wunder, dass sich Presse und Gäste mit Lob über das Park Lane Guest House förmlich überschlagen.

ROOMS: 4 COTTAGES
SPECIALTIES: POOL, MASSAGES,
CONSERVATION OF RESOURCES
(E.G. SOLAR POWER,
EV CHARGING STATION)

PARK LANE GUEST HOUSE
221 PARK LANE
78704 AUSTIN
USA
WWW.PARKLANEGUESTHOUSE.COM
+1 512 447 7460

ZIMMER: 4 COTTAGES
BESONDERHEITEN: POOL, MASSAGEN,
RESSOURCENSCHONUNG
(U.A. SOLARENERGIE,
E-AUTO-LADESTATION)

BLACK HILLS
HEALTH & EDUCATION CENTER

HERMOSA, SOUTH DAKOTA

In western South Dakota, the Black Hills could easily be referred to as the "Red Hills," because the landscape of canyons, cliffs, lakes, and rivers is characterized by the same kind of red rock that so many associate with the USA. The region is famous for Mount Rushmore, a sculpture of four US presidents that is carved into the granite mountain face and depicts them gazing off into the distance. Although a considerable amount of gold was mined here in the early 20th century, the treasure that can be found in the Black Hills today cannot be measured in gold: tranquility, relaxation, health, and growth.

Secluded in the heart of nature, the Black Hills Health & Education Center is situated on the plateau of a fire-red canyon. Words do not exist that can adequately describe this unique spot.

In this setting, two things that would be mutually exclusive anywhere else effortlessly join together in the most beautiful way possible: work and relaxation. The Black Hills Center is more than a hotel. Here guests can not only learn how nutrition and the proper lifestyle can help to address illnesses, but they can also come here to complete certified training courses in the healthcare field. Yet this is far more than an education center: Here, in the midst of the tranquility and seclusion of untouched nature, guests can come to rejuvenate themselves.

Walking trails on the grounds beckon guests to let their feet and minds wander. This is a place of recreation, education, change, and of growth, and one where visitors will leave invigorated. The Black Hills Center has offered this unique blend of services for more than 30 years.

Die Black Hills im Westen von South Dakota müssten eigentlich „Red Hills" heißen, denn die Landschaft aus Canyons, Felsen, Seen und Flüssen ist geprägt von jenem roten Gestein, das viele im Geiste mit den USA verbinden. Die Region ist berühmt für ihren Mount Rushmore, von dem vier große US-Präsidenten in die Weite blicken. Anfang des 20. Jahrhunderts wurde hier eine beträchtliche Menge Gold gefördert. Den Schatz, den man heute in den Black Hills finden kann, lässt sich jedoch mit Gold nicht aufwiegen: Ruhe, Erholung, Gesundheit und Wachstum.

Hier, auf dem Plateau eines feuerroten Canyons, liegt abgeschieden mitten in der wilden Natur das Black Hills Health & Education Center. Um diesen einzigartigen Ort richtig zu beschreiben, müsste man eigentlich ein neues Wort erfinden.

Mühelos und auf schönste Weise verbinden sich hier zwei Aspekte, die einander andernorts eigentlich kategorisch ausschließen: Arbeit und Erholung. Das Black Hills Center ist mehr als ein Hotel, weil man hier nicht nur lernen kann, mit Ernährung und der richtigen Lebensweise Krankheiten in den Griff zu bekommen, sondern auch zertifizierte Ausbildungen im Gesundheitssektor absolvieren kann. Und es ist so viel mehr als eine Akademie, da man inmitten von Stille, Abgeschiedenheit und unberührter Natur wunderbar neue Kraft tankt.

Die Spazierwege auf dem Gelände laden dazu ein, die Füße gemeinsam mit dem Geist umherwandern zu lassen. Ein Ort der Erholung, Bildung, Veränderung und des Wachstums also, den die Besucher gestärkt wieder verlassen – seit mehr als 30 Jahren bietet das Black Hills Center diese einzigartige Mischung.

ROOMS: 11
SPECIALTIES: HOLISTIC HEALTH PROGRAMS, MASSAGE, BIBLICAL RESPONSE THERAPY® (BRT), COOKING CLASSES, HIKING, ACCESSIBLE FOR DISABLED PEOPLE

**BLACK HILLS
HEALTH & EDUCATION CENTER
13815 BATTLE CREEK ROAD
57744 HERMOSA
USA
WWW.BHHEC.ORG
+1 605 255 4101**

ZIMMER: 11
BESONDERHEITEN: GANZHEITLICHE GESUNDHEITSPROGRAMME, MASSAGE, BIBLICAL RESPONSE THERAPY® (BRT), KOCHKURSE, WANDERN, BEHINDERTENGERECHT

SEWALL HOUSE YOGA RETREAT

ISLAND FALLS, MAINE

In the late 1800s, William Sewall, a naturalist and the great grandfather of the current owner, welcomed a pale and thin young man as a regular summer guest to Sewall House. At the time Sewall could not have imagined that this young Harvard student with a weak heart named Theodore Roosevelt would later become the 26th President of the United States. Sewall and Roosevelt enjoyed a lifelong friendship as well as joint adventures, and Sewall House, situated in the enchanting landscape of northern Maine, was destined to become a safe harbor that would welcome people in search of relaxation and healing.

In 1997, well-known yoga teacher and nutritionist Donna Sewall Davidge became the fifth generation of her family to manage this historic house when she decided to purchase it and transform it into a yoga retreat. Northern Maine is the perfect place for a retreat, situated as it is along the Canadian border and featuring forests, lakes, abundant wildlife, the Katahdin Woods and Waters National Monument, Baxter State Park, hiking trails, and healthy fresh air. Just as in the past, guests can look forward to escaping from everyday life and enjoying the solitude and tranquility, the beauty and the healing forces of nature, much like Theodore Roosevelt. The retreat center offers different styles of yoga with expert and personalized instruction. Healthy vegetarian meals—with vegan and gluten-free options available upon request—promote healing. The beneficial recipes of Chef Nadja Waxenegger have already been immortalized in the *Sewall House Cookbook*.

Als der Urgroßvater der heutigen Betreiberin, der Naturkundler William Sewall, einen dünnen und blassen jungen Harvard-Studenten mit schwachem Herzen namens Theodore Roosevelt mehrere Sommer im Sewall House zu Gast hatte, konnte er wahrlich nicht ahnen, dass dieser einige Jahre später der 26. Präsident der USA werden würde. Sewall und Roosevelt konnten später auf eine lebenslange Freundschaft und gemeinsame Abenteuer zurückschauen, und das Sewall House in der bezaubernden Landschaft Nord-Maines sollte noch für viele Menschen ein sicherer Hafen zur Erholung und Heilung werden.

Die bekannte Yogalehrerin und Ernährungsberaterin Donna Sewall Davidge führt das historische Haus seit 1997 in der nunmehr fünften Generation und wandelte es in ein Yoga-Retreat um. Der Norden Maines an der Grenze zu Kanada, mit seinen Wäldern, Seen, einer reichen Tierwelt, dem Nationaldenkmal Katahdin Woods and Waters, dem Baxter State Park, Wanderwegen und gesunder frischer Luft scheint dafür der perfekte Ort zu sein. Heute wie damals kann man die Ruhe und Einsamkeit fernab des Alltags, die Schönheit und heilenden Kräfte der Natur genießen, ganz im Stile Theodore Roosevelts. Das Retreat-Zentrum bietet verschiedene Formen des Yogas mit fachkundiger und persönlicher Anleitung, und auch die gesunden vegetarischen, auf Wunsch veganen und glutenfreien Gerichte, sorgen für eine heilende Wirkung. Die wohltuenden Rezepte von Köchin Nadja Waxenegger wurden bereits in einem eigenen Kochbuch, dem *Sewall House Cookbook* verewigt.

ROOMS: 6
SPECIALTIES: YOGA, MEDITATION, MASSAGE, SAUNA, JACUZZI, HIKING, BIKE RENTALS

SEWALL HOUSE YOGA RETREAT
1027 CRYSTAL ROAD
ME 04747 ISLAND FALLS
USA
WWW.SEWALLHOUSE.COM
+1 646 316 5151

ZIMMER: 6
BESONDERHEITEN: YOGA, MEDITATION, MASSAGE, SAUNA, JACUZZI, WANDERN, FAHRRADVERLEIH

THE DREAMCATCHER

SAN JUAN, PUERTO RICO

Caution: follow the Dreamcatcher's Instagram account and you are bound to catch a severe case of vacation fever. And you would not be the only one, since this very special bed & breakfast was voted the best hotel in Puerto Rico four years in a row. Guests and the press outdo each other with enthusiasm. *New York Magazine* wrote, "Everything about this inn promotes relaxation." Including the incense, mediation music in the background, bubbling fountains, and the Native American dreamcatchers that inspired the name and hang in every corner to drive away bad dreams.

Located a mere two hundred meters from Ocean Park Beach, right in the middle of the hippie quarter, the only vegetarian bed & breakfast in San Juan is famous, not least, for its legendary vegetarian and vegan brunch. Innkeeper Sylvia virtually hired Chef Jerome directly away from his food truck and brought him to The Dreamcatcher after she had sampled his terrific cabbage wraps with salsa, avocado, and cashews. Jerome's culinary creations, such as his raw vegan mousse au chocolat, are certainly one reason why the guests praise their stay here in such glowing terms. Many other attributes, however, also make sure that you never want to leave the hotel again: the vintage look of the rooms, designed by the owners Sylvia and Stephan, the yoga and meditation classes with first-rate instructors, and the magnificent location. Indeed, the most important reason why you will fall completely in love with The Dreamcatcher is not immediately apparent, although it can be felt—the incredible passion with which Sylvia, Stephan, and their team have turned the inn into an unforgettable place.

Vorsicht: Wer dem Instagram-Account von The Dreamcatcher folgt, wird unweigerlich große Urlaubssehnsucht bekommen. Damit wäre man allerdings auch nicht alleine, denn dieses ganz besondere Bed & Breakfast wurde unter anderem vier Jahre in Folge zum besten Hotel Puerto Ricos gewählt. Gäste und Presse überschlagen sich vor Begeisterung, das *New York Magazine* schrieb: „Jedes Detail in diesem Gästehaus verspricht Entspannung" – inklusive Räucherstäbchen, Meditationsmusik im Hintergrund, plätschernden Brunnen und den indianischen Traumfängern, auf die der Name zurückgeht und die in jeder Ecke hängen, um böse Träume zu vertreiben.

Nur zweihundert Meter vom Ocean Park Beach und inmitten des Hippieviertels liegt das einzige vegetarische Gästehaus San Juans, das nicht zuletzt für seinen legendären vegetarisch-veganen Brunch berühmt ist. Chefkoch Jerome wurde von Gastgeberin Sylvia quasi direkt aus seinem Foodtruck heraus für The Dreamcatcher verpflichtet, nachdem sie seinen fantastischen Kohlwrap mit Salsa, Avocado und Cashews genossen hatte. Jeromes kulinarische Kreationen, wie seine roh-vegane Mousse au Chocolat, tragen ganz sicher zur Begeisterung der Gäste über ihren Aufenthalt bei. Aber auch die von den Besitzern Sylvia und Stephan im Vintagelook gestalteten Zimmer, die Yoga- und Meditationskurse mit erstklassigen Lehrern und die herrliche Lage – all das sorgt dafür, dass man am liebsten gleich hier bleiben möchte. Der wichtigste Grund The Dreamcatcher komplett zu verfallen, ist allerdings nicht sofort sichtbar, aber er ist spürbar – es ist diese unglaubliche Leidenschaft, mit der Sylvia, Stephan und ihr Team das Gästehaus zu einem unvergesslichen Ort machen.

ROOMS: 12 ROOMS & SUITES
SPECIALTIES: YOGA, EXCLUSIVE TOURS, BIKE RENTAL, SALSA CLASSES, PADDLE BOARDING, TAROT READING

THE DREAMCATCHER
2009 CALLE ESPANA
00911 SAN JUAN
PUERTO RICO
WWW.DREAMCATCHERPR.COM
+1 787 455 8259

ZIMMER: 12 ZIMMER & SUITEN
BESONDERHEITEN: YOGA, EXKLUSIVE TOUREN, FAHRRAD-VERLEIH, SALSAKURSE, STAND-UP-PADDLING, TAROTKARTEN LEGEN

WILLKA T'IKA
ESSENTIAL WELLNESS

URUBAMBA, CUSCO

The Sacred Valley of the Incas is a locality shrouded in myths. Its original inhabitants, the Quechua, have deep and grateful connection to this region and its fertile soil, situated between Cusco, the picturesque former capital of the Incan Empire, and the legendary citadel of Machu Picchu. When Carol Cumes arrived here for the first time in the 1980's from the USA, she not only experienced the sincere hospitality of the people who live here but also sensed the powerful energy that fills the valley. She kept returning over the years, finally purchasing the land for Willka T'ika in 1994. With help from the locals, she worked with great reverence for nature to achieve her vision of a luxurious retreat, one that would combine the essence of Andean culture with the philosophy of yoga. Today, her guests stroll along paths that wind through the seven energy-giving Chakra Gardens, at the crown of which grows a thousand-year-old Lucuma tree. Three greenhouses, an herb and vegetable garden, and protein-rich Andean superfoods form the foundation of Willka T'ika's delicious gourmet organic vegetarian cuisine.

Yoga group events, wellness retreats, and conferences are hosted in the hotel's beautiful facilities that include two light-filled yoga rooms. Retreat guests enthusiastically participate in traditional Andean rituals and healing sessions, which leave a particularly deep impression in these unique surroundings. Overnight guests find Wilka T'ika to be an ideal sanctuary for exploring the local region—Pisaq, Moray, Machu Picchu. In the evening, guests can relax in solar baths, carved out of rock and fragrant with blossoms and medicinal herbs, while gazing into the Milky Way.

Das heilige Tal der Inkas ist ein Ort mit mythischer Ausstrahlung. Seine Ureinwohner, die Quechua, haben eine tiefe und dankbare Verbundenheit mit dieser Region und ihren fruchtbaren Böden, die zwischen der malerischen ehemaligen Hauptstadt des Inka-Imperiums, Cusco, und der sagenumwobenen Zitadelle von Machu Picchu liegt.

Als Carol Cumes in den 1980er-Jahren zum ersten Mal aus den USA hierher kam, spürte sie nicht nur die aufrechte Freundlichkeit der Menschen, sondern auch die starke Energie des Tals. Sie kehrte immer wieder zurück, bis sie 1994 schließlich ein geeignetes Stück Land für Willka T'ika kaufte. Mit Hilfe der Einheimischen realisierte sie mit viel Aufwand und großem Respekt vor der Natur ihre Vision eines luxuriösen Retreats, das sowohl die Essenz der Kultur der Anden als auch die Philosophie des Yoga zum Ausdruck bringt. Heute durchstreifen Gäste auf verschlungenen Pfaden die sieben Energie spendenden Chakra-Gärten, in deren Zentrum ein eintausend Jahre alter Lucumabaum thront. Drei eigene Gewächshäuser, ein Kräuter- und Gemüsegarten sowie proteinreiches Andengetreide bilden die Grundlage der kraftspendenden vegetarischen Biogourmetküche des Willka T'ika.

In den beiden lichtdurchfluteten Yogaräumen finden Yogaseminare, Wellnessretreats und kleine Konferenzen statt. Die Gäste sind immer wieder begeistert von der Teilnahme an traditionellen Andenritualen und Heilsitzungen, die in dieser einzigartigen Umgebung einen besonders tiefen Eindruck hinterlassen. Von Willka T'ika aus, lässt sich die Region – Písac, Moray, Machu Picchu – wunderbar erkunden. Zur Nacht können Gäste in den aus Stein gehauenen Solarbädern ein Blumen- und Heilkräuterbad nehmen und sich vom Anblick der Milchstraße überwältigen lassen.

ROOMS: 28
SPECIALTIES: YOGA, MEDITATION, ANDEAN SPA TREATMENTS INCLUDING CRYSTAL LIGHT THERAPY, SOLAR BATH THERAPY, & CONSERVATION OF RESOURCES (E.G. SOLAR POWER)

WILLKA T'IKA
PARADERO RUMICHAKA
08660 URUBAMBA
CUSCO, PERU
WWW.WILLKATIKA.COM
+1 805 884 1121

ZIMMER: 28
BESONDERHEITEN: YOGA, MEDITATION, ANDEAN-SPA-BEHANDLUNGEN WIE KRISTALL-LICHTTHERAPIE, SOLARBADTHERAPIE, & RESSOURCENSCHONUNG (U.A. SOLARANLAGE)

ANDEAN SPIRIT LODGE
LIMATAMBO VALLEY, CUSCO

Oda and Armando, the two owners of the Andean Spirit Lodge in the Peruvian Andes, are firmly convinced that they did not find this place—it found them. The views of the snow-capped peak of Mount Humantay; the magnificent old Pisonay tree at the foot of the garden; the variety of birds, including hummingbirds, rare owls, and majestic condors that can be appreciated nearby; and the peaceful location in the midst of nature—it was love at first sight. This was the precise spot where they wanted to build their home.

Not long after their house was finished, they began to feel the need to share this relaxing place with others. They built additional guest bungalows and a large space for practicing yoga and meditation. They also put in an organic garden to grow vegetables and herbs so they could spoil guests with vegetarian and vegan specialties from the Andes and from around the world. Situated at an elevation of 7,874 feet (2,400 meters), the Andean Spirit Lodge is a very personal place for guests who enjoy a wide variety of interests, whether they are birdwatchers or nature lovers, whether they wish to practice yoga or meditation, or perhaps they are simply in search of tranquility. It is also the perfect spot for people who love delicious food as well as those who want to follow in the footsteps of the Incas. For more than twenty years, Oda and Armando have been organizing vegetarian/vegan adventure tours in Peru that provide authentic insights into the country's culture—and for that, the Andean Spirit Lodge is also the perfect starting point. It is no surprise that guests frequently fall in love with this magical spot!

Oda und Armando haben diesen Ort nicht gefunden – er hat sie gefunden, davon sind die beiden Betreiber der Andean Spirit Lodge in den peruanischen Anden überzeugt. Der Blick auf den schneebedeckten Humantay, den majestätischen Pisonay-Baum am Fuße des Gartens, die Vogelvielfalt mit Kolibris, seltenen Eulen und riesigen Kondoren, die in der Nähe zu sehen sind sowie die ruhige Lage inmitten der Natur – es war Liebe auf den ersten Blick. Genau an dieser Stelle wollten und sollten sie ihr Zuhause bauen.

Als ihr Haus fertig war, entstand schnell der Wunsch, diesen erholsamen Ort auch mit anderen Menschen zu teilen. Und so errichteten sie zusätzliche Gästebungalows und einen großen Raum für Yoga- und Meditationsübungen. Gleichzeitig wurde ein biologischer Gemüse- und Kräutergarten angelegt, um die Gäste mit vegetarischen und veganen Spezialitäten aus den Anden und der ganzen Welt zu verwöhnen. Die auf 2400 Metern Höhe gelegene Andean Spirit Lodge ist ein ganz persönlicher Ort für Naturliebhaber und Vogelbeobachter, für Yogis und Meditierende, für Ruhesuchende sowie für Menschen, die genussvolles Essen lieben und für solche, die auf den Spuren der Inkas wandern möchten. Oda und Armando organisieren in Peru seit über 20 Jahren vegetarisch-vegane Abenteuertouren, die einen authentischen Einblick in die Kultur des Landes vermitteln. Auch dafür ist die Andean Spirit Lodge der perfekte Startpunkt. Es sollte einen also nicht wundern, wenn man sich selbst in diesen magischen Ort verliebt!

ROOMS: 4 BUNGALOWS
SPECIALTIES: MEDITATION, YOGA, HIKING, SMALL LIBRARY, BIRD WATCHING

ANDEAN SPIRIT LODGE
SECTOR PICHUIMARCA
LIMATAMBO VALLEY
PERU
WWW.ANDEANSPIRITLODGE.COM
+51 984 763 109

ZIMMER: 4 BUNGALOWS
BESONDERHEITEN: MEDITATION, YOGA, WANDERN, KLEINE BIBLIOTHEK, VOGELBEOBACHTUNGEN

WELLNESSHAUS LODGE & SPA

CUNCO, CAUTÍN PROVINCE

Professional astronomers aren't the only ones who appreciate Chile's night sky, one of the clearest and darkest in the world. Picture yourself relaxing in an outdoor hot-water jacuzzi made of wood, taking in deep breaths of incredibly pure air, and admiring the endless expanse of the star-studded sky—all in complete silence.

The town of Cunco in Cautín Province is home to a very special refuge of this kind. Halfway between mighty Andean mountain ridges and the long beaches of southern Chile, the Wellnesshaus Lodge & Spa is surrounded by numerous rivers and lakes, with nature reserves, volcanos, and popular tourist destinations all nearby.

Visitors from all over the world come to this hospitable hotel, whose holistic wellness concept includes massages, steam baths, and a variety of detox treatments as well as an entirely vegan cuisine. All aspects of the program are intended to help you rid yourself of unwanted baggage. Along with workshops on mental, physical, and spiritual health, the lodge also offers vegan cooking classes. Most of the ingredients are harvested from the hotel's own garden, and nothing could be more organic than this region's pristine nature.

Innkeeper Alicia Packard's personal experiences motivated her to open a wellness hotel. More than 30 years ago, she discovered the enormous influence of a healthy diet—since then, it has been her mission to share this knowledge with others. The Wellnesshaus Lodge & Spa provides the heavenly backdrop for turning her vision into reality.

Dass der chilenische Nachthimmel zu den klarsten und dunkelsten der Welt zählt, wissen nicht nur professionelle Astronomen. Man stelle sich einfach mal vor, man entspannt im Freien, in einem Heißwasserwhirlpool aus Holz, atmet tief die unglaublich reine Luft ein und bestaunt die Unendlichkeit des Sternenmeeres am Firmament – all das bei kompletter Stille.

Das Städtchen Cunco in der Provinz Cautín ist Heimat eines ebensolchen Refugiums der besonderen Art. Auf halbem Weg zwischen mächtigen Andenausläufern und den langen Stränden Südchiles liegt das Wellnesshaus Lodge & Spa, umgeben von zahlreichen Flüssen und Seen, in der Nähe von Naturreservaten, Vulkanen und beliebten Touristenzielen.

Besucher aus aller Welt kommen in dieses gastfreundliche Haus. Zum ganzheitlichen Wellnesskonzept gehört neben Massagen, Dampfbädern und verschiedenen Detox-behandlungen auch die komplett vegane Verpflegung. Alle Komponenten sollen dabei helfen, zusätzlichen Ballast abzuwerfen. So stehen Workshops zur geistigen, körperlichen und spirituellen Gesundheit ebenso auf dem Programm wie Kochkurse für vegane Ernährung. Die Zutaten werden größtenteils im eigenen Garten geerntet und mehr bio als aus der unberührten Natur dieser Region geht wohl kaum.

Die Motivation ein Wellnesshaus zu eröffnen, erwuchs bei Gastgeberin Alicia Packard aus den eigenen Erfahrungen: Alicia lernte bereits vor über 30 Jahren, welch großen Einfluss eine gesunde Ernährung hat. Seitdem verfolgt sie die Mission, anderen Menschen diese Erkenntnisse weiterzugeben. Das Wellnesshaus Lodge & Spa bildet den entsprechend traumhaften Rahmen dazu.

ROOMS: 10
SPECIALTIES: COOKING CLASSES, SOLAR POOL, STEAM BATH, JACUZZI, MASSAGES, HORSE RIDING, HIKING, WINTER AND WATER SPORTS, ROOFTOP TERRACE FOR SUNBATHING

WELLNESSHAUS LODGE & SPA
FAJA 8000 SUR CAMINO A CUNCO
CUNCO
CHILE
WWW.WELLNESSHAUS.CL
+56 989 005 988

ZIMMER: 10
BESONDERHEITEN: KOCHKURSE, SOLAR-POOL, DAMPFBAD, JACUZZI, MASSAGEN, REITEN, WANDERN, WINTER- UND WASSERSPORT, DACHTERRASSE ZUM SONNENBADEN

ERANDIA MARARI AYURVEDA BEACH RESORT

ALLEPPEY, KERALA

Ayurveda is the oldest holistic healing art known to man, and if you've ever been treated by an Ayurvedic practitioner, you will know how wonderful it feels afterwards—just like being reborn. Ayurveda can be found in many places in the South Indian state of Kerala, but few of them are as authentic as the Erandia Marari Ayurveda Beach Resort while simultaneously offering such a stylish ambience.

The resort was built right on the heavenly, mile-long Marari Beach, with its countless numbers of coconut palms, to create a thoroughly personal retreat for all those who see a holistic Ayurvedic spa experience based on ancient principles. Panchakarma, the queen of Ayurvedic disciplines, removes toxic substances from the body to strengthen the immune system and mobilize life forces, bringing body and soul back into balance.

Personalized care is part of the concept here, and each guest gets their own vegetarian meals prepared individually according to Ayurvedic principles. Erandia Marari is Green Leaf-certified, the highest distinction for Ayurvedic centers in Kerala, and for good reason. The resort's unique modern architecture combines western minimalism with Indian style elements, and guests can open up their light-suffused suites to the elements and enjoy an ocean view, depending on their mood.

Those who wish to can take off their shoes on arrival and never put them back on until they depart—true barefoot luxury. Incidentally, Alappuzha, the "Venice of India," is the gateway to the famous Kerala backwaters, which run for hundreds of miles through the back country.

Ayurveda ist die älteste ganzheitliche Heilkunst der Menschheit, und wer einmal eine Ayurveda-Kur erlebt hat, kennt das großartige Gefühl, sich anschließend wie neugeboren zu fühlen. Im südindischen Bundesstaat Kerala wird die Kunst des Ayurveda an unzähligen Orten angeboten, doch so authentisch und gleichzeitig in einem solch stylishen Ambiente wie im Erandia Marari Ayurveda Beach Resort nur selten.

Direkt am traumhaften kilometerlangen Marari-Strand mit seinen zahllosen Kokospalmen wurde mit dem Resort ein überaus persönlicher Rückzugsort für alle geschaffen, die auf der Suche nach einer ganzheitlichen Ayurveda-Kur im Sinne der alten überlieferten Prinzipien sind. Während einer Panchakarma-Kur, der Königsdisziplin des Ayurveda, werden Schlacken aus dem Körper ausgeleitet, das Immunsystem gestärkt und die Lebenskräfte mobilisiert – Leib und Seele werden wieder in Balance gebracht.

Die ganz persönliche Betreuung gehört hier zum Konzept, selbst die nach ayurvedischen Prinzipien zubereiteten vegetarischen Mahlzeiten werden für jeden Gast individuell gekocht. Nicht umsonst bekam Erandia Marari mit der Green-Leaf-Zertifizierung bereits die höchste Auszeichnung für Ayurveda-Zentren in Kerala. Die einzigartig moderne Architektur des Resorts kombiniert westlichen Minimalismus mit indischen Stilelementen, und die lichtdurchfluteten Suiten können je nach Stimmung zu einem offenen Zuhause mit Meerblick gemacht werden.

Wer mag, zieht seine Schuhe bei der Ankunft aus und erst bei der Abreise wieder an – das ist wahre Barefoot Luxury. Übrigens: Alappuzha, das Venedig Indiens, ist Tor zu den berühmten Backwaters, die sich Hunderte von Kilometern durch das Hinterland ziehen.

ROOMS: 13 ROOMS IN 6 BUNGALOWS
SPECIALTIES: AYURVEDA TREATMENTS, YOGA, MEDITATION, COOKING CLASSES, POOL

ERANDIA MARARI AYURVEDA BEACH RESORT
MARARI BEACH SOUTH, KATTOOR
688546 ALLEPPEY
INDIA (INDIEN)
WWW.ERANDIAMARARI.COM
+91 965 655 2200

ZIMMER: 13 ZIMMER IN 6 BUNGALOWS
BESONDERHEITEN: AYURVEDA-BEHANDLUNGEN, YOGA, MEDITATION, KOCHKURSE, POOL

The specially designed louvered doors made of teak, which completely
enclose each bungalow, are a unique feature of this hotel.
Guests can adjust the partitions to suit their mood—and thus organize
the 144 square feet (44 square meters) of space according to their own
preferences. Closing the doors turns the terrace into a living room,
which is separated from the sleeping area by large sliding glass doors.
Leave the entryways open, on the other hand, and you cannot fail
to feel as though you were "outdoors," with an unobstructed view
of the sea.

Eine Besonderheit sind die eigens entworfenen Jalousietüren
aus Teakholz, die jeden Bungalow vollständig umschließen.
Je nach Stimmung können Gäste ihre Trennelemente individuell
einstellen – und damit den 44 Quadratmeter großen Raum selbst
gestalten. So wird bei geschlossenen Jalousien aus der Terrasse
ein Wohnraum, der mit großen Glasschiebetüren vom Schlafbereich
getrennt werden kann. Sind diese Zugänge hingegen offen, entsteht
unweigerlich ein Gefühl von „draußen sein" mit freiem Blick aufs Meer.

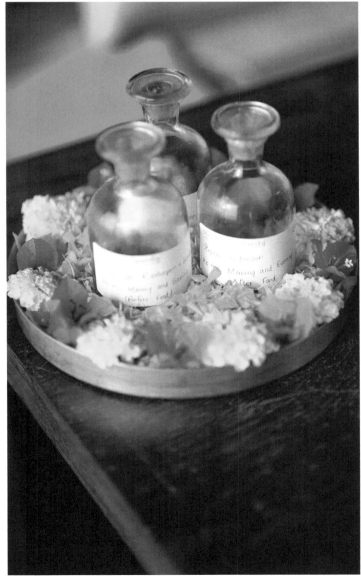

TEN AYURVEDA TIPS FOR DAILY LIFE

IF YOU INCORPORATE SOME AYURVEDIC PRACTICES INTO YOUR DAILY ROUTINE, THEN YOUR BODY, MIND, AND SOUL WILL STAY IN A STATE OF HEALTH.

1. Be an early bird and rise with the sun. When you awake, sink into the tranquility of nature and calm your senses. Avoid late nights.

2. Start your day by drinking a glass of warm water with 2 teaspoons of fresh lemon juice and a teaspoon of honey stirred in. This helps to detoxify and stimulate your digestive system.

3. Set aside time to have a regular bowel movement every day.

4. Pamper yourself with a warm herbal oil rub in the morning. This will rejuvenate your body at a cellular level and improve your blood circulation. Use any Ayurvedic oil and wait for half an hour before taking a warm shower.

5. Have a close look at what you eat during the day. Try to eat fresh, seasonal, organic fruits and vegetables. Keep away from oily food and junk food, as much as possible. If possible do not eat later than 7:00 pm.

6. Use herbs and spices like basil, coriander, fresh ginger, turmeric, garlic, cumin seeds, and black pepper in your cookings.

These herbs reduce bad cholesterol and protect your vital organs by supporting your immune system.

7. Include cycling, yoga, or any other aerobic exercise in your daily regimen. A good 30 minutes of exercise will enhance your blood circulation, help you maintain a healthy weight, and help keep disease at bay.

8. Take a "just-for-me" break as often as you can during the day. Close your eyes, disconnect from the outer world, and tune in to your own self. Complement this with slow and deep breathing.

9. Take a warm bath before bed with essential oils such as lavender, sesame, or sandalwood; it will help to calm your senses.

10. Try to meditate every day. It's fine if you meditate only for 5 minutes but it should be part of your daily routine. Short meditations every day are much more effective than longer meditations once in awhile.

ZEHN AYURVEDA-TIPPS FÜR DEN ALLTAG

WER EINIGE AYURVEDA-PRAKTIKEN IN SEINEN ALLTAG INTEGRIERT, HÄLT KÖRPER, GEIST UND SEELE GESUND.

1. Morgenstund' hat tatsächlich Gold im Mund: Stehen Sie mit der Sonne auf. Versinken Sie nach dem Aufwachen in der Gelassenheit der Natur und beruhigen Sie Ihre Sinne. Bleiben Sie nicht bis spät nachts auf.

2. Trinken Sie gleich nach dem Aufstehen ein Glas warmes Wasser mit 2 Teelöffeln frischem Zitronensaft und einem Teelöffel eingerührtem Honig. Das entgiftet und regt Ihr Verdauungssystem an.

3. Nehmen Sie sich Zeit für eine regelmäßige Darmentleerung.

4. Verwöhnen Sie sich morgens, indem Sie sich mit warmem Kräuteröl einreiben. Das verjüngt die Körperzellen und verbessert die Blutzirkulation. Verwenden Sie ein Ayurveda-Öl. Warten Sie anschließend eine halbe Stunde, bis Sie warm duschen.

5. Essen Sie bewusst. Versuchen Sie frisches, saisonales Biogemüse und -obst zu sich zu nehmen. Lassen Sie nach Möglichkeit die Finger von fetten Speisen und Fastfood. Essen Sie nach 19 Uhr nichts mehr.

6. Verwenden Sie in der Küche Kräuter und Gewürze wie Basilikum, Koriander, frischen Ingwer, Kurkuma, Knoblauch, Kreuzkümmel

und schwarzen Pfeffer. Sie senken das schlechte Cholesterin und schützen Ihre Organe, indem Sie Ihr Immunsystem stärken.

7. Integrieren Sie Radfahren, Yoga oder eine andere aerobe Betätigung in Ihren Tagesablauf. 30 Minuten Sport verbessern den Kreislauf, helfen Ihnen, ein gesundes Gewicht zu halten, und senken das Krankheitsrisiko.

8. Legen Sie in Ihrem Tagesablauf so oft wie möglich „Zeit-für-mich"-Pausen ein. Schließen Sie die Augen, lösen Sie sich von der Außenwelt und wenden Sie sich Ihrem Selbst zu. Unterstützen Sie dies durch langsames, tiefes Atmen.

9. Nehmen Sie vor dem Zubettgehen ein warmes Bad mit essenziellen Ölen wie Lavendel, Sesam oder Sandelholz. Es hilft Ihnen Ihre Sinne zu beruhigen.

10. Versuchen Sie täglich zu meditieren. Schon fünf Minuten reichen – Hauptsache, die Meditation wird fester Bestandteil Ihres Tagesablaufs. Eine kurze Meditation jeden Tag ist wesentlich effektiver als eine lange Meditation hin und wieder.

SVATMA HERITAGE RESIDENCE

THANJAVUR, TAMIL NADU

The Svatma Heritage Residence is far more than just a marvelously beautiful boutique hotel. It is devoted entirely to everything that makes the ancient traditions of Tamil Nadu, the southernmost state in India, so distinctive: its rich art and cultural traditions, its timeless, unforgettable architecture, and even its culinary heritage. The current owners of this 150-year-old former residence of a ruling family carefully and lovingly renovated the hotel over a period of ten years, restoring old furniture and collecting art. These objects fill every corner of the establishment with a special ambience. There are no standard rooms here; instead, each one is unique.

Guests who wish to explore ancient Tamil Nadu in greater depth can participate in guided thematic programs, from trips to temples and instruction in ancient Indian dance to chamber concerts with Carnatic music or discover antique handicrafts.

The nearby Brihadishvara Temple in Thanjavur, which is one thousand years old, is not only a UNESCO World Heritage Site but also one of the most impressive examples of South Indian temple architecture. Many other sights, such as the royal palace, are also worth visiting.

The Svatma Heritage Residence will transport you far away from the city's hustle and bustle and immerse you in meditative tranquility and serenity far from your everyday cares. The spa and yoga center, along with two vegetarian restaurants and a rooftop bar, contribute to this ambience, ready to pamper you with health-conscious, traditional Tamil cuisine. The days you spend here are not just a trip into Tamil Nadu's past but also a journey of self discovery—after all, "svatma" means "the soul."

Die Svatma Heritage Residence ist viel mehr als ein beeindruckend schönes Boutiquehotel, es ist die pure Hingabe an alles, was die uralten Traditionen Tamil Nadus, des südlichsten indischen Bundesstaats, auszeichnet: seine reichhaltige Kunst und Kultur, seine zeitlos beeindruckende Architektur und auch sein kulinarisches Erbe. Zehn Jahre lang wurde die 150 Jahre alte Residenz einer Herrscherfamilie behutsam und mit viel Liebe restauriert, alte Möbel aufgearbeitet und Kunst gesammelt. Objekte, die jeden Winkel des Hauses so besonders erscheinen lassen. Jeder Raum ist hier einzigartig, Standardzimmer gibt es nicht.

Der Gast kann, wenn er mag, durch geführte Themenmodule noch tiefer in das alte Tamil Nadu eintauchen – von Tempelbesuchen über Einführungen in die altindischen Tanzstile zu Kammerkonzerten mit karnatischer Musik oder zur Entdeckung antiker Kunsthandwerke.

Der nicht weit entfernte eintausend Jahre alte Brihadishvara-Tempel in Thanjavur ist als UNESCO-Weltkulturerbe eines der beeindruckendsten Beispiele südindischer Tempelarchitektur. Aber auch zahlreiche weitere Sehenswürdigkeiten, wie der Königspalast, sind einen Besuch wert. Thanjavur ist schließlich eine der ältesten Städte Indiens.

In der Svatma Heritage Residence spürt man wenig vom geschäftigen Treiben der Stadt, hier herrscht meditative Stille und alltagsferne Gelassenheit. Dafür sorgen auch das Spa und das Yogazentrum sowie gleich zwei vegetarische Restaurants und eine Rooftop-Bar, die mit gesundheitsbewusster, traditioneller tamilischer Küche verwöhnen. Die Tage hier sind nicht nur eine Reise in die Vergangenheit Tamil Nadus, sondern auch eine Reise zum Selbst – „Svatma" bedeutet übrigens „die eigene Seele".

ROOMS: 38
SPECIALTIES: COOKING CLASSES, MANTRA CLASSES, ART CLASSES, GYM, YOGA, MEDITATION, MASSAGES, POOL, JACUZZI

SVATMA HERITAGE RESIDENCE
NO.4/1116, BLAKE HIGHER
SECONDARY SCHOOL ROAD
613001 THANJAVUR
INDIA (INDIEN)
WWW.SVATMA.IN
+91 436 227 3222

ZIMMER: 38
BESONDERHEITEN: KOCHKURSE, KURSE ZUM MANTRASINGEN, MALKURSE, FITNESSRAUM, YOGA, MEDITATION, MASSAGEN, POOL, JACUZZI

PULIYODHARAI
TAMARIND RICE

INGREDIENTS
SERVES 2

Puliyodharai Powder
3 dried red chiles
2 tbsp bengal gram (split chickpeas,
  also called chana dal)
1 tbsp coriander seeds
¼ tsp fenugreek seeds
1 tbsp white sesame seeds
1½ tsp black pepper

Tamarind Paste
1 lemon-sized piece of tamarind,
  soaked for 30 minutes in 2 cups/
  470 ml warm water
7 tbsp/100 ml sesame oil
3 dried red chiles
¼ cup/50 g peanuts
1 tbsp cashews
1 tbsp black gram
1 tbsp bengal gram
1½ tsp mustard seeds
¾ tsp asafetida
1 sprig curry leaves
Pinch ground turmeric
Salt
1 tsp brown sugar

2 cups/300 g steamed rice, cooled

ZUTATEN
FÜR 2 PERSONEN

Puliyodharai-Pulver
3 getrocknete rote Chilischoten
2 EL Bengal Gram (Chana Dal,
  getrocknete, halbierte Kichererbsen)
1 EL Koriandersamen
¼ TL Bockshornkleesamen
1 EL weiße Sesamsamen
1½ TL schwarzer Pfeffer

Tamarindenpaste
1 zitronengroßes Stück Tamarindenfleisch, 30 Minuten in 500 ml
  warmem Wasser eingeweicht
100 ml Sesamöl
3 getrocknete rote Chilischoten
50 g Erdnüsse
1 EL Cashewkerne
1 EL schwarzes Gram (Urad Dal)
1 EL Bengal Gram

1½ TL Senfkörner
¾ TL Asant-Pulver
1 kleiner Zweig Curryblätter
1 Prise gemahlene Kurkuma
Salz
1 TL Rohrzucker

Zum Servieren
300 g gedämpfter Reis, abgekühlt

METHOD

Puliyodharai powder: In a dry skillet, toast the chiles, bengal gram, coriander seeds, and fenugreek seeds over medium-high heat until you get a nice aroma. Transfer to a spice grinder. Toast the sesame seeds and transfer to the grinder.
Add the pepper and grind everything together into a powder. Set aside.
Tamarind paste: Strain the tamarind pulp mixture through a fine-mesh strainer into a bowl, pressing on the pulp to extract as much juice as possible. Set aside.
Heat the oil over medium heat and add the chiles, peanuts, cashews, black gram, bengal gram, mustard seeds, curry leaves, and asafetida. When the mixture turns golden brown, add the tamarind liquid, turmeric, and salt to taste and bring to a boil.
Add the sugar and cook until the consistency becomes like a thick paste and the oil separates out, about 20 minutes. Add the puliyodharai powder and stir to combine. Let the mixture rest for 30 minutes. Mix with the cool rice gently (without breaking the rice). Serve.

ZUBEREITUNG

Für das Puliyodharai-Pulver Chilis, Bengal Gram, Koriander- und Bockshornklee-samen in einer Pfanne ohne Öl bei mittlerer bis starker Hitze rösten, bis es fein duftet. In eine Gewürzmühle geben. Den Sesam rösten und zugeben. Den Pfeffer zufügen und alles pulverfein zermahlen.
Für die Tamarindenpaste die eingeweichten Tamarinden durch ein feines Sieb streichen und dabei gut ausdrücken, um möglichst viel Saft auszupressen. Das Öl bei mittlerer Hitze erhitzen. Chilis, Erdnüsse, Cashewkerne, schwarzes und Bengal Gram, Senfkörner Senfkörner, Asant und Curryblätter darin goldbraun rösten. Dann Tamarindensaft und Kurkuma zugeben, mit Salz abschmecken und aufkochen. Den Zucker zufügen und alles etwa 20 Minuten köcheln lassen, bis eine dicke Paste entsteht und das Öl austritt. Das Puliyodharai-Pulver einrühren und die Paste 30 Minuten durchziehen lassen. Die Tamarindenpaste unter den kalten Reis heben, den Tamarindenreis auf zwei Tellern anrichten und servieren.

KAIRALI –
THE AYURVEDIC HEALING VILLAGE
PALAKKAD DISTRICT, KERALA

What does Ayurveda actually mean? "Ayur" stands for "life" and "veda" for "science." Kairali—the Ayurvedic Healing Village in the South Indian state of Karala, is dedicated entirely to Ayurveda, India's 5,000-year-old "science of life," which can perform veritable miracles on the human body. The multiple prize-winning wellness resort works to alleviate and heal all kinds of complaints with a holistic and personalized approach, and it does this in an ambiance that comes very close to paradise. Surrounded by 60 acres (24 hectares) of lush vegetation, the 30 exclusive villas blend marvelously with their natural surroundings, filled with medicinal plants, coconut palms, and mango trees. The villa rooms are designed according to the principles of "vastu shastra," India's version of feng shui, and also according to ancient Ayurvedic recommendations. Every guest can be assigned the right villa, based on that individual's personal astrological and physical constitution. They can even get a glimpse of the future with the help of the hotel's own astrologer and palm reader.

Kairali's ambitious mission is to help its guest detoxify, cleanse, and heal their bodies in the comfort of a luxury retreat. This includes an organic, entirely vegetarian cuisine, cooking courses, yoga, and mediation, with panchakarma, the all-around cleansing cure, as the crowning jewel. The Ayurvedic healing village is one of the leading Ayurvedic health centers in Asia and one of the best wellness centers in the world, and for good reason. Many a guest has rated their stay here as a life-changing experience.

Was bedeutet eigentlich Ayurveda? „Ayur" steht für „Leben" und „Veda" für „Wissenschaft". Kairali – The Ayurvedic Healing Village im südindischen Bundesstaat Kerala hat sich voll und ganz dem Ayurveda verschrieben, Indiens 5000 Jahre alter Wissenschaft vom Leben, die wahre Wunder für den menschlichen Körper bewirken kann. Ganzheitlich und individuell wird in dem vielfach prämierten Gesundheitsresort an der Linderung und Heilung von Beschwerden jeglicher Art gewirkt, und das in einem Ambiente, das wahrlich paradiesisch anmutet. Inmitten 24 Hektar üppiger Vegetation fügen sich die 30 exklusiven Villen wunderbar in die natürliche Umgebung mit ihren Heilpflanzen, Kokospalmen und Mangobäumen ein. Die Raumgestaltung der Villen entspricht den Prinzipien des Vastu Shastra, der indischen Version des Feng-Shui, und gleichzeitig den alten ayurvedischen Empfehlungen. So kann für jeden Besucher die passende Villa ausgewählt werden, basierend auf der persönlichen astrologischen und physischen Konstitution. Mit dem hauseigenen Astrologen und Handleser darf sogar ein Blick in die Zukunft gewagt werden.

Entgiften, reinigen und heilen, begleitet vom Komfort eines Luxusretreats – das ist die anspruchsvolle Mission Kairalis. Dazu gehört auch eine hundertprozentig vegetarische Bioküche, Kochkurse, Yoga sowie Meditation und als Krönung die umfassende Reinigungskur Panchakarma. Das ayurvedische Heilungsdorf ist zu Recht eines der führenden ayurvedischen Gesundheitszentren Asiens und eines der besten Wellnesszentren weltweit. So mancher Gast bewertete seinen Aufenthalt hier als lebensverändernd.

ROOMS: 30 VILLAS
SPECIALTIES: DETOXIFICATION PROGRAMS, YOGA, AYURVEDA TREATMENTS, MEDITATION, POOL, COOKING CLASSES

KAIRALI – THE AYURVEDIC HEALING VILLAGE
P.O. OLASSERY, KODUMBU
678 551 DIST. PALAKKAD
INDIA (INDIEN)
WWW.AYURVEDIC HEALINGVILLAGE.COM
+91 9999 23 1117

ZIMMER: 30 VILLEN
BESONDERHEITEN: DETOX-PROGRAMME, YOGA, MEDITATION, AYURVEDA-BEHANDLUNGEN, POOL, KOCHKURSE

The resort's founders have been sharing their knowledge of authentic, traditional Ayurveda all over the world since 1989. This original form of Ayurveda has been taught by a physician's family over the course of many generations—a family heritage that uses knowledge of traditional therapies to promote good health and long life. The first wellness retreat of the Kairali Ayurvedic Group, located in Kerala, was followed by Ayurvedic centers across India and the World.

Seit 1989 teilen die Gründer ihr Wissen über den authentischen, traditionellen Ayurveda auf der ganzen Welt. Die ursprüngliche Form des Ayurveda wurde von einer Ärztefamilie über viele Generationen hinweg weitervermittelt – ein Familienerbe, welches traditionelles Heilwissen anwendet, um Gesundheit und ein langes Leben zu fördern. Dem ersten Wellnesszentrum der Kairali Ayurvedic Group in Kerala folgten Ayurveda-Zentren in ganz Indien und der Welt.

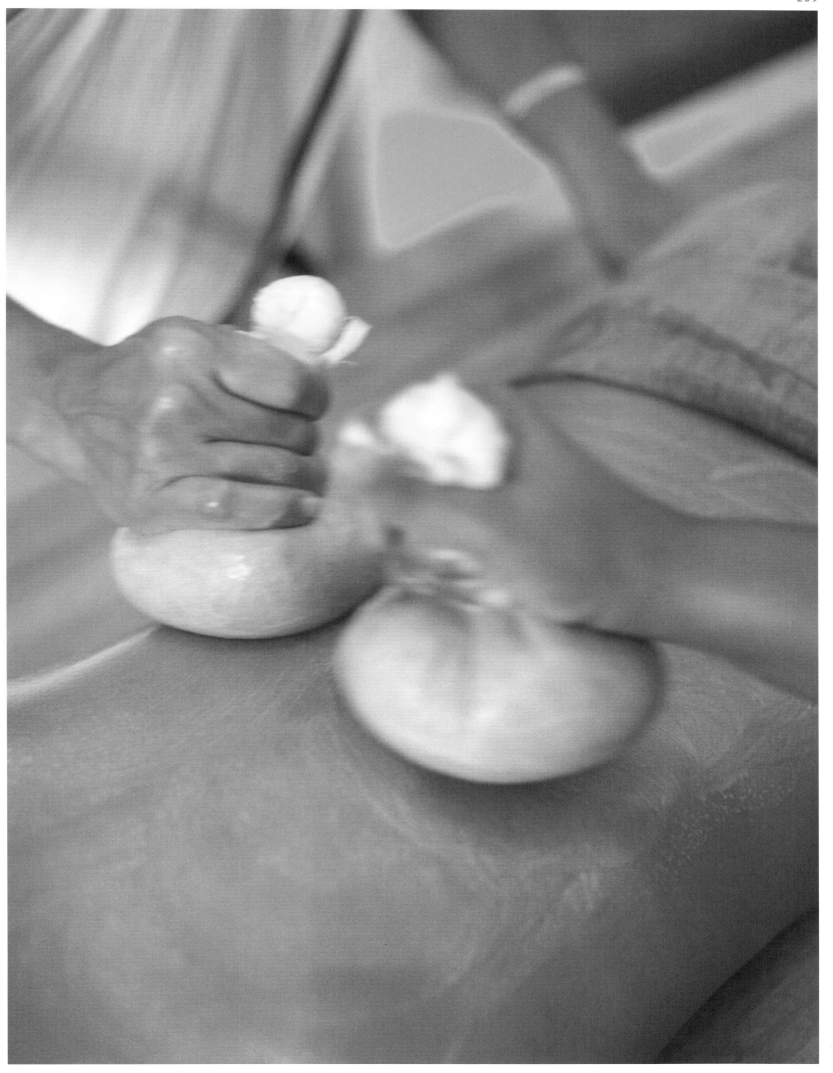

SAMBHAR
TRADITIONAL VEGETABLE STEW

SAMBAR
SÜDINDISCHER GEMÜSEEINTOPF MIT TAMARINDE

INGREDIENTS
SERVES 2 TO 3

Stew
2 small eggplants, sliced 1 inch thick
1 carrot, peeled and cut into 1-inch-thick pieces
½ cup/100 g dried mung beans (moong dal),
  washed thoroughly
1 onion, sliced
2 green chiles, chopped
½ tsp ground turmeric
4 oz/115 g tamarind pulp, soaked in 1 cup/
  235 ml warm water for 30 minutes
1 tbsp vegetable oil

7 oz/200 g okra, trimmed and cut into
  1-inch-thick pieces
salt
1 tbsp/15 g sambhar powder

Tempering
1 tsp vegetable oil
1 dry red chile, broken
8–10 curry leaves
1½ tsp mustard seeds
¼ tsp asafetida powder

ZUTATEN
FÜR 2–3 PERSONEN

Eintopf
2 kleine Auberginen, in 1 cm dicke
  Scheiben geschnitten
1 Möhre, in 1 cm dicke Scheiben
  geschnitten
100 g getrocknete Mungobohnen
  (Moong Dal), gewaschen
1 Zwiebel, in Scheiben geschnitten
2 grüne Chilischoten, gehackt
½ TL gemahlene Kurkuma
115 g Tamarindenfleisch, 30 Minuten in
  235 ml warmem Wasser eingeweicht
1 EL Öl
200 g Okraschoten, in 1 cm dicke
  Scheiben geschnitten
Salz
1 EL Sambar-Pulver

Tempering
1 TL Öl
1 getrocknete rote Chilischote, zerbröselt
8–10 Curryblätter
1 ½ TL Senfkörner
¼ TL Asant-Pulver

This traditional South Indian meal is a lentil-based vegetable stew cooked with tamarind broth. If you don't have a pressure cooker, a pot or Dutch oven can be used.

METHOD
Stew: Combine the eggplants and carrot with the mung beans in a pressure cooker. Add the onion and green chiles, turmeric, and 2 cups/475 ml water and cook. Allow just one whistle and remove from the heat.
While the beans and vegetables cook, strain the tamarind mixture through a fine-mesh strainer, pushing on the pulp to extract as much juice as possible. Set aside. Heat the oil in a skillet; fry the okra lightly. Transfer the okra to the pressure cooker, add the strained tamarind juice, season with salt to taste, and bring to a simmer. Add the sambhar powder and continue to simmer for 5 minutes.
Tempering: Heat the oil in a skillet; add the red chile, curry leaves, mustard seeds, and asafetida. Pour this into the sambhar and stir well. Serve hot.

ZUBEREITUNG
Für den Eintopf Auberginen, Möhre und Mungobohnen in einen Dampfkochtopf geben. Zwiebel, Chilis, Kurkuma und 475 ml Wasser zufügen, verschließen und aufkochen. Den Topf kurz pfeifen lassen, dann vom Herd nehmen.
Während das Gemüse gart, die eingeweichten Tamarinden durch ein feines Sieb streichen und dabei gut ausdrücken, um möglichst viel Saft auszupressen. Das Öl in einer Pfanne erhitzen und die Okras darin anbraten. Den Dampfkochtopf abdampfen lassen, öffnen und Okras und Tamarindensaft zum Eintopf geben.
Mit Salz abschmecken und zum Köcheln bringen. Das Sambar-Pulver einrühren und den Eintopf noch 5 Minuten weiterköcheln lassen. Inzwischen für das Tempering das Öl in einer Pfanne erhitzen. Chili, Curryblätter, Senfkörner und Asant-Pulver einrühren. Das Würzöl in den Sambar rühren und den Eintopf heiß servieren.

Tipp: Wenn Sie keinen Dampfkochtopf besitzen, verwenden Sie stattdessen einen Bräter, Dutch Oven (Feuertopf) oder einen normalen Topf.

SHREYAS RETREAT

BANGALORE, KARNATAKA

Bangalore—India's busy IT metropolis, home to eight million inhabitants, is a city of skyscrapers, western consumerism, and never-ending hustle. But only 35 kilometers northwest of downtown, a place of serenity nestles up to the picturesque, southern Indian plateau: Shreyas Retreat. This special hotel is nothing less than the world's most luxurious ashram, where your stay is organized around yoga and meditation. The establishment maintains the standards of a five-star hotel. Twelve guest bungalows, an infinity pool, lounging spaces, meditation huts, and tiny hideaways are surrounded by an extensive green garden landscape permeated by the scent of blossoms.

Shreyas Retreat is where you can leave behind the daily rat race of work and hectic activity for a time and embark on a journey of self discovery without distractions. Yoga instructors from all over the world accompany you along the way by offering classes for all levels of proficiency. However, the gourmet Ayurvedic, vegetarian meals, a large spa zone, and the entire property also help you relax by combining modern design and traditional Indian elements into a unique atmosphere. This mix of amenities is not the only surprising aspect of Shreyas Retreat, for here you don't practice yoga with your body alone. Because community service is also part of yoga practice, hotel guests are invited to take part in social activities. For example, the retreat supplies a nearby orphanage with fresh, healthy meals, and every guest is welcome to help serve the children. The unique character of Shreyas Yoga Retreat is found in this combination of complete serenity on the outskirts of a big city, physical yoga practice and relaxation, luxury and asceticism, community and seclusion.

Bangalore – das ist die quirlige IT-Metropole Indiens, mit acht Millionen Einwohnern, Wolkenkratzern, westlicher Konsumwelt und allgegenwärtiger Betriebsamkeit. Doch nur 35 Kilometer nordwestlich des Stadtzentrums schmiegt sich ein Ort der Ruhe ins malerische südindische Tafelland: Shreyas Retreat. Dieses besondere Hotel ist nicht weniger als einer der luxuriösesten Aschrams der Welt. Yoga und Meditation stehen im Zentrum des Aufenthalts. Das Haus selbst hat den Standard eines Fünfsternehotels. Zwölf Gästebungalows, ein Infinity-Pool, Meditationshütten und versteckte kleine Rückzugsorte werden von einer mit Blütenduft durchzogenen, grünen Gartenlandschaft umrahmt.

Im Shreyas Retreat kann man für eine Weile das tägliche Hamsterrad aus Arbeit und Hektik verlassen und ohne Ablenkung den Weg zum eigenen Selbst beschreiten. Dabei helfen Yogalehrer aus aller Welt, die Übungsstunden für alle Niveaustufen anbieten. Aber auch die ayurvedisch-vegetarische Gourmetküche, ein großer Spa-Bereich sowie die ganze Anlage selbst, mit ihrer Kombination von modernem Design und traditionellen indischen Elementen, tragen zur besonderen Atmosphäre bei. Nicht die einzige Mischung, die überrascht. Im Shreyas Retreat wird Yoga nicht nur mit dem Körper praktiziert. Da Dienst an der Gemeinschaft Teil der Yogalehre ist, sind auch die Hotelbesucher eingeladen, sich bei sozialen Aktivitäten zu engagieren. Das Retreat versorgt zum Beispiel ein nahegelegenes Waisenhaus mit frischem, gesundem Essen und jeder Gast kann gerne bei der Versorgung der Kinder mithelfen. In dieser Verbindung aus vollkommener Ruhe am Rande der Großstadt, yogischer Körperarbeit und Erholung, Luxus und Askese, Gemeinschaft und Zurückgezogenheit liegt die Besonderheit des Shreyas Yoga Retreats.

ROOMS: 12 COTTAGES
SPECIALTIES: AYURVEDA TREATMENTS (E.G. PANCHAKARMA), YOGA, MEDITATION, COOKING CLASSES, INFINITY POOL, JACUZZI, STEAM BATH, LIBRARY, GYM, ACCESSIBLE FOR DISABLED PEOPLE

SHREYAS RETREAT
SANTOSHIMA FARM,
GOLLAHALLI GATE NELAMANGALA
562123 BANGALORE
INDIA (INDIEN)
WWW.SHREYASRETREAT.COM
+91 80 2773 7102 | +91 99161 17773

ZIMMER: 12 BUNGALOWS
BESONDERHEITEN: AYURVEDA-BEHANDLUNGEN (U.A. PANCHAKARMA), YOGA, MEDITATION, KOCHKURSE, INFINITY-POOL, JACUZZI, DAMPFBAD, BIBLIOTHEK, FITNESS-RAUM, BEHINDERTENGERECHT

FIVELEMENTS

BANJAR BATURNING, BALI

Bali—paradise island. A good many people (day) dream of escaping to this place in order to take a break from their everyday lives at least for a while. We associate Bali with something mystical and archaic but also with tropical nature, green rice paddies, and heavenly beaches—a bit of paradise, in fact. It is therefore the perfect setting for a wellness retreat like the truly exotic Fivelements not far from Ubud. The exclusive, spacious guest suites built from bamboo, with their own terraces and outdoor bathtubs, were placed in a divine setting right on the banks of the sacred Ayung River.

The Fivelements is famous in part for its extensive range of holistic therapies and healing rituals, inspired by the Balinese lifestyle and administered by local healers, whose skills were handed down within their families over the course of many generations.

You can choose from innovative wellness treatments, meditation, gentle bodywork, Balinese fire and water ceremonies, and even authentic Healing Journeys in order to ground yourself and get in touch with your inner self. New paths to achieving good health are offered here in a beautiful ambience.

This includes wholesome cuisine. Many of the dishes served in the prize-winning Sakti Dining Room™ are made from vital raw foods, which are especially nutritious and filled with healing power (*shakti*). Even fans of the finest gourmet gastronomy will be surprised at how wonderful the artfully prepared dishes look and taste. It is not for nothing that raw foods are also called "living nourishment," and the Fivelement's refined cuisine is known far beyond Indonesia for very good reason. Balinese traditions and healing arts, paired with heavenly luxury—this place has every right to call itself paradise.

Sehnsuchtsort Bali – hierher entfliehen nicht wenige in ihren (Tag)träumen, um zumindest für eine Weile aus dem Alltag auszusteigen. Mit Bali verbindet man etwas Mystisches, Archaisches, aber auch tropische Natur, grüne Reisfelder und Traumstrände – etwas Paradiesisches eben. Es ist also das perfekte Setting für ein Wellnessretreat wie das wahrlich exotisch anmutende Fivelements nahe Ubud. In traumhafter Lage wurden die exklusiven großzügigen Gästesuiten aus Bambus, mit eigener Terrasse und Freiluftbadewanne, direkt am Wasserlauf des heiligen Flusses Ayung platziert.

Berühmt ist das Fivelements unter anderem für sein umfangreiches Angebot an ganzheitlichen Therapien und Heilritualen, die von der balinesischen Lebensweise inspiriert sind und von einheimischen Heilern durchgeführt werden, deren Gabe über viele Generationen innerhalb ihrer Familien weitergegeben wurde. Innovative Wellnessanwendungen, Meditation, einfühlsame Körperarbeit, balinesische Feuer- und Wasserzeremonien, selbst authentische Healing Journeys kann man wählen, um sich zu erden und mit tieferen Seinsschichten in Kontakt zu treten. Neue Wege der Regeneration dürfen hier in wunderschönem Ambiente begangen werden.

Dazu gehört natürlich auch eine heilsame Küche. Im preisgekrönten Restaurant Sakti Dining Room™ besteht ein Großteil der Gerichte aus vitaler Rohkost, die besonders reich an Nährstoffen und Heilkraft (*Shakti*) ist. Auch Liebhaber der gehobenen Gourmetgastronomie werden beim Anblick und Geschmack der kunstvoll zubereiteten Speisen noch überrascht. Nicht umsonst nennt man Rohkost auch „lebendige Nahrung", und nicht ohne Grund ist die raffinierte Küche des Fivelements weit über die Grenzen Indonesiens hinaus bekannt. Balinesische Traditionen und Heilkunst, gepaart mit paradiesischem Luxus – dieser Sehnsuchtsort darf sich zweifellos so nennen.

ROOMS: 9 SUITES
SPECIALTIES: POOL, BEAUTY TREATMENTS, MEDITATION, YOGA, AIKIDO, DETOX RETREATS

FIVELEMENTS
PURI AHIMSA BANJAR BATURNING
MAMBAL, 80352 BALI
INDONESIA (INDONESIEN)
WWW.FIVELEMENTS.ORG
+62 361 469 260

ZIMMER: 9 SUITEN
BESONDERHEITEN: POOL, BEAUTY-BEHANDLUNGEN, MEDITATION, YOGA, AIKIDO, DETOX-RETREATS

BEINGSATTVAA

UBUD, BALI

The bustling town of Ubud is the cultural and artistic center of Bali, the island of the gods. The area around Ubud is also made up of different municipalities, each of which is dedicated to a particular handicraft or art. Ubud draws many people like magic: artists, escapists, backpackers, hippies, and often even conventional vacationers who want to immerse themselves in this tropical world as an antidote to their mundane everyday lives.

It is therefore not entirely by chance that a large number of fabulous restaurants, spas, and resorts can be found in Ubud and its environs. One of them is BeingSattvaa, which was built a short distance outside the town in the middle of rice paddies. Ten pavilion-like villas set in a lushly overgrown Balinese garden filled with the island's native plants make guests feel like they are living in a treehouse. The hotel's unique and environmentally friendly architecture seamlessly blurs the boundaries between indoor and outdoor areas, leaving the impression that one is connected to the tropical surroundings even in the rooms. The luxurious spa area, with its view of the rainforest, offers treatments and remedies based on a blend of traditional Balinese and Ayurvedic medicine. From the yoga pavilion to the spa, the undulating over-flow pool to the delicious, healthy cuisine made with ingredients from the hotel's own organic fruit and vegetable garden, BeingSattvaa has absolutely everything you need to regain a sense of balance and lightness of being. Special retreat packages are offered to guests as well. And if the peace and quiet gets to be too much for you, just head for the town and immerse yourself in the hustle and bustle of Ubud.

Die quirlige Stadt Ubud auf Bali, der Insel der Götter, ist das kulturelle und künstlerische Zentrum der Insel. Und auch die Umgebung setzt sich aus verschiedenen Kommunen zusammen, die sich jeweils einem speziellen Handwerk oder einer Kunst widmen. Ubud zieht viele Menschen magisch an: Künstler, Aussteiger, Backpacker, Hippies und oft auch traditionelle Urlauber, die als Kontrastprogramm zu ihrem Alltag einmal in diese tropische Welt eintauchen wollen.

Nicht ganz zufällig findet man deshalb in Ubud und Umgebung zahlreiche fantastische Restaurants, Spas und Resorts, wie das BeingSattvaa, welches, umgeben von Reisfeldern, etwas außerhalb der Stadt gebaut wurde. In einem üppig-bewachsenen balinesischen Garten voller inseltypischer Pflanzen geben zehn Pavillon-artige Villen dem Besucher das Gefühl, in einem Baumhaus zu wohnen. Die einzigartige und umweltfreundliche Architektur des BeingSattvaa lässt die Übergänge zwischen Innen- und Außenbereichen nahtlos erscheinen und vermittelt den Eindruck, dass man auch in den Räumen mit der tropischen Umgebung verbunden bleibt. Im luxuriösen Spa mit Blick auf den Regenwald darf man Anwendungen und Heilmittel, basierend auf einer Mischung aus traditionellen balinesischen und Ayurveda-Behandlungen, in Anspruch nehmen. Spezielle Retreatpakete, ein Yogapavillon, der Overflow-Pool und eine gesund-köstliche Küche mit Zutaten aus dem eigenen Biogemüsegarten – an nichts fehlt es hier, um Balance und Leichtigkeit wiederzuentdecken. Und falls es doch einmal weniger ruhig zugehen darf, taucht man einfach ins geschäftige Treiben von Ubud ein.

ROOMS: 11 PAVILIONS, VILLAS & JOGLO HOUSES
SPECIALTIES: POOL, MASSAGES, VARIOUS HEALTH TREATMENTS (E.G. AYUERVEDIC), YOGA, MEDITATION, COOKING CLASSES, ACCESSIBLE FOR DISABLED PEOPLE

BEINGSATTVAA RETREAT
JALAN RAYA KENDRAN, BANJAR KEPITU
DESA KENDRAN UBUD
80561 BALI
INDONESIA (INDONESIEN)
WWW.BEINGSATTVAA.COM
+65 9111 5642 | +62 813 3825 3958

ZIMMER: 11 PAVILLONS, VILLEN & TRADITIONELLE JOGLO-HÄUSER
BESONDERHEITEN: POOL, MASSAGEN, VERSCHIEDENE GESUNDHEITSBEHANDLUNGEN (U.A. AYURVEDISCH), YOGA, MEDITATION, KOCHKURSE, BEHINDERTENGERECHT

WATERMELON GAZPACHO
WITH MINT AND CILANTRO

WASSERMELONEN-GAZPACHO
MIT MINZE UND KORIANDER

INGREDIENTS
SERVES 2 TO 3

1 cup/265 g pureed watermelon,
  plus ½ cup/80 g diced seeded
  watermelon
½ large cucumber, peeled, seeded,
  and diced
¼ cup/40 g diced yellow bell pepper
1 scallion, minced
¼ cup fresh mint leaves, minced
¼ cup fresh cilantro leaves, minced,
  plus cilantro sprigs for serving
½ jalapeño chile, seeded and minced
1 tbsp lime juice
½ tsp grated fresh ginger
½ tsp Himalayan pink salt
½ tsp ground cumin, toasted
Freshly ground black pepper

ZUTATEN
FÜR 2–3 PERSONEN

265 g Wassermelone, püriert
80 g Wassermelone, entkernt und
  in Würfel geschnitten
½ große Salatgurke, geschält, entkernt
  und in Würfel geschnitten
40 g gelbe Paprikaschote,
  in Würfel geschnitten
1 Schalotte, gehackt
3 EL frisch gehackte Minze
3 EL frisch gehacktes Koriandergrün,
  plus einige Zweige zum Garnieren
½ Jalapeño-Chilischote, entkernt
  und gehackt
1 EL Limettensaft
½ TL frisch geriebener Ingwer
½ TL rosa Himalajasalz
½ TL gemahlener Kreuzkümmel, geröstet
schwarzer Pfeffer

METHOD
In a large bowl combine the watermelon puree with the diced watermelon, cucumber, bell pepper, scallion, mint, cilantro, and chile. Add the lime juice, ginger, salt, and cumin and stir.

Refrigerate for 30 minutes.

Sprinkle with pepper, garnish with cilantro sprigs, and serve.

ZUBEREITUNG
Wassermelonenpüree, Wassermelonenwürfel, Gurke, Paprika, Schalotte, Minze, Koriandergrün und Chili in einer großen Schüssel verrühren. Limettensaft, Ingwer, Salz und Kreuzkümmel untermischen.

Die Mischung 30 Minuten im Kühlschrank durchziehen lassen.

Die Gazpacho danach portionweise in Schalen anrichten. Mit frisch gemahlenem Pfeffer bestreuen, mit Korianderzweigen garnieren und servieren.

THANYAPURA
HEALTH & SPORTS RESORT

THALANG, PHUKET

If you're up for swimming morning laps in the olympic-size pool at the Health & Sports Resort, don't be bothered if other swimmers on your right and left leave you in their wake—they could very well be professional athletes on an Olympic team. No other resort in Asia offers such an unparalleled combination of wellness and sports facilities designed to Olympic standards. The hotel has created a unique concept, based on the pillars of health, spirituality, sports, and teaching, all of them intended to help you reach your full potential.

The establishment offers an impressive range of training opportunities, fitness courses, detox programs, meditation and yoga classes, massages, personal coaching with bona fide professionals—the options for activities and R&R on Thailand's gorgeous Phuket Island seem practically endless. The resort even has its own medical department, where you can undergo physical examinations and a wide range of therapies. The place is a veritable hot spot for those who enjoy an active lifestyle!

But this doesn't mean that guest who prefer a casual vacation experience get the short end of the stick here. The resort is embedded in the pristine nature of the Khao Phra Thaeo Nature Park, and only 20 minutes away you will find a great many enchanting beaches that invite you to spend the day sunbathing, swimming, or snorkeling. Upon returning to the hotel with a healthy appetite, you can enjoy a bountiful, wholesome feast in good conscience, perhaps by dining on the raw vegan delicacies served in the DiLite restaurant.

Wer im Thanyapura Health & Sports Resort morgens seine Bahnen im 50-Meter-Becken zieht, sollte sich nicht ärgern, wenn er rechts und links überholt wird, denn da könnten durchaus Profis einer Olympiamannschaft an einem vorbeischwimmen. Kein Resort in Asien bietet diese beispiellose Kombination aus Wellness und Sportanlagen nach olympischen Vorgaben. Hier wurde ein einzigartiges Konzept – basierend auf den Säulen Gesundheit, Geist, Sport und Unterricht – geschaffen, das dabei helfen soll, sein eigenes Potenzial zu optimieren.

Ein beeindruckendes Angebot an Trainingsmöglichkeiten, Fitnesskursen, Detoxprogrammen, Meditations- und Yogakursen, Massagen, Personal Coachings mit echten Profis – die Optionen für Aktivitäten und Erholung scheinen hier auf Thailands wunderschöner Insel Phuket unbegrenzt. Sogar eine resorteigene medizinische Abteilung, die Untersuchungen und unterschiedlichste Behandlungsmethoden anbietet, gibt es vor Ort. Ein absoluter Hotspot für aktive Menschen!

Doch das heißt nicht, dass die ungezwungene Urlaubsfreude hier zu kurz kommen muss: Nur 20 Minuten entfernt vom Resort, das in die unberührte Natur des Nationalparks Khao Phra Thaeo eingebettet ist, entdeckt man zahlreiche fantastische Traumstrände, die zum Sonnenbaden, Schwimmen oder Schnorcheln einladen. Kehrt man anschließend hungrig ins Resort zurück, darf man mit gutem Gewissen ausgiebig gesund schlemmen, zum Beispiel die rohveganen Köstlichkeiten des Restaurants DiLite.

ROOMS: 114
SPECIALTIES: POOL (OLYMPIC-SIZE & 2 X 27 YARDS), BIKE RENTAL, PERSONAL TRAINER, TENNIS, GYM, TRACK, YOGA, MEDICAL DEPARTMENT, MEDITATION, NUTRIONAL PLANNING, CHIROPRACTIC, PHYSIOTHERAPY, ACCESSIBLE FOR DISABLED PEOPLE

THANYAPURA HEALTH & SPORTS RESORT
120, 120/1 MOO 7, T. THEPKASATTRI
THALANG
THAILAND
WWW.THANYAPURA.COM
+66 763 36000

ZIMMER: 114
BESONDERHEITEN: POOL (50 METER & 2 X 25 METER), FAHRRADVERLEIH, SPORTPLATZ, PERSONAL TRAINER, TENNIS, FITNESS TRAINING, LEICHT-ATHLETIK, YOGA, MEDIZINISCHE ABTEILUNG, MEDITATION, ERNÄHRUNGS-BERATUNG, CHIRO- & PHYSIOTHERAPIE, BEHINDERTENGERECHT

DETOX JUICES • DETOX-SÄFTE

INGREDIENTS
SERVES 1

BREAKFAST IN A BOTTLE
⅔ cup/100 g chopped mango
⅔ cup/100 g chopped papaya
½ cup/120 ml water
½ cup/15 g spinach leaves
1 tbsp peanut butter
1 tbsp vanilla extract
1 tbsp almond meal
1 tsp flaxseeds

SHREK
1 cup/30 g kale leaves
½ cup/15 g spinach leaves
1 small celery stalk
1½ green apples, cored and cut into
  large pieces
1 kiwi, peeled
¼ small cucumber, peeled
1 tbsp lemon juice
1 tsp flaxseeds

UP BEET
2 red apples, cored and cut into large pieces
1 medium beet (about 6 oz/190 g), peeled and
  cut into large pieces
1 medium celery stalk

THE BUTTON BLEND
½ cup/120 ml coconut juice
5 pitted dates, chopped
2 tbsp vanilla or plain protein powder
2 tbsp almond meal
1 tbsp chia seeds
Pinch salt

ZUTATEN
FÜR 1 PERSON

FRÜHSTÜCK AUS DER FLASCHE
100 g Mangofruchtfleisch, gehackt
100 g Papayafruchtfleisch, gehackt
15 g Spinat
1 EL Erdnusscreme
1 EL Vanilleextrakt oder Mark
  von 1 Vanilleschote
1 EL gemahlene Mandeln
1 TL Leinsamen
120 ml Wasser

SHREK
30 g Grünkohl
15 g Spinat
1 kleine Stange Staudensellerie
1 ½ grüne Äpfel, entkernt und
  in große Stücke geschnitten
1 Kiwi, geschält
¼ kleine Gurke, geschält
1 EL Zitronensaft
1 TL Leinsamen

ROTE-BETE-BOOSTER
2 rote Äpfel, entkernt und
  in große Stücke geschnitten
1 mittelgroße Rote Bete (ca. 190 g),
  geschält und in große Stücke geschnitten
1 mittelgroße Stange Staudensellerie

BUTTON BLEND
120 ml Kokoswasser
5 Datteln, entsteint und gehackt
2 EL Eiweißpulver, natur oder
  Vanillegeschmack
2 EL gemahlene Mandeln
1 EL Chiasamen
1 Prise Salz

METHOD

BREAKFAST IN A BOTTLE: The perfect way to start your day, this drink is full of vitamins and nutrients that will help with digestion and flush out toxins. While the spinach gives this smoothie its color, all the flavor comes straight from mango, papaya, peanut butter and vanilla extract, resulting in a flavorful and super nutrient-dense breakfast. Combine all the ingredients in a high-speed blender and process until smooth.

SHREK: Spinach, kale, and flaxseeds are superfoods that make this smoothie "green." Apple, celery, cucumber, kiwi, and lemon juice are there for an extra health benefit. The apple adds sweetness without adding too much sugar while the cucumber adds coolness. Combine all the ingredients in a high-speed blender and process until smooth.

UP BEET: This refreshing juice is an ideal way of detoxifying your body. It helps to flush out toxins from the blood, liver, gallbladder, kidneys, intestine, lymphatic system, and digestive system, as well as boosting the immune system. Process the ingredients one at a time through a juicer, following the manufacturer's directions.

THE BUTTON BLEND: This tasty smoothie was designed by Formula One driver Jenson Button when he trained here at Thanyapura. The mixture of nutritious foods make this drink perfect for training, cleansing, and nourishing your body. Coconut juice, also called coconut water, hydrates your body and provides it with essential electrolytes to keep your energy up. Combine all the ingredients in a high-speed blender and process until smooth.

ZUBEREITUNG

Für FRÜHSTÜCK AUS DER FLASCHE, SHREK und BUTTON BLEND jeweils alle Zutaten in den Standmixer füllen und cremig pürieren. Für ROTE-BETE-BOOSTER alle Zutaten nacheinander im Entsafter nach Gebrauchsanleitung entsaften.

Tipp: Das schmackhafte und gesunde FRÜHSTÜCK AUS DER FLASCHE ist der perfekte Start in den Tag. Der Power-Smoothie mit vielen Vitaminen und Nähr-stoffen fördert die Verdauung und spült Gifte aus dem Körper. Spinat gibt dem Smoothie seine Farbe, Mango, Papaya, Erdnussbutter und Vanille seinen Geschmack. Der SHREK punktet mit Spinat, Grünkohl und Leinsamen. Sie zählen zu den Super-foods und färben diesen Smoothie grün. Apfel, Sellerie, Gurke, Kiwi und Zitronensaft machen ihn noch ein gutes Stück gesünder. Die Äpfel süßen ohne Industriezucker, die Gurke gibt ihm eine kühlende Wirkung.

Der erfrischende ROTE-BETE-BOOSTER ist eine Detoxkur für sich. Er spült Gifte aus Blut, Leber, Gallenblase, Nieren, Lymph- und Verdauungssystem und stärkt gleichzeitig das Immunsystem.

Den köstlichen BUTTON-BLEND-SMOOTHIE erfand Formel-Eins-Pilot Jenson Button während eines Trainingsaufenthalts in Thanyapura. Mit seiner ausgewogenen Mischung aus nährstoffreichen Zutaten eignet er sich perfekt für Work-outs sowie zum Reinigen und Kräftigen des Organismus. Kokoswasser versorgt den Körper mit Flüssigkeit und wichtigen Elektrolyten, die einer Ermüdung vorbeugen.

THE FARM AT SAN BENITO

CITY OF LIPA, BATANGAS

Enjoy prize-winning vegan meals of the very first order, surrounded by lush, tropical vegetation. Who would not find this a heavenly experience? The only five-star wellness hotel and retreat in the Philippines makes this dream come true. The Farm at San Benito is only a 90 minutes drive from the bustling metropolis of Manila, and yet the two are worlds apart. Situated on the heavenly tropical grounds of a 124-acre (50-hectare) coconut plantation, the hotel promises an extraordinary and holistic vacation experience. The place is vibrantly green, peaceful and vast, filled with the scent of exotic plants. You can hear birds chirping and water bubbling while you take in the breathtaking view of majestic mountains.

Thirty-three villas comfortably furnished in a contemporary, tropical style, lie hidden among the palms and mango trees. This harmonic blend of nature, luxury, and therapeutic treatments in one of Asia's best wellness resorts helps bring body, mind, and soul back into harmony. You will relax and heal in idyllic, natural surrounding with holistic wellness programs known as "healing retreats."

Nature and a vegan diet lie at the heart of The Farm's philosophy—after all, the purely vegan restaurant is called "Alive!" The kitchen staff turns revitalizing, organic food, most of it grown in the hotel's own garden, into healthy yet tasty meals of mainly raw foods, prepared with innovative techniques. You will not find any environmentally harmful animal ingredients here. The private paradise has won many international awards, including the "World's Best Medical Wellness Resort."

Preisgekrönte vegane Küche auf höchstem Niveau genießen und das inmitten reichhaltiger tropischer Vegetation, für wen wäre das nicht traumhaft? Im einzigen Fünfsterne-Gesundheitsretreat der Philippinen wird dieser Traum Wirklichkeit. The Farm at San Benito ist nur 90 Minuten von der geschäftigen Millionenstadt Manila entfernt, und doch liegen Welten zwischen der Großstadt und dieser auf einer Kokosplantage errichteten, 50 Hektar umfassenden tropisch-paradiesischen Anlage, die eine außergewöhnliche und ganzheitliche Urlaubserfahrung verspricht. Üppig grün ist es hier, ruhig und weitläufig, es riecht nach exotischen Pflanzen, man hört Vögel zwitschern und Wasser fließen, und der Blick auf die majestätischen Berge ist einfach atemberaubend.

Zwischen Palmen und Mangobäumen verstecken sich 33 Villen mit tropisch-modernem Komfort. Diese harmonische Vereinigung von Naturerleben, Luxus und Behandlungen in einem der besten Wellnessresorts Asiens hilft, Körper, Geist und Seele wieder in Einklang zu bringen. Mit ganzheitlichen Gesundheitsprogrammen, den Healing Retreats, gelingt das Entspannen und Heilen in natürlicher, idyllischer Umgebung.

Die Natur und eine vegane Ernährungsweise sind Herzstück der Philosophie von The Farm – nicht umsonst trägt das rein vegane Restaurant den Namen Alive!. Nahrungsmittel, die belebend wirken, biologisch und hauptsächlich aus dem eigenen Garten sind, werden mit innovativen Küchentechniken zu gesund-schmackhaften, meist rohköstlichen Kreationen veredelt. Auf belastende tierische Inhaltsstoffe wird hier komplett verzichtet. Das private Paradies ist vielfach international ausgezeichnet worden, unter anderem als Bestes Medizinisches Wellnessresort der Welt.

ROOMS: 33 VILLAS
SPECIALTIES: VARIOUS POOLS, YOGA, MEDITATION, COOKING CLASSES, GYM, HEALING BODY TREATMENTS (E.G. ALKA, OZONE, DETOXIFYING, FOUR HANDS YIN YANG PURI), SAUNA, STEAM BATH

THE FARM AT SAN BENITO
119 BARANGAY TIPAKAN
4217 LIPA
PHILIPPINES (PHILIPPINEN)
WWW.THEFARMATSANBENITO.COM
+63 2 884 8074

ZIMMER: 33 VILLEN
BESONDERHEITEN: MEHRERE POOLS, YOGA, MEDITATION, KOCHKURSE, FITNESSRAUM, GESUNDHEITSBEHANDLUNGEN (U.A. ALKA, OZON, DETOX, YIN-YANG-4-HAND-MASSAGE), SAUNA, DAMPFBAD

लोकाः समस्ताः सुखिनो भवन्तु

Lokāḥ samastāḥ sukhino bhavantu

YOGA, VEGGIE
& THE PATH TO HAPPINESS
YOGA, VEGGIE & DAS GLÜCK

"Lokāḥ samastāḥ sukhino bhavantu – May all beings be happy." This well-known Vedic mantra is also extremely popular among Western yogis. When the wise Indian scholar, Maharishi Patanjali, formulated the fundamentals of yoga philosophy in the distant past, he based them on universal principles. One such principle is "ahimsa" (do no harm), which forms the basis for the concept of nonviolence.

So it's hardly surprising that yoga and a vegetarian diet complement each other perfectly. When we refrain from eating animals, we also go a long way toward doing no harm to other sentient beings in their desire to be happy. "Do unto others as you would have them do unto you"—the Golden Rule underscores the principle of practical ethics and, in this case, quite naturally covers animals as well.

Inspired by the booming popularity of yoga in recent years, millions of people now study one of yoga's many disciplines even outside its country of origin. An estimated three million people practice yoga in Germany, and this figure is likely 25 – 30 million in the United States. The various forms of practice include all variations of traditional yoga teachings, from the especially popular, physical Hatha Yoga to the many schools of meditation and mindfulness, which also trace their origins back to the same spiritual source. What they all have in common is the recommendation that students favor a vegetarian diet.

Yoga is often described as a journey of self-discovery, one that is supposed to bring body and spirit into healthy harmony. In yoga, therefore, a healthy diet not only strengthens our bodies but is also necessary for an alert mind. Yogis therefore recommend a diet of light, unadulterated food. Within the yoga community, one often encounters the concept of a "sattvic diet." In Sanskrit, sattva means "purity." This means that a diet compatible with yoga practices

„Lokāḥ samastāḥ sukhino bhavantu – Mögen alle Wesen Glück erfahren", besagt ein bekanntes vedisches Mantra, welches sich auch in der westlichen Yogawelt großer Beliebtheit erfreut. Als der weise, indische Gelehrte, Maharishi Patanjali, in grauer Vorzeit die Grundzüge der Yogaphilosophie formulierte, gründete er diese auf universelle Prinzipien. Eines davon lautet „Ahimsa" – zu Deutsch „Nicht-Verletzen", woraus sich das Konzept der Gewaltlosigkeit ableitet.

Kein Wunder also, dass sich Yoga und vegetarische Ernährung sinnvoll ergänzen: Verzichtet man darauf, Tiere zu verzehren, leistet man einen wichtigen Beitrag dazu, das Glücksstreben anderer fühlender Wesen nicht zu verletzen. „Behandle andere so, wie du von ihnen behandelt werden willst", lautet die Goldene Regel, ein Grundsatz der praktischen Ethik und die bezieht in diesem Fall eben auch ganz selbstverständlich Tiere mit ein.

Inspiriert durch den Yoga-Boom der letzten Jahre praktizieren auch außerhalb des Ursprungslandes Indien Millionen Menschen eine der vielen Varianten des Yoga. In Deutschland geht man von etwa drei Millionen Praktizierenden aus, in den USA sollen es 25–30 Millionen sein. Zu den verschiedenen Ausübungsformen zählen alle Varianten der ursprünglichen Yogalehre, angefangen vom besonders populären, körperbezogenen Hatha Yoga bis hin zu den vielen Schulen der Meditation und Achtsamkeit, die sich ebenfalls auf dieselben spirituellen Grundlagen berufen. Allen gemeinsam ist die Empfehlung an die Schüler, eine vegetarische Ernährungsweise zu bevorzugen.

Yoga wird oft auch als Weg zum eigenen Selbst bezeichnet, der zu einem harmonischen und gesunden Zusammenspiel von Körper und Geist führen soll. Gesunde Ernährung bedeutet im Yoga folgerichtig, dass sie nicht nur unseren Körper stärkt, sondern auch für einen

should be freshly prepared, rich in vital nutrients, and without any harmful substances. Because yogis also consider the subtler qualities of sustenance, meat, fish, and eggs are not sattvic foods, since they require taking a life.

People who adopt a harmonized attitude toward life through yoga and meditation often seem to naturally migrate toward a vegetarian diet, which, in turn, supports their progress in mastering yoga practice. Countless numbers of yoga schools and meditation centers around the world therefore point out the benefits of a vegetarian diet—largely without taking a dogmatic stance. This has also likely fueled the veggie boom over the past few years.

It is therefore no coincidence that many VeggieHotels and VeganWelcome establishments provide space for yoga or meditation as a matter of course. Vegetarianism, yoga, and happiness simply make for a perfect fit.

wachen Geist förderlich ist. Deshalb werden in Yogakreisen leichte, unbelastete Lebensmittel empfohlen. Im yogischen Sprachgebrauch wird auch häufig von „sattvischer Ernährung" gesprochen. Das Sanskritwort Sattva bedeutet „Reinheit". Eine der Yogapraxis zuträgliche Ernährung sollte demnach frisch zubereitet, vitalstoffreich und frei von Schadstoffen sein. Da auch die subtileren Qualitäten der Nahrung berücksichtigt werden, zählen Fleisch, Fisch und Eier nicht zu den sattvischen Lebensmitteln, denn sie setzen die Zerstörung von Leben voraus.

Häufig ist zu beobachten, dass Menschen mit einem durch Yoga und Meditation harmonisierten Lebensgefühl ganz natürlich zu einer vegetarischen Ernährung tendieren und diese wiederum die Fortschritte auf dem Weg des Yoga begünstigt. In unzähligen Yogaschulen und Meditationszentren auf der ganzen Welt wird deshalb – überwiegend undogmatisch – auf die Vorteile einer vegetarischen Ernährungsweise hingewiesen. Auch das dürfte den Veggie-Boom der letzten Jahre zusätzlich befeuert haben.

Es ist also kein Zufall, dass in vielen VeggieHotels und VeganWelcome-Häusern Yoga- oder Meditationsräume ganz selbstverständlich dazugehören: Vegetarismus, Yoga und das Glück passen einfach wunderbar zusammen.

Veggie Hotels
100% VEGETARISCH/VEGAN

IN ALPHABETICAL ORDER

Vegan Welcome

**SELECTION OF
VEGAN FRIENDLY HOTELS**

IN ALPHABETICAL ORDER

WWW.VEGAN-WELCOME.COM

RECIPES
REZEPTE

PHOTO CREDITS

IMPRINT

© 2017 teNeues Media GmbH & Co. KG, Kempen

PUBLISHER
teNeues Media GmbH & Co. KG

EDITED & COMPILED
Karen Klein, Thomas Klein, Peter Haunert
VeggieHotels® & VeganWelcome®

TEXTS
Patrick Bolk

ART DIRECTION
Martin Graf, teNeues Media GmbH & Co. KG

GRAPHIC DESIGN
Christin Steirat, Sophie Franke,
teNeues Media GmbH & Co. KG

PROJECT MANAGEMENT
Regine Freyberg, Arndt Jasper, Nadine Weinhold,
teNeues Media GmbH & Co. KG

PROOFREADING
Karen Klein, Petra Teetz, Nadine Weinhold (German),
Cheryl Redmond, Romina Lais & Anja Hemming-Xavier,
WeSwitch Languages GmbH & Co. KG (English)

TRANSLATIONS
Reinhardt Ferstl (German), Heidi Holzer, Heather Bock,
WeSwitch Languages GmbH & Co. KG (English)

PHOTO EDITING
David Burghardt, www.db-photo.de

PREPRESS
Jens Grundei,
teNeues Media GmbH & Co. KG

PRODUCTION
Nele Jansen,
teNeues Media GmbH & Co. KG

ISBN 978-3-96171-045-4

Printed in the Czech Republic

MIX
Papier aus verantwortungsvollen Quellen
Paper from responsible sources
FSC
www.fsc.org
FSC® C005833

PUBLISHED BY TENEUES PUBLISHING GROUP
teNeues Media GmbH & Co. KG
Am Selder 37, 47906 Kempen, Germany
Phone: +49 (0)2152 916 0
Fax: +49 (0)2152 916 111
e-mail: books@teneues.com

teNeues Media GmbH & Co. KG
Munich Office
Pilotystraße 4, 80538 Munich, Germany
Phone: +49 (0)89 443 8889 62
e-mail: bkellner@teneues.com

Press department: Andrea Rehn
Phone: +49 (0)2152 916 202
e-mail: arehn@teneues.com

teNeues Publishing Company
350 7th Ave., Suite 301, New York, NY 10001, USA
Phone: +1 212 627 9090
Fax: +1 212 627 9511

teNeues Publishing UK Ltd.
12 Ferndene Road, London SE24 0AQ, UK
Phone: +44 (0)20 3542 8997

teNeues France S.A.R.L.
39, rue des Billets, 18250 Henrichemont, France
Phone: +33 (0)2 48 26 93 48
Fax: +33 (0)1 70 72 34 82

www.teneues.com

The paper TAURO used for this book, produced by
Sappi Fine Paper Europe in Stockstadt, is vegan.
Das für dieses Buch verwendete und von
Sappi Fine Paper Europe in Stockstadt produzierte
Papier TAURO ist vegan.